中國古代印刷史圖冊

An Illustrated History of Printing in Ancient China

中國印刷博物館編
羅樹寶主編
陳善偉　譯

Compiled by The Printing Museum of China
Edited by Luo Shubao
Translated by Chan Sin-wai

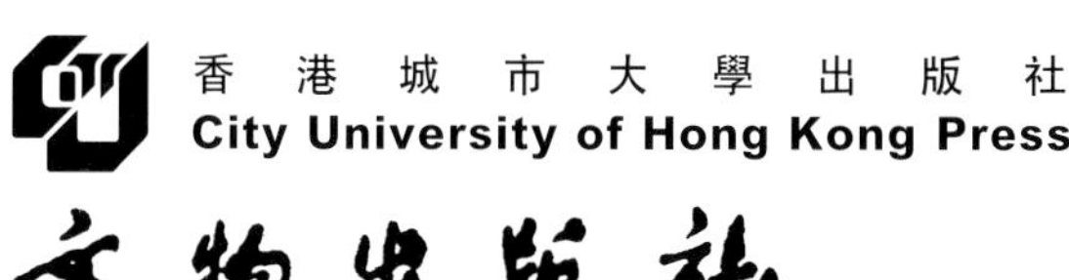

國際統一書號：962-937-032-8

出版：香港城市大學出版社
香港九龍達之路 83 號
香港城市大學
互聯網：www.cityu.edu.hk/upress/
電郵：upress@cityu.edu.hk

文物出版社
中國北京東城區
五四大街 29 號　100009

承印：深圳 中華商務聯合印刷
(廣東) 有限公司

ISBN: 962-937-032-8

Publishers: City University of Hong Kong Press
83 Tat Chee Avenue,
Kowloon, Hong Kong
Internet: www.cityu.edu.hk/upress/
E-mail: upress@cityu.edu.hk

Cultural Relics Publishing House
29 Wusi Dajie,
Beijing, 100009 China

Printed by: C & C Joint Printing Co.,
(Guangdong) Ltd., Shenzhen, China

鳴　謝

為弘揚中華民族輝煌的印刷文化史，我們在各方面的關心和支持下，編輯出版了這本圖冊。

本圖冊以圖為主，並附以簡要的文字說明，以便讀者直觀地系統了解中國古代的印刷術從起源、發明到發展的過程。圖冊中以歷代有代表性的印刷品圖錄為主，從中可以看出歷代印刷品的風貌，以及當時的刻版印刷水平。對印刷史上有貢獻的人物，我們也作了簡要介紹。

圖冊的起源部分十分重要，沒有這些印刷術出現前的文化史，就不可能有印刷術的發明。本圖冊的這種形式，我們過去還沒有出版過，經驗不足，還請讀者看後提出意見。

本冊的編輯出版過程中，得到張伯海、周興華先生、楊瑾女士等的指導和支持，得到中國印刷博物館魏志剛教授及業務部同仁的協助，我們謹致謝意。香港城市大學出版社及文物出版社大力支持給予出版，在此亦致謝意。

中國印刷博物館

Acknowledgements

This book chronicles the glorious history of printing in China. We have received wide and warm support from various quarters.

The book's illustrations enable readers to visually and systematically understand the entire process of printing in ancient China, from its origin to its later development. Representative examples of printing form the bulk of the book, providing an overview of the styles and characteristics of printing throughout various dynasties, including the level of block printing reached at those times. Historical figures who contributed to the history of printing are introduced.

The part on the origins of printing is very important, for without the various cultural developments prior to the invention of printing, printing could not have come into being. The format of this book has not been used before and since we are rather inexperienced, we wish to receive suggestions from our readers.

In editing this book for publication, we have been benefitted by the guidance and support of Mr Zhang Bohai, Mr Zhou Xinghua and Ms Yang Jin and we have also been greatly assisted by Professor Wei Zhigang and staff of the Business Section at The Printing Museum of China. Our gratitude also goes to the City University of Hong Kong Press and the Cultural Relics Publishing House for their great assistance in the production of this book.

The Printing Museum of China

目　錄

Contents

Introduction 序言

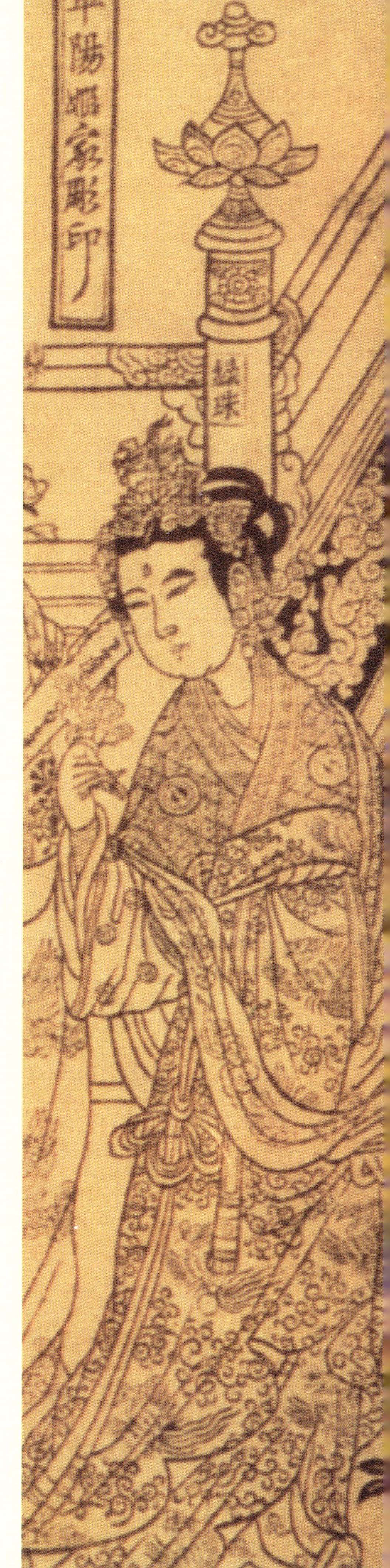

序言

印刷術是中國古代四大發明之一。它的發明、發展和向世界的傳播，對人類文明和社會進步，做出了巨大的貢獻。

本書的編輯宗旨就是以中國印刷博物館的“源頭古代館”的布展內容和時代順序為基礎，採用大量翔實的圖片資料，附以簡要的文字說明，從而更形象、更具體地再現中國印刷術的起源、發明和發展過程，使讀者更清晰地了解中國古代印刷文明和印刷文化的輝煌成就。

印刷術的發明，是文化、技藝、物質材料長期發展和積累的結果。一般認為，發明印刷術必須具備四個方面的條件：一、必須有成熟、定型、規範的文字。文字是印刷的主要對象，沒有文字的廣泛應用，就不具備發明印刷術的條件。二、必須有熟練的文字雕刻技藝，這是雕刻印版的基礎技藝。三、必須有印刷不可缺少的工具和物質材料，主要是筆墨和紙張。四、必須有社會的需要。當社會文化發展到一定水平時，讀書人越來越多了，需要大量文字、圖像的複製品，傳統的用手抄寫書籍方式，已不能滿足社會的需要，作為圖文複製的印刷術就應運而生。

文字

中國漢字經歷了長期的發展演變過程，早在新石器時代的彩陶上，就出現一些記事符號，一些專家認為這就是漢字的原始形態。公元前 13–14 世紀的商代甲骨文，已有四千多個單字，可以用來記述複雜的事件，被認為是成熟的漢字。西周時期的青銅器銘文，比甲骨文又向前發展一步，稱為大篆。秦始皇時，在簡化大篆統一文字的基礎上，發布了一種新字體，即小篆。漢代通行隸書，是漢字書體的一次較大改革。在使用隸書的同時，為了書寫方便，人們又創造了一種更簡便的書體——章草。東漢末期，出現楷書，從而完成了漢字書體的發展和演變。印刷術發明後的很長一段時期，楷書成為雕版印刷的主要字體。

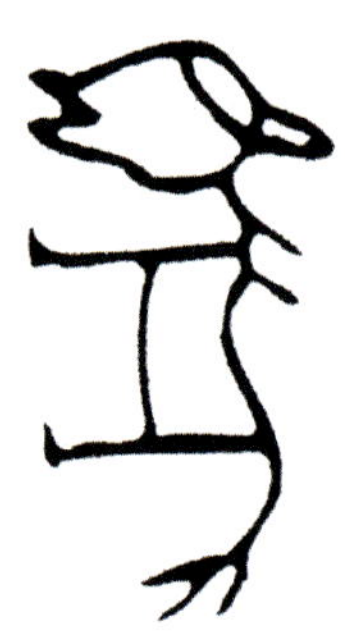
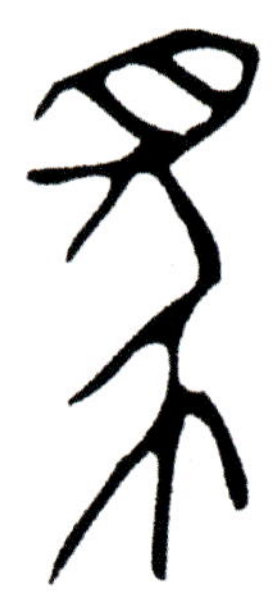
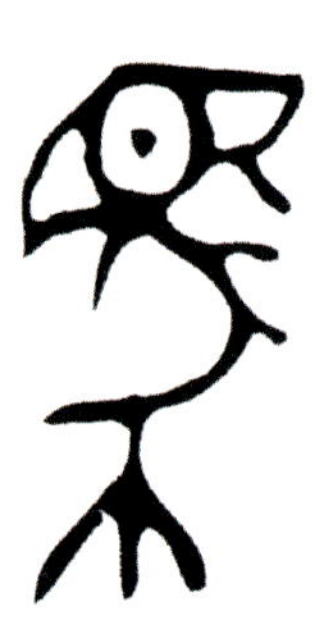
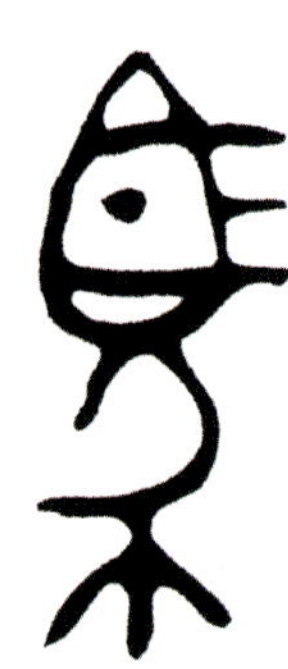

年代 Timeline	5000 BC	2000 BC	1800 BC	1600 BC	1400 BC	1200 BC
朝代 Dynasty		夏 Xia 2100–1600 BC		商 Shang 1600–1066 BC		
印刷大事 Printing in China	約公元前 4000 年 c. 4000 BC 陶器符號 Symbols on pottery	c. 2700 BC 絲之使用 Use of silk			c. 1600–1066 BC 甲骨文、印章、凸版字、銘文 Bone oracles, seals, relief characters, and stone inscriptions	
世界大事 World History	約公元前 4000 年 c. 4000 BC 新石器時代末 End of the Neolithic Age	c. 2700 BC 金字塔 Egyptian pyramids	c. 1800 BC 楔形文字(巴比倫)出現 Cuneiform writing (Babylon)	c. 1600 BC 字母(中東出現) Alphabets appear in the Middle East		1280–1250 BC 猶太人出埃及 Exodus of the Jews from Egypt

Printing is one of the four major inventions of ancient China. Its invention, development and dissemination to other parts of the world contributed significantly to human civilization and social progress.

This book is basically a pictorial record of the exhibits at the Ancient Sources Hall of The Printing Museum of China. Many pictures of other artefacts unavailable in the Museum have been added. From the artefacts and captioned illustrations, which visually and solidly show the history of Chinese printing from its origin to its later development, readers will be able to appreciate the magnificence of printing culture in the civilization of ancient China.

The invention of printing resulted from the development and accumulation of culture, techniques and materials over a long period of time. It is believed that there are four prerequisites for the invention of printing. Firstly, the existence of fixed and standardized written words. This prerequisite would not have been met in the absence of widespread use of written words. Secondly, there should be considerable experience in character-carving techniques which are the basic techniques for woodblock carving. Thirdly, there should be materials and tools for printing, namely the writing brush, ink and paper. Fourthly, there should be social needs. When a society has developed to a certain level, more people can read, and the demand for the reproduction of words and drawings increases enormously, thus giving rise to printing as traditional ways of copying books by hand failed to meet demand.

Writing System

The writing system of China went through a long process of development. As early as the New Stone Age, symbols recording events appeared on painted pottery. According to experts, these were probably the prototypes of Chinese characters. More than four thousand single characters have been found in oracle bone inscriptions of the thirteenth and fourteenth centuries B.C. They could be used to record complicated events and are believed to be mature Chinese characters. Bronze inscriptions of the Western Zhou Dynasty were a significant advancement and became known as *great-seal scripts*. During the reign of the First Emperor of Qin, efforts to unify and simplify the great-seal scripts led to the formation of a new script known as the *small-seal script*. The *clerical script* that was popular in the Han Dynasty was the result of another large-scale reform in Chinese characters. Parallel to the use of clerical script was a simpler form of script, the *running script*, which was invented to make writing more convenient. Towards the end of the Eastern Han Dynasty, the *regular script* emerged, and this completed the development of the various scripts of Chinese characters. After the invention of printing, the regular script became the major typeface for woodblock printing.

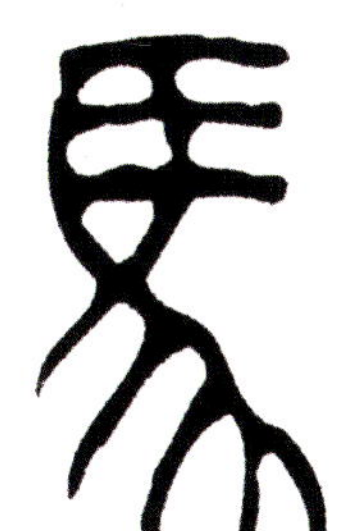

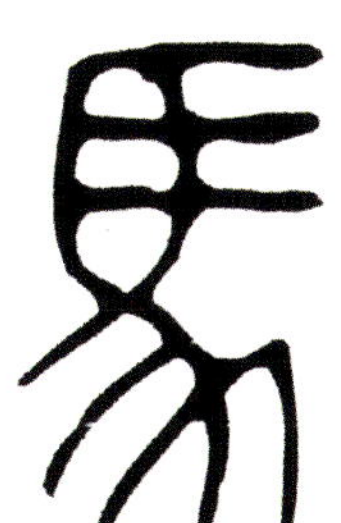

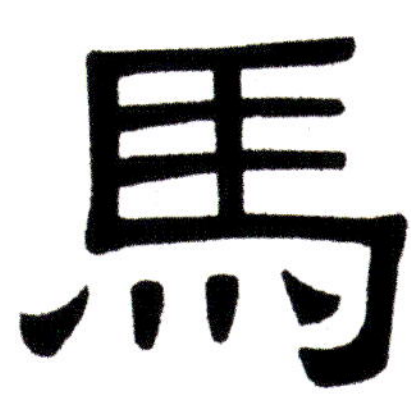

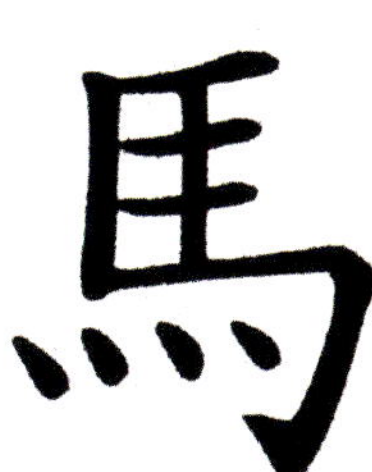

1200 BC | 1000 BC | 800 BC | 600 BC | 400 BC | 200 BC | 0

商 Shang 1600–1066 BC

西周 Western Zhou 1066–771 BC

東周 Eastern Zhou 770–256 BC

春秋 Spring and Autumn Period 722–481 BC

戰國時代 Warring States Period 403–221 BC

秦 Qin 221–206 BC

西漢 Western Han 206 BC – AD 23

c. 1066–771 BC
銅銘文、泥范、大篆
Bronze inscriptions, earthen moulds and great-seal scripts.

c. 700–476 BC
帛書出現
Words in ink written on fabrics

c. 604– c. 531 BC
老子 Lao Zi

551–479 BC
孔子
Confucius

c. 344–256 BC
《石鼓文》大篆
Great-seal script on drum-shape stones

219–212 BC
秦始皇石刻
Stone inscriptions of the Qin Emperor

c. 206 BC – AD 23
《爾雅》
Erya, the first Chinese dictionary

c. 1000 BC
絲經波斯傳入埃及
Chinese silk reaches Egypt via Persia

c. 800 BC
羊皮紙
Parchment

c. 565– c. 486 BC
釋迦牟尼
Buddha

c. 427–47 BC
柏拉圖 Plato

356–323 BC
亞歷山大大帝
Alexander the Great

c. 250 BC
埃及文書籍販賣
Egyptian books sold

59–44 BC
凱薩當權
Julius Caesar in power

雕刻技術

文字的雕刻技藝，是發明印刷術不可缺少的基礎技術，這種技術也經歷了長期發展過程。新石器時代的陶器上，就有雕刻的符號。商周時期的青銅器銘文，大多為鑄造，在澆鑄之前要製造泥笵，而泥笵文字也是雕刻而成的。

石刻文字起源於岩壁符號的雕刻。《墨子・天志》中說：“書其事於竹帛，鏤之金石，琢之盤盂，傳遺後世子孫…”可見以石刻來記載重大事件，早已有之。現存最早的石刻文字是《石鼓文》，為公元前344–256年秦國之物。它將文字刻於10個近似鼓形的石頭上，每鼓約70字。公元前219–211年，秦始皇巡遊天下，先後在嶧山、泰山、瑯玡台、芝罘、碣石等處刻石，所用字體均為小篆。

歷史上最著名的文字石刻當屬東漢的《熹平石經》，它開雕於漢靈帝熹平四年（175年），完成於光和六年（183年），共刻《易經》、《尚書》、《詩經》、《儀禮》、《春秋》、《公羊傳》、《論語》七經，計20餘萬字。《熹平石經》刻成之後，立於洛陽太學門前，供人們閱讀、傳抄和校刊，是一種傳播文化的手段。它也説明，文字雕刻技術至此已十分成熟。以後，石經的雕刻歷代不斷。著名的有魏《正始石經》，唐《開成石經》以及五代的《蜀石經》等。

在文字雕刻技術中，有一種反向字體和凸形字體。這更近似於印版的雕刻，因為印版的要求，不但文字是凸形的，而且文字是反向的。最早的反向文字的雕刻是印章，它出現於商代。早期的印章主要用於封泥，佩飾物及權力的象徵。紙張出現後，才主要用於着色鈐印。印章除了容納文字少外，其工藝已十分近似於印刷。在南北朝時期的碑刻上，出現了反向文字和陽凸文字，這説明，印刷所需要的文字雕刻技術，已經成熟。

簡策和帛書是印刷術發明前書籍的主要載體形式。中國古代的很多著作，主要靠這種形式而流傳至今。它在印刷術發明過程中，起到了積累文化和經驗的作用。

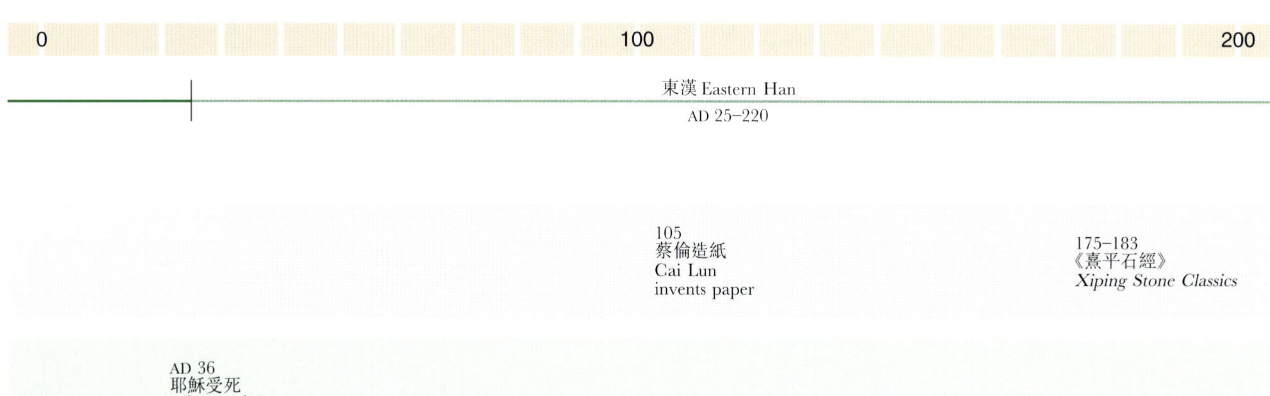

Carving Skills

The techniques of character-carving are basic skills indispensable for the invention of printing. Carving techniques have also gone through a long period of development. On the painted pottery of the New Stone Age were some carved signs. The inscriptions on the bronzes of the Shang and Zhou Dynasties were mostly made by casting. They were carved on a clay mould which was made before casting the bronze. Stone inscriptions were originated from the engraving of signs on cliffs. In the chapter entitled "The Will of Heaven" in *Mozi*, it is said that "records of bad service were written on bamboo and silk, engraved on metal and stone, inscribed on basins and bowls for transmission to posterity so that later generations would know about them." It can be seen that using stone inscriptions to keep records of important events has a long history in China. The earliest stone inscriptions existing today are the *Drum-shaped Stone Inscriptions* of the Qin State (344–256 B.C.). Each of the ten drum-shaped stones is inscribed with 70 characters. In 219–211 B.C., when the First Emperor of Qin made an inspection tour of the country, he made inscriptions on stones in Yishan, Taishan, Langyatai, Zhifu, Jieshi and other places. The type of characters he used was *small-seal script*.

The most famous stone inscriptions in history are those of the *Xiping Stone Classics*. The carving was begun in the fourth year of the Xiping period of Emperor Hanling of the Eastern Han Dynasty (A.D. 175) and was completed in the sixth year of the Guanghe period (A.D. 183). The seven classics —*The Book of Changes, The Book of History, The Book of Odes, The Book of Rites, The Spring and Autumn Annals, The Gong-Yang Commentary on the Spring and Autumn Annals*, and *The Analects of Confucius*—were inscribed, totalling more than 200,000 characters. When the *Xiping Stone Classics* were completed, the stone was erected at the main entrance of the Imperial College in the capital, Luoyang, for the public to read, copy, and to compare with other texts. The stones served as a means of cultural transmission. The event also indicates that character-engraving skills were extremely refined. From then on, stone inscriptions of the classics continued throughout the dynasties. Prominent among them are the inscriptions of the classics like the *Zhengshi Stone Classics* during the Wei Dynasty, *Kaicheng Stone Classics* during the Tang Dynasty, and *Stone Inscriptions of the State of Shu* during the Five Dynasties period.

One kind of character-carving technique is a form of reverse relief characters, similar to letterpress printing. The earliest reverse-character carving was used in seals which emerged in the Shang Dynasty. Seals were used mainly in clay-sealing and ornaments and were a symbol of power and authority. With the emergence of paper, they were used mainly for stamps. Apart from a limited number of characters, seals were very close to printing as far as the techniques are concerned. On stone tablet inscriptions of the Northern and Southern Dynasties (420–581) were some reverse relief characters along with regular ones, indicating that these techniques were already highly developed.

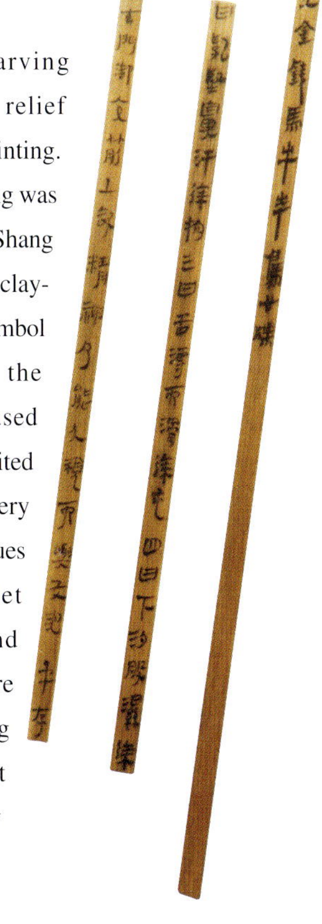

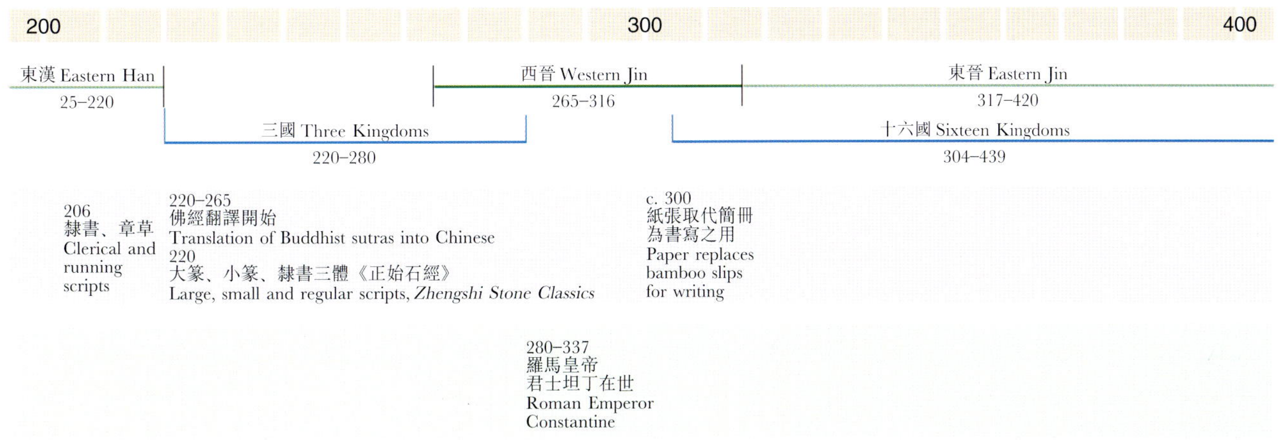

序言

物料和工具

紙張、筆、墨等是印刷的主要物料和工具。墨和筆的使用，約起源於商代。春秋戰國間，筆墨的質量大為提高，長沙左家公山戰國墓出土的毛筆，其外形和製作工藝已十分先進。

紙張的發明和推廣應用，為書籍提供了優質、輕便、廉價的載體，同時紙張也是印刷術不可缺少的承印材料。出土實物證明，早在西漢初年，就開始使用紙，西漢時期的文獻上也有用紙的記載。東漢和帝時，蔡倫改良了造紙工藝，擴大造紙原材料的範圍，造出了優質紙張。從此，紙張的使用量逐漸增大。到公元 4 世紀，紙張已經代替了簡策，成為書寫的主要材料，書籍進入了紙寫本的時代。西晉至隋代，紙寫本大量使用，使書籍的造價更低，從而加快了文化傳播的速度，促進了社會、文化的進步，為印刷術的發明，提供了良好的社會條件。至此發明印刷術的各種條件都已具備，只要社會對批量、快速複製書籍有強烈的需求，印刷術就會誕生。

印刷發明

雕版印刷術發明的具體年代，學術界還沒有統一的看法，這是因為目前最早的印刷實物，還沒有被發現。但是，根據社會文化發展的進程，以及有關的文獻記載，我們大體可以勾勒出一個輪廓，即明代胡應麟在《少室山房筆叢》中所說的："雕本肇於隋時，行於唐世"。關於唐代的雕版印刷，不但有多處文獻記載，而且有多種印刷實物流傳至今。例如，明代人邵經邦的《弘簡錄》一書中有，"太宗后長孫氏，洛陽人，……遂崩，年三十六，上為之慟。及宮司上其所撰《女則》十篇。……帝覽而嘉嘆，以後此書足垂後代，令梓行之。"這是政府使用印刷術的最早記載。此事發生在貞觀十年（636 年）。唐末馮贄《雲仙散錄》中說：玄奘"以回鋒紙印普賢像，施於四眾，每歲五馱無餘。"由此可見玄奘於貞觀十九年（645 年）取經回國後的印刷活動。佛教宣傳品用量很大，最適宜採用印刷的方法。

1974 年西安郊區出土 7 世紀初印品梵文陀羅尼經，為現存最早的印品實物。

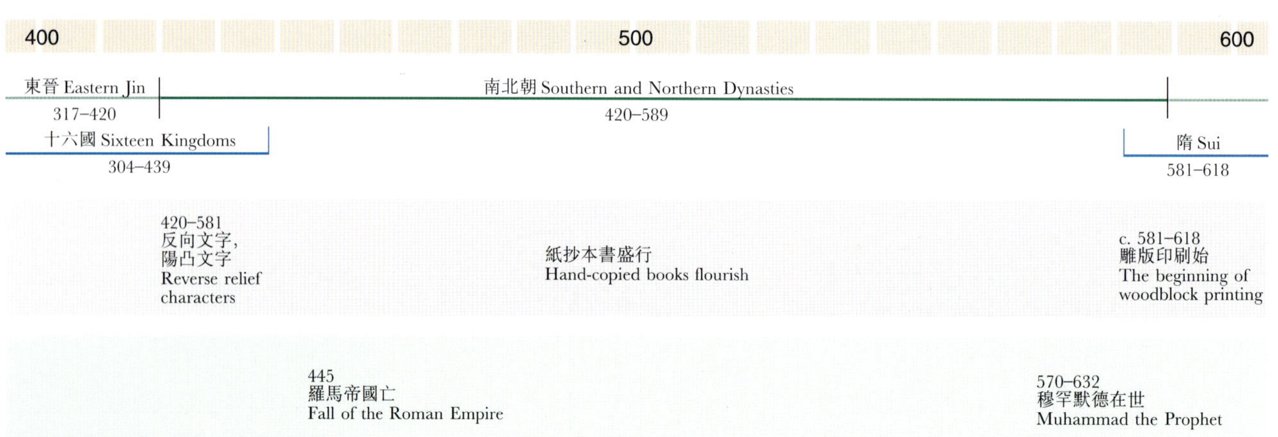

Before the invention of printing, bamboo slips and silk were the principal media used for books. Many ancient Chinese books, thanks largely to these media, have survived to the present. In the process which led to the invention of printing such books served as a fund of cultural experience.

Materials and Tools

Paper, writing brushes and ink were the major materials and tools needed for printing. The use of ink and writing brushes began around the Shang Dynasty.

During the Spring and Autumn and the Warring States periods, the quality of brushes and ink greatly improved. From the brushes unearthed from a tomb of the Warring States Period in Zuojiagong Hill, Changsha, we can see that the appearance and manufacturing technology of brushes were already very advanced.

The invention and wide application of paper provided a high quality, convenient and inexpensive medium for books. Paper also became an indispensable material for printing. Unearthed objects prove that as early as the beginning of the Western Han Dynasty, paper was already in use, and in the literature of the period the use of paper is mentioned. During the reign of Emperor Hedi of the Eastern Han Dynasty, Cai Lun improved on the paper making techniques and extended the range of raw materials for producing good quality paper. From then on, the amount of paper used gradually increased. By the fourth century, paper had replaced bamboo slips and became the major material for writing. Books entered into the era of paper. From the Western Jin Dynasty (265–316) to the Sui Dynasty (581–618), as the volume of paper books increased, their prices fell, leading to the more rapid dissemination of culture. In turn, the social and cultural progress provided the ideal social conditions for the invention of printing. With the various conditions for the invention of printing in place, all that was needed was strong demand for a large quantity and fast reproduction of books.

Invention of Printing

The exact year in which woodblock printing was invented is still very much debated in academic circles because no artefacts or documentary records related to the earliest printing have been discovered. Nevertheless, judging from the pace of social and cultural developments and relevant documentary evidence, we can draw a rough outline. As the Ming scholar Hu Yinglin puts it in his *Notes from Shaoshishan Studio*: "Woodblocks were first used in the Sui Dynasty and became popular in Tang Dynasty." As to woodblock printing in the Tang Dynasty (618–907), plenty of documentary records and printing artefacts have survived to the present. In *A History of the Tang and Song Dynasties, Including Liao, Jin and Western Xia* by Shao Jingbang of the Ming Dynasty, for example, it is recorded that "The wife of Tang Dynasty Emperor Taizong, nee Zhangsun, was a native of Luoyang. ... She passed away at the age of thirty-six and the emperor was deeply sorrowful. Palace officials later submitted to the emperor her ten essays on *Paradigm of Womanhood* ... When the emperor read them, he praised her and believed that the book could set a good example for posterity, so he ordered that the essays be printed." This is the earliest record of the official use of printing. The incident took place in the tenth year of the period Zhenguan (636).

Feng Zhi of late Tang said in his *Notes by Yunxian* that "Xuan Zang used *huifeng* paper to print *Portraits of the Various Saints* and distributed them free to the public. Each year, five packs were distributed and none remained." Xuan Zang undertook this printing work after he returned to China with Buddhist scriptures in the nineteenth year of the Zhenguan period (645). Given the large amount of Buddhist promotional materials, printing was the most appropriate method of reproduction.

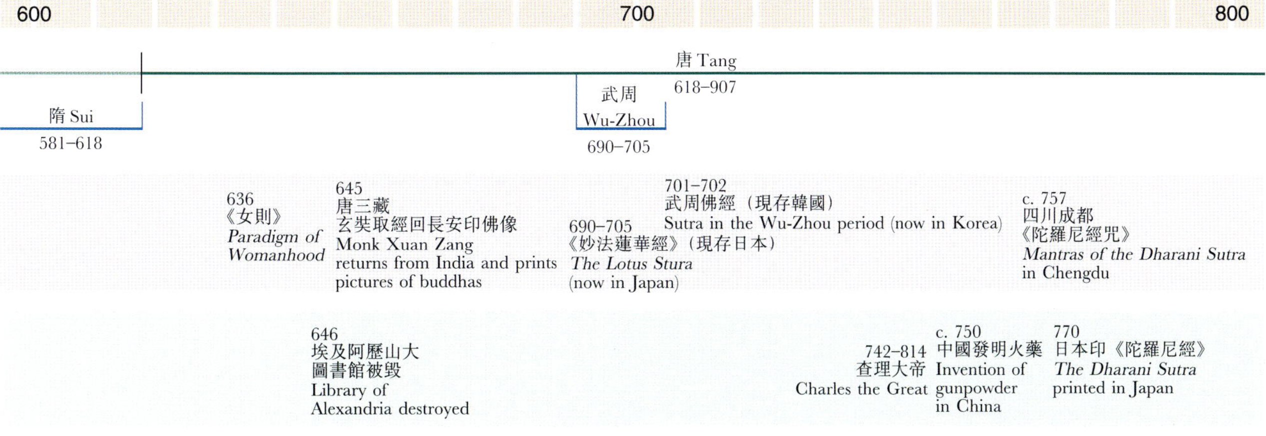

早期印刷文物

關於早期的印刷品實物，流傳至今者十分稀少。至今發現的早期印刷品為《妙法蓮華經》卷五、《如來佛壽品第十六》殘卷及《分別功德品第十七》全卷。此印經於1906年發現於中國新疆吐魯番，現藏於日本。據有關學者考證，此印經為武周時期之物。1966年於韓國慶州佛國寺釋迦塔內發現一件雕版印刷品《無垢淨光大陀羅尼經》，此印經內使用了幾個武周制字。據我國學者多人考證，此經為武周末年（701–702年）於中國洛陽刻印，隨後傳至新羅。唐代的雕版印刷品流傳至今的還有：成都唐墓出土的成都府成都縣龍池坊卞家雕印的《陀羅尼經咒》，約為唐至德二年（757年）前後刻印。咸通九年（868年）王玠刻印了《金剛經》。這一時間民間刻印的曆書，有多種實物流傳至今。從以上文獻記載和實物流傳證明，雕版印刷術是中國古代的偉大發明，"肇於隋時，行於唐世"的說法是可信的。

唐代中後期，出現了印刷術發明後的第一次高潮，除佛教界最積極使用印刷術外，道家也開始印書。印刷地域也從京城長安、東都洛陽，發展到四川、淮南、敦煌等地。民間印刷業也開始興盛。據文獻記載，當時四川、淮南一帶，民間大量刻印日曆，在市場上銷售，政府曾下令禁止民間印刷日曆。柳玭於唐中和三年（883年）親自見到在成都的書肆上，有各種印刷品出售，其中有：陰陽雜記、占夢、相宅、九宮、五緯、字書、小學等。可見當時印書的品種很多。

五代十國時期（907–960年），雖然出現各地割據，朝代更迭頻繁的動亂局面，但印刷術的應用，仍在擴大，佛經、佛像的刻印仍十分興盛。但最能代表這一時期印刷發展特點的是，政府開始組織大量刻印儒家經典總集《九經》。發起組織這一刻印工程的是歷任五朝宰相的馮道。在他的倡導下，經最高統治者的批准，自後唐長興三年（932年）起，至後周廣順三年（953年）止，歷時22年，完成了這一巨大的印書工程。所刻印的書包括了儒家的九種經典和《經典釋文》。五代時，另一位組織刻印較多書籍的是任蜀國宰相的毋昭裔。他自己出資雇工刻印了《文選》、《初學記》、《白氏六帖》等書。他還經蜀主孟昶批准，組織刻印過《九經》及歷史著作。五代的這些印書活動，為宋代印刷的擴大和發展創造了條件。

800 … 900

唐 Tang
618–907

835
四川民間曆書
Almanacs from Sichuan

868
王玠印《金剛經》
Wang Jie's prints
The Diamond Sutra
Earliest complete book extant

883
成都書市
(柳玭)
Book market in Chengdu
(Liu Pin)

806
日本僧空海回國並創
日本文字平假名
Japanese monk returns to Japan after three years in China and invents *Kana* script

890
維京人入侵英國
Viking invasion of England

Relics of Early Prints

Actual examples of early printed materials which have survived to the present are extremely rare. The earliest publications discovered to date are Volume 5 of the *Saddharma Pundarika Sutra* and the entire volume of *Different Merits Sutra No. 17*. This printed sutra was discovered in Turpan in Xinjiang, China in 1906 and is now in Japan. According to the study of some scholars, this printed sutra dates from the period of Wu-Zhou (690–705). In 1966, a Wu-Zhou woodblock-carved publication entitled *Dharani Sutra*, in which a few words of the Wu-Zhou Dynasty administration were used, was found in the Sokka Pagoda at Pulguk-sa Monastery in Kyongju, Korea. According to several scholars in China, this sutra was printed in the late Wu-Zhou period (circa 701–702) in Luoyang, China and later found its way to Xin Luo (ancient Korea). Other woodblock-carved publications from the Tang Dynasty that are extant today include such works as *Mantras of the Dharani Sutra*, carved by the Bian family around the second year of the Zhide period (757) and unearthed in a Tang-period tomb at the Dragon Pool Square in Chengdu, and the *Diamond Sutra* carved by Wang Jie in the ninth year of the Xiantong period (868). Many almanacs of those days survived to today. The above documentary records and artefacts prove that woodblock carving was a great invention in ancient China and that the statement that "printing began in the Sui Dynasty and became popular in the Tang Dynasty" is a credible one.

In the latter part of the Tang Dynasty, printing reached its first high tide since its invention. Apart from the Buddhists who actively used printing, the Taoists also began to print books. The production centres of printing also spread from the capital city of Chang'an and Luoyang (the eastern capital) to places such as Sichuan, Huainan, and Dunhuang. Private printing houses also began to prosper. According to documentary records, at that time, in the areas of Sichuan and Huainan, private printers published a large number of almanacs that were sold in the market, but then the government passed a law prohibiting people from printing the almanacs. In the third year of the Zhonghe period (883), Liu Pin recorded that he personally saw in the bookshops of Chengdu various kinds of publications on sale, including books on *yinyang*, divination by interpreting dreams, *fengshui*, music scores, and the five fortune telling texts, wordbooks, and philology. From this can be seen the great variety of books printed at that time.

During the Five Dynasties and Ten Kingdoms Period (907–960), despite the disunity caused by rival principalities and the chaotic situation created by the frequent changes of dynasties, the scope of printing kept expanding, and the printing of Buddhist scriptures and Buddhist images was still extremely popular. But the feature which best represented the development of printing in this period was that the government began to coordinate the mass printing of a collection of Confucian classics, known as *The Nine Classics*. The person who initiated this organized effort to print the classics was Feng Dao, who served as prime minister for five short-lived dynasties. Under his guidance, and with the approval of the highest rulers, the huge endeavour began in the third year of the Changxing period of the Later Tang Dynasty (932) and ended in the third year of the Guangshun period of the Later Zhou Dynasty (953), a period of 22 years. The books printed included the nine classics of the Confucian school and *Explanations and Glosses of the Classics*. During the Five Dynasties period, another person who organized the printing of a considerable number of books was Wu Zhaoyi, the Prime Minister of the state of Shu. He personally bore the cost of hiring people to print A *General Anthology of Prose and Verse*, *A Primer for Learning* and *Bai's Six Models of Calligraphy*. He also sought the approval of Meng Chang, the King of Shu, and organized the printing of *The Nine Classics* and historical writings. These book printing activities during the Five Dynasties created the conditions

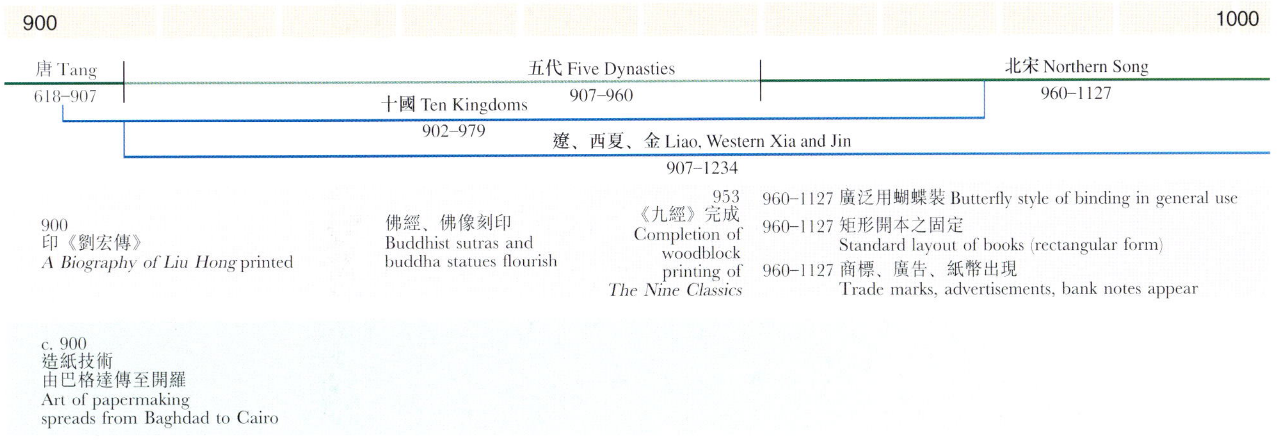

宋代（960–1279年）

宋代的印刷業十分興盛，主要標誌是：政府部門從中央到地方大都從事過印書活動，民間印刷業規模擴大，印坊遍及各地，形成了建寧、杭州、益州、江西等幾個印刷業較集中的地區；印刷品種齊全，經、史、子、集各類書都有印刷；佛經印刷規模擴大，多次刻印佛經總集；除書籍印刷外，還出現了紙幣印刷和商標廣告印刷等新品種。

宋代雕版印刷技術已達到很高水平。歷代版本學家認為，宋版書雕版精良、紙質上乘、墨色醇厚。在書籍的裝幀工藝方面，廣泛使用蝴蝶裝，從而開創了書籍的冊頁矩形開本的裝幀形式。

宋代在印刷技術上的重大貢獻是活字版的發明。據沈括《夢溪筆談》一書記載，北宋慶曆年間（1041–1048年）布衣畢昇用活字版印書。這一發明，開創了活字版印刷的歷史，是印刷史上的偉大里程碑。

與宋同時的還有遼、西夏、金等幾個少數民族建立的政權。這些地區的印刷水平，與中原及南方地區的水平相似，在某些方面還有所突破。近年山西應縣木塔內發現了一批遼代印刷品，除著名的《契丹藏》外，還有其他書籍，從刊印質量看，已經達到很高的水平。其中有幾幅印刷敷彩佛像，是經印刷黑白輪廓綫條後，再以手工塗彩而成，是迄今發現最早的紙印刷敷彩工藝。金代的印刷業也很繁榮，最著名的是平陽的印刷業，當時，這裏集中了幾十家印刷作坊，還有一批刻版工匠被寺院所雇用，刻印佛經。平陽的印刷品，幾乎包括經、史、子、集等各門類，而以醫學類書最為著名。這裏所刻印的《金藏》，是北方地區繼《遼藏》之後，又一部規模宏大的佛經總集。平陽的圖版雕刻技藝也很精良，平陽姬家刻印的《四美圖》，刻工精細，綫條流暢，人物生動，被認為是現存最早的家庭裝飾畫。

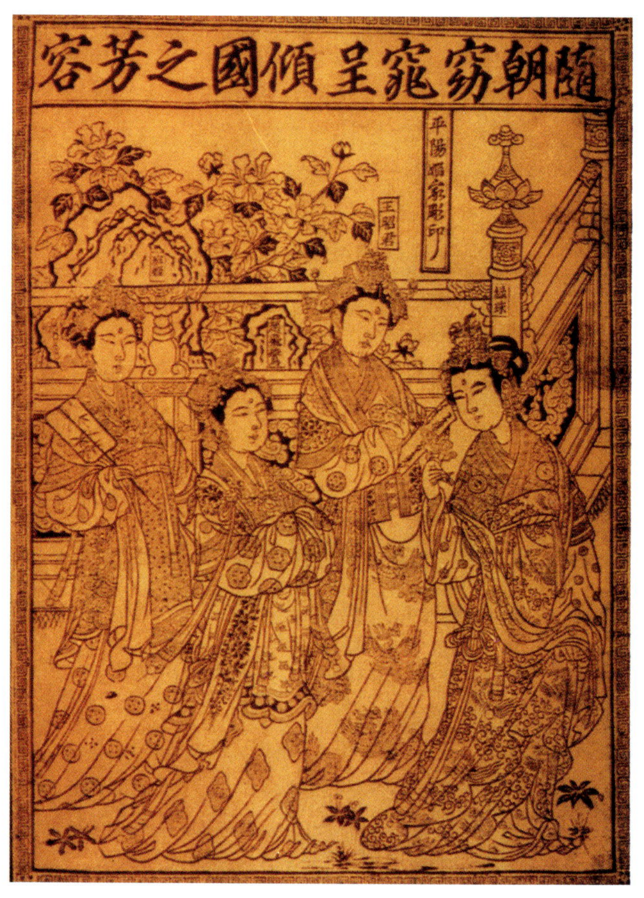

1000	1100

北宋 Northern Song
960–1127

遼、西夏、金 Liao, Western Xia and Jin
907–1234

1023
紙幣由中央銀行印刷
Issue of money centralized by government banks

1041–1048
沈括提及畢昇用活字
Bi Sheng's use of movable type mentioned by Shen Kuo

1066–1084
司馬光編《資治通鑑》
Compilation of *Comprehensive Mirror to Aid in Government* by Sima Guang

1001
維京人由格陵蘭航抵北美洲紐芬蘭
Leif Erikson sails from Greenland to Newfoundland

1066
諾曼人征服英國
Norman Conquest of England

for the expansion and development of printing in the Song Dynasty.

Song Dynasty (960–1279)

The printing industry thrived during the Song Dynasty. Government departments from the central to the local level engaged in printing activities. The private printing industry expanded, leading to the existence of printing houses throughout the country, and the creation of a few areas of concentration such as at Jianning, Hangzhou, Yizhou and Jiangxi. All types of texts were printed including Confucian classics, history, philosophy and *belles-lettres*. The scale of Buddhist publications was considerably larger and collections of Buddhist scriptures were printed several times. Apart from the printing of books, new items appeared, including the printing of paper money and trademark advertisements.

Techniques of woodblock printing in the Song Dynasty reached a high level of achievement. Throughout the following dynasties, printing plate specialists recognized the fine quality of the plates, the high grade paper, and the richness of the colour found in Song printing plates. As regards the craft of bookbinding, the butterfly style was widely used, which in turn gave rise to the rectangular format of binding found in painting and calligraphy albums.

An important revolution of printing technology of the Song Dynasty was the invention of movable-type printing. According to Shen Kuo's *Dream Pool Jottings*, a commoner by the name of Bi Sheng used movable-type blocks for printing during the Qingli years (1041–1048) of the Northern Song. This invention ushered in an era of movable-type printing and is a significant milestone in the history of printing.

Contemporary with the Song Dynasties were the regimes of ethnic minorities such as the Liao, Western Xia and Jin. The level of printing in these areas was on a par with that of Central and Southern China. In some respects, breakthroughs were also made. In recent years, a batch of publications of the Liao Dynasty (907–1125) was found in a wooden pagoda in Ying County, Shanxi Province. Apart from the famous *Qidan Tripitaka*, there were other books and, judging from the quality of printing, a very high level was attained. Among them were a few hand-coloured Buddha images. The colour was painted by hand after the black and white outlines had been printed. To date, this is the earliest colour application technique for printing on paper. Printing in the Jin Dynasty (1115–1234) also flourished, with the most famous printing industry found in Pingyang. At that time, several dozen printing houses concentrated in this city, and artisans were also employed by temples to engrave blocks for printing Buddhist scriptures. Publications produced in Pingyang included classics, history, philosophy, *belle-lettres* as well as other topics, but Pingyang became famous for its medical texts. Following the *Liao Tripitaka* of the Northern Region, the *Jin Tripitaka* was another large-scale collection

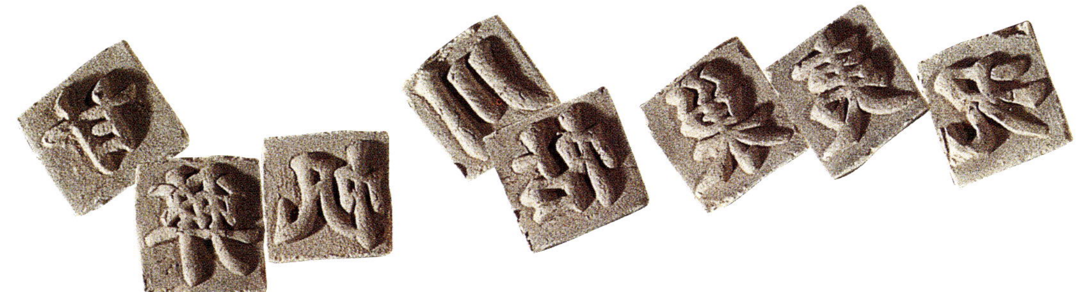

1100 1200

北宋 Northern Song 960–1127

南宋 Southern Song 1127–1279

遼、西夏、金 Liao,Western Xia and Jin 907–1234

1107
套色紙幣印行
Bank notes in multiple colours

1115–1234
（金代）早期出版之醫書
Early medical book in China (Jin Dynasty)
c. 1115
金代平陽印《四美圖》
Picture of Four Beauties printed in Pingyang, during the Jin Dynasty

1193
《玉堂雜記》
最早之銅版活字印本
Earliest book printed with bronze moveable type

1100–1109
造紙生產術傳至摩洛哥
Papermaking techniques spreads to Morocco

1150
歐洲第一間
造紙作坊（西班牙）
First papermaking workshop in Europe (Spain)

1189
法國建立造紙廠
First government papermaking workshop in France

都城設於興慶府（今寧夏銀川）的西夏國，是黨項族建立的政權，西夏建國初期，經常從南宋和金購買書籍，後來他們也從事印刷。所刻印的書籍除佛經外，還有曆書、字書、史書、醫書及詩文集等。1991年，於寧夏賀蘭縣拜寺溝方塔中，發現了西夏文佛經《吉祥遍至口合本續》9冊，為蝴蝶裝。經考古學家研究和有關專家鑑定確認，此件為西夏後期（即12世紀下半葉）木活字版印本。這一印本是現存最早的木活字版印本。在中國古代印刷發展史上具有重要意義。

元代（1271–1368年）

元朝的建立，使中國又出現了統一的局面，印刷業有了進一步發展。北方的主要印刷基地在平陽和大都，南方仍以杭州、建陽為中心。在今天江蘇、江西及兩湖地區，也分布着較多的印刷作坊。由於國家的統一，為印刷術向偏遠地區的傳播創造了條件，在今西藏、新疆等地也有一定規模的印刷業。

元代學校的印刷十分活躍，最有名的是西湖書院，它除存有南宋國子監的印版外，還在各地收集了大量印版，所印書量很大。學校印刷的另一特點是幾所學校聯合，分工刻印大部頭書籍。這樣可以在較短時間內完成整部書的印刷。例如大德年間，由江東九路儒學分工刻印了《十七史》，大約兩年多就完成了這一龐大工程。其中太平路儒學承印的《漢書》，共刻版2775塊，只用了八個月就完成了。為使各家所印的書形式統一，還規定了統一規格的版式和開本尺寸。

元代在印刷技術方面也有很大的發展，最主要的有：一、在書籍裝訂方面，繼蝴蝶裝之後，又出現了包背裝，這種形式使書籍的裝幀又向前發展了一步。二、雙色套印源於宋代，但只見記載，未見實物，元至正元年（1341年），中興路資福寺刻印的《金剛經注》，為朱墨雙色套印。三、出現了配有插圖的書籍封面。

元代在印刷技術方面最大的成就是王禎對木活字版工藝的改革。他在任旌德縣尹期間（1298年）雇工刻木活字，設計了轉輪排字盤，按韻存放活字，並用這種工藝排印了《旌德縣志》。他將自己對木活字工藝的改良，寫成《造活字印書法》一文，附入所著《農書》中。這是最早記述木活字工藝的著作。在王禎之前不久還有人使用過錫活字，這可能是歷史上最早的金屬活字。

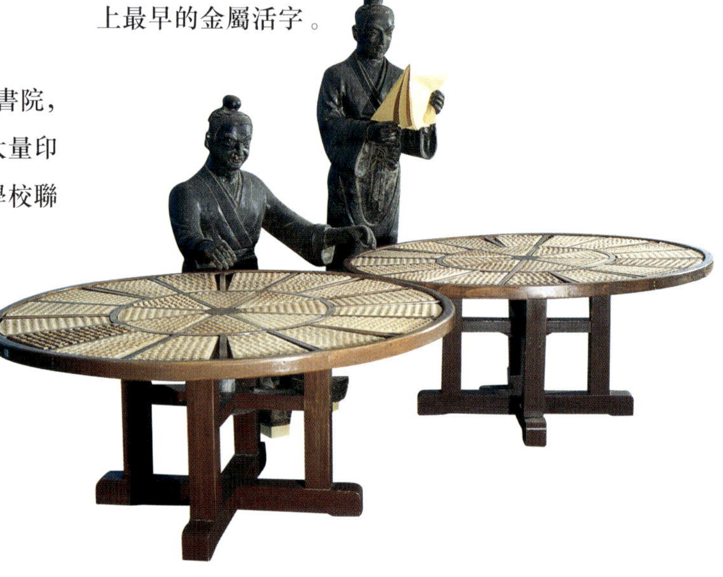

1200 — 1300

南宋 Southern Song 1127–1279

遼、西夏、金 Liao, Western Xia and Jin 907–1234

元 Yuan 1271–1368

c. 1200
西夏文佛經《吉祥遍至口合本續》
為現存最早之木活字版印本
Propitiousness Has Spread to Everywhere
is the earliest book printed with wooden movable type

12世紀末
回鶻文木活字
Wooden movable-type in Uighur script, end of 12th century

1279–1368
合作印書之始（各路儒學）
Collaborative production of large sets of books (at different academies)

1215
英國大憲章簽署
Magna Carta signed

1250–1533
印加帝國（秘魯）
Inca Empire (Peru)

of Buddhist books printed in Pingyang. The graphic carving craft of Pingyang was also extremely sophisticated. *A Picture of Four Beauties* carved by the Ji family in Pingyang, and believed to be the earliest extant decorative family drawing, showed meticulous craftmanship with its graceful lines and lifelike figures.

Western Xia, whose captial was located in Xingqing (present-day Yinchuan, Ningxia), was established by the Dangxiang tribe. In the early period of its establishment, Western Xia frequently bought books from the Southern Song and the Jin areas. Later, they also engaged in the business of printing. Besides the Buddhist scriptures, they also printed almanacs, wordbooks, history books, medical books, and collections of poetry and essays. In 1991, a nine-volume Buddhist scripture entitled *Propitiousness Has Spread to Everywhere*, which was written in Western Xia characters and bound in butterfly format, was found in a square pagoda at Baishigou in Helan County, Ningxia Autonomous Region. Archaeologists and experts have determined that these volumes were printed in the latter part of the Western Xia (second half of the 12th century) using wooden movable type. This scripture has been taken to be the earliest extant example of wooden movable-type printing and it occupies an important position in the history of Chinese printing.

Yuan Dynasty (1271–1368)

With the founding of the Yuan Dynasty, China was again reunified, and great strides were made in printing. In the north, major printing areas centred around Pingyang and Dadu; while in the south, Hangzhou and Jianyang remained the important centres. There were also a number of printing houses scattered across the areas of present-day Suzhou, Jiangxi, Hunan and Hubei. Owing to the national unity, favourable conditions existed for the spread of printing to remote areas. Areas such as present-day Tibet and Xinjiang also had sizeable printing industries.

In the Yuan Dynasty, printing in academies was extremely active. Most famous of all was the West Lake Academy, which, in addition to storing the woodblocks of the National Academy of the Southern Song, also collected a large number of printing plates and published a huge volume of books. Another characteristic of academy printing was that several of them joined forces and divided the labour in the printing of voluminous works. This allowed shorter time to complete the printing of the entire work. During the Dade period, for example, nine routes of Confucian scholars divided work among themselves and carved and printed *The Seventeen Dynastic Histories*, thereby taking a little more than two years to complete this enormous task. The Taiping Route of Confucian scholars were responsible for the printing of *The History of Han*. They carved 2,775 plates and it took them only eight months to complete the work. To achieve unity in the books printed by the various branches, a united format, layout and book-size were stipulated.

Great progress was made in printing techniques during the Yuan Dynasty. Some of the major improvements were: Firstly, in bookbinding, following the butterfly binding, there emerged the wrapped-ridge binding, which pushed bookbinding a step further. Secondly, while two-colour printing originated in the Song Dynasty, there are only documentary records and no actual examples of this. But in the first year of the Zhizheng period (1341) of the Yuan Dynasty, the *Commentaries on the Diamond Sutra* was carved by the Zifu Temple in the Zhongxing Route, and was printed in red and black. Thirdly, book jackets with illustrations appeared in the Yuan Dynasty.

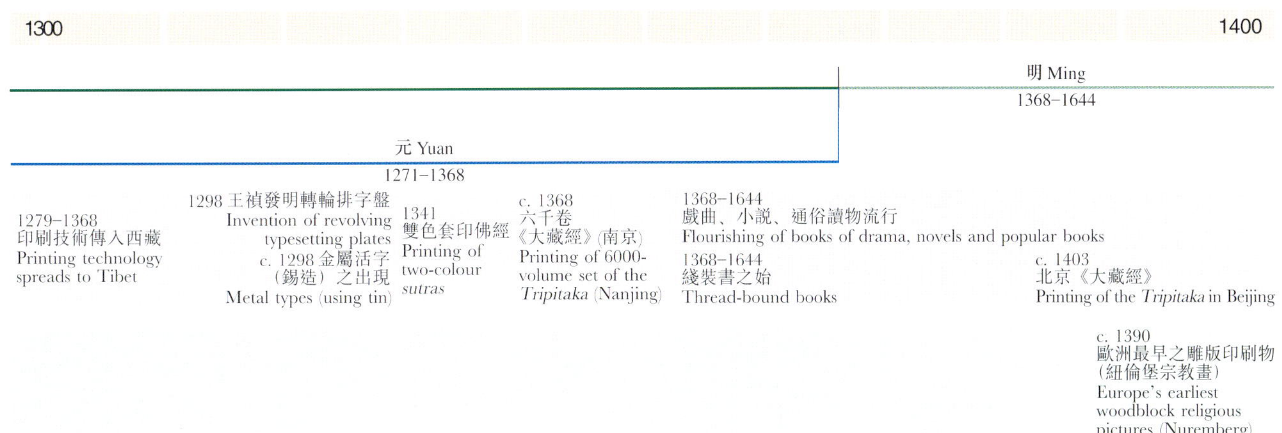

明代（1368-1644年）

明代是中國印刷史上最輝煌的時代，其主要標誌是：一、前代所開創的雕版、木活字版、金屬活字版、整體金屬版、多色套印技術等，在明代都有應用，而技藝更為精湛。二、紙墨及雕版技藝等都達到前所未有的水平。三、印刷的規模、品種和數量達到歷史最高水平。除經、史、子、集等傳統書籍大量印刷外，地方誌、科技書、技藝類書、通俗讀物、啟蒙讀物、戲曲、小説等也大量印刷。四、印刷專用字體——宋體字更為成熟，並廣泛應用。五、首創木版彩色印刷，並完善了這一工藝。

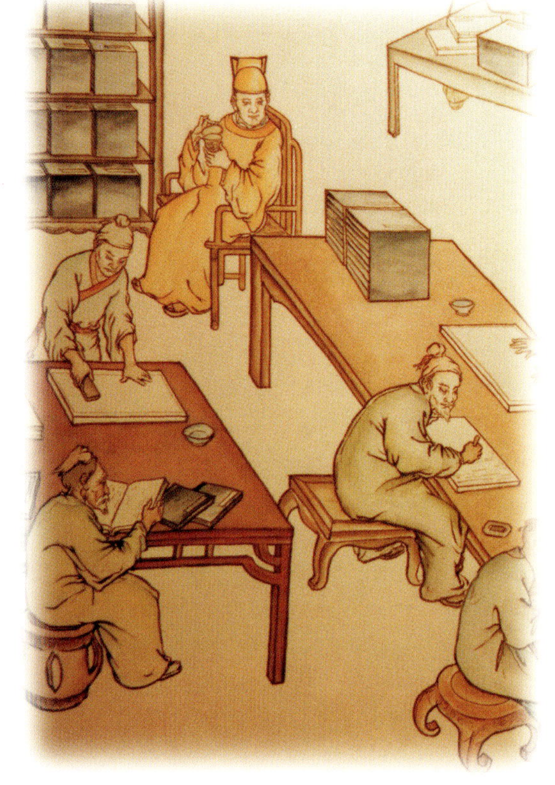

明代政府的最大印刷工場為司禮監經廠，永樂十九年（1421年）開始建立，到嘉靖年間，已有刻版、刷印、裝訂、製墨、製筆等工匠近1,000人，是歷史上最大的印刷工場。政府的很多出版物，都由經廠承印。欽天監也設有印刷作坊，主要承印每年度的曆書樣本。國子監也是政府的主要印書機構。有南京國子監和北京國子監，南監規模比北監大，它收集了元代西湖書院以及各儒學的存版，再加上新刻本朝書，所印書籍約有270多種。北監刻印書籍約有85種，著名的是《十三經注疏》和《二十一史》。

明代的宗教印刷規模很大，最著名的有明初刻印於南京的《大藏經》和永樂年間刻印於北京的《大藏經》，萬曆年間又刻印《藏文大藏經》，其規模都超過6,000卷。正統年間，還刻印了《道藏經》，計5,000多卷。

藩王府印書是明代的特有現象。由於這些藩王多無實際職務，又有較多資金，因而著作、刻印書籍成風。據不完全統計，各藩王刻印書籍超過500多種。有些書如棋書、樂書、茶書等，填補了書籍品種的空白。地方誌的印刷起源於宋代，到明代形成一種風氣。各地區，各州縣幾乎都刻印了當地的方誌。由於這些書籍的出版，留下了大量珍貴的歷史資料。

1400 — 1500

明 Ming
1368–1644

1404–1408
《永樂大典》
古代最大之百科全書
The Yongle Encyclopedia,
largest in ancient China

1444–1447
《正統道藏》
最早之道教總匯
The Taoist Tripitaka,
earliest complete
collection of Taoist texts

1452–1519
達芬奇在世
（佛羅倫薩）
Leonardo da Vinci
(Florence)

1455
古騰堡聖經
Gutenberg Bible

1457
歐洲雙色印刷（紅、藍）
Colour printing in Europe (Peter Shoeffer)

1492
哥倫布
發現美洲大陸
Columbus
arrives in America

The greatest achievement in the printing techniques of the Yuan Dynasty was Wang Zhen's innovation of the wooden movable type technology. When he served as magistrate in Shengde County (1298), he hired people to carve movable wooden types, and designed a revolving typesetting plate to store the movable types according to the order of the rhymes. He made use of this technique to typeset and print *The Annals of Shengde County*. Wang Zhen wrote about his improvements to the craft of wooden movable type printing in his article "Making Movable Types to Print Books," which was included in his book *A Treatise on Agriculture*. This is the earliest work recording wooden movable type technology. Not too long before Wang Zhen's time, some people also used tin movable type, possibly the earliest use of metal movable type in history.

Ming Dynasty (1368–1644)

The Ming Dynasty (1368–1644) is the most glorious period in the history of printing in China. The main indications of this include: Firstly, all the inventions of previous dynasties — woodblock carving, wooden movable type, metal movable type, whole metal plates, and techniques of multi-colour printing — were used in the Ming Dynasty, and, moreover, the technical skills became exquisite. Secondly, paper, ink and woodblock carving techniques attained an unprecedented standard.Thirdly, the scope, variety and volume of printing reached the highest level in history. Besides printing traditional books, such as the classics, history, philosophy and *belle-lettres,* in large quantities, the gazetteers, books on science and technology, books on craftsmanship, popular readers, primers, plays, and novels were also printed in great number. Fourthly, the type of characters used specially for printing — the Song typeface — became more refined and was widely used. Fifthly, with the invention of woodblock colour printing, the craft of printing was perfected.

The largest printing house operated by the Ming court was the factory run by the Directorate of Ceremonies. Construction of the factory began in the nineteenth year of the Yongle period (1421), and by the Jiajing period, it had around one thousand artesans working on woodblocks, printing, binding, ink-making and brush-making. It was the largest printing factory in Chinese history. Many government publications were put out by the factory. The Imperial Observatory also had a printing house whose main duty was to print the annual sample almanac. The National Academy was also the government's major book-printing unit. The Academy was divided into the Nanjing National Academy and the Beijing National Academy, and the former was larger in size than the latter. The Nanjing National Academy collected the printing plates made during the Yuan Dynasty at the West Lake Academy and the Confucian works extant. Combined with the newly printed books of the Ming Dynasty, there were more than 270 series of printed books. The Beijing National Academy carved and printed about 85 series of books, of which the most famous were *Commentaries on the Thirteen Classics* and *The Twenty-one Dynastic Histories*.

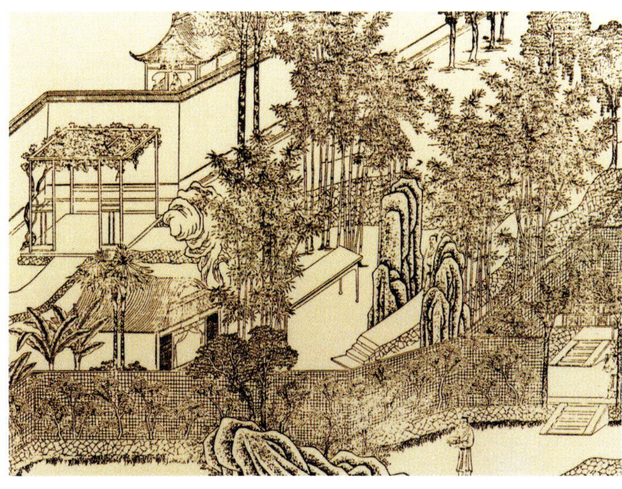

1500 1600

明 Ming
1368–1644

1502
拉丁美洲第一間
印刷所（墨西哥）
First printing workshop
in Latin America (Mexico)

1543
哥白尼出版
《天體運行論》
Copernican
revolution
in astronomy

1564–1642
伽利略在世
Galileo Galilei

1567–1619
印刷體
(宋體)出現
"Song typeface"
appeared

1573–1619
《藏文大藏經》
(萬曆年間)
Tibetan Tripitaka
(during the
Wanli period)

1584
利瑪竇出版
《畸人十規》(中文)
Jesuit M. Ricci
published his book in Chinese

1596–97
日本最早木活字
字版書藉
Earliest wooden
movable-type
book in Japan

明代的民間印刷規模宏大，除原有的印刷基地外，南京、蘇州、北京等地也成為新興的印刷基地。民間所需的各種戲曲小說、通俗讀物、啟蒙讀物等，得到了大量印刷。書籍的流通更為活躍，發行到全國各地。

明代在印刷技術上的新突破，是首創了木版彩色印刷，它採用分色勾描，分色刻版，逐色套印的工藝，印出近似於原作的彩色圖畫。明代中期，徽派刻印工匠，首先在一整塊圖版上，刷塗不同的顏色，一次刷印出彩色印刷品。但用這種方法印出的印刷品，效果還不理想。明代後期，畫家胡正言與徽派工匠合作，採用餖版方法，刻印了《十竹齋畫譜》四卷，隨後又刻印了《十竹齋箋譜》，在《箋譜》中，首次使用了拱花技術，這是一種無色壓凸印刷。

明代的書籍裝幀，已由包背裝演變為綫裝，使書籍的裝幀形式更為完美。

清代（1644–1911年）

清代是中國古代印刷事業發展的又一個高峰期。首先是印刷規模的擴大。清代逐漸形成了從中央到地方、從作坊到私家的出版印書網。除了大量印刷出版歷代典籍外，還印刷了大量當代的著作。據有關出版史、書史、版本學和目錄學文獻的記載，有清一代，所印書籍的品種和數量，都遠遠超過以往任何時代。其次是印刷技術的發展和印刷工藝的改進。我國古代發明和發展的各種印刷技術，在清代都有使用，有些技術還有所改進和發展。特別是活字版印刷，不但使用比例大大超過任何時代，而且各種活字都有使用。木活字、銅活字、泥活字等都達到很高的技術水平。雕版彩色印刷不但更普及，而且印刷質量更精美。年畫印刷發展成為一個規模很大的行業門類，印刷網點遍及全國很多地區，印刷產品進入千家萬戶，使印刷產品的普及率達到歷史的最高水平。因此，就傳統的印刷技術應用而言，清代實際上達到了頂峰。

清政府的編印機構是武英殿。清順治年間，主要使用明朝沿用之經廠所留下的技術力量，以雕版印刷為主。康熙後期，開始製作銅活字，到雍正年間，完成了《古今圖書集成》的排印。乾隆年間，武英殿在金簡主持下，刻製棗木活字大小各一副，共25萬個，用以排印了《武英殿聚珍版叢書》。金簡所編的《武英殿聚珍版程式》一書，全面介紹了武英殿木活字工藝技術，是古代珍貴的印刷技術專著。

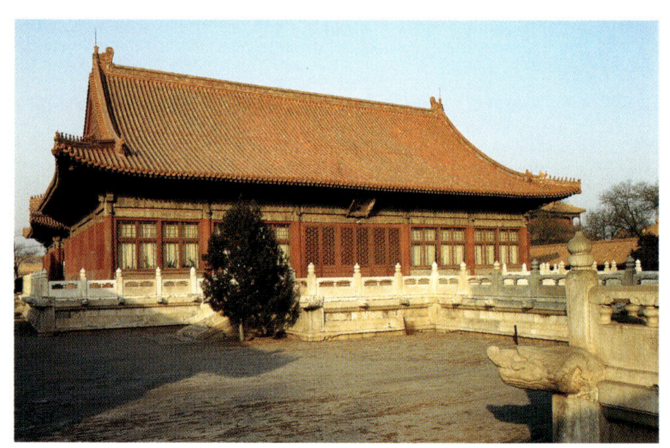

1600 — 1650

明 Ming
1368–1644

1596
李時珍《本草綱目》
Li Shizhen's medical book, *The Great Pharmacopoeia*

1603–1607
徐光啟與利馬竇合譯《幾何原理》出版
Translation and publication of a geometry book into Chinese by M. Ricci and Xu Guangqi

c. 1600 各種裝幀完備
Bookbinding methods well developed

1620
西方最早官方出版社（路易十三）
First royal printer in Europe (Louis XIII)

1627–44
胡正言彩印《十竹齋畫譜》
Hu Zhengyan prints his *Painting Manual of the Ten-bamboo Studio* in colour

1638
美國最早之印刷所
S. Day's printshop in Cambridge (Mass.), first in America

c. 1644
拱花技術之使用
Bind stamping technique used

1645–1660
英國革命
Cromwell and the English Revolution

The scale of religious printing in the Ming Dynasty was very large. The most famous works included *The Chinese Tripitaka* printed in Nanjing during the early Ming, *The Chinese Tripitaka* printed in Beijing during the Yongle years, and *The Tibetan Tripitaka*, printed during the Wanli years. The size of each of the above exceeded six thousand volumes. During the Zhengtong years, *The Taoist Tripitaka*, containing more than five thousand volumes, was printed.

Printing by Provincial Commanders' Offices was a phenomenon characteristic of the Ming Dynasty. As most of these commanders did not have any real administrative responsibilities and as they were wealthy, it became a fashion for them to engage in writing and printing. According to some incomplete statistics, the provincial commanders printed more than five hundred books. Some of these were books on chess, music and tea, adding variety to the books printed. The publication of local gazetteers originated in the Song Dynasty, and became a fashion in the Ming. Districts and prefectures all printed their own gazetteers. Thanks to the publication of these books, a large amount of valuable historial material has been passed on.

The scale of private printing in the Ming was also large. Besides the old centres, places such as Nanjing, Suzhou and Beijing emerged as new centres. Types of books read by the masses, such as dramatic novels and musicals, popular literature and primers, were printed in large quantities. The circulation of books became more dynamic and they were distributed to places throughout the country. A breakthrough that came during the Ming Dynasty was the creation of woodblock colour printing. It used the techniques of colour separation delineation, colour separation block engraving, and trapping to produce reproductions of colour paintings that closely resemble the originals. In the mid-Ming Dynasty, Hui School carvers initiated the process of putting different colours on the entire printing frame to print colour pressed reproductions. But what was produced by this method was far from satisfactory. In the latter part of the Ming Dynasty, Hu Zhengyan, a painter, collaborated with the Hui School carvers and used the watercolour block printing method to produce four volumes of *Painting Manual of the Ten-bamboo Studio*, followed by *Letter-paper Designs of the Ten-bamboo Studio*. This was the first use of the blind stamping technique, a kind of colourless dye stamping. Bookbinding in the Ming changed from wrapped-ridge binding to thread binding, which was a great improvement.

Qing Dynasty (1644–1911)

Printing in ancient China reached yet another peak during the Qing Dynasty. First of all, the scale of printing production greatly expanded not only in the capital but also in regional centres of China. Networks of private printers and workshops were developed. The varieties of publications increased too. Classics from ancient times and contemporary works were printed in huge quantities. Present-day studies on bibliography and on the history of books and publication have established that the Qing Dynasty indeed surpassed all previous Chinese dynasties in terms of the quantity and variety of publications.

Another advance made during the 267-year Qing Dynasty was in the development of printing technology. All printing techniques known then continued to be in use and new ones were devised. Special mention must be made about movable type. The proportion of publications utilising movable type rose steadily. Fonts and sizes of movable type proliferated. Be they made with wood, bronze or clay, movable type attained very high standards in quality.

1650 1700

清 Qing
1644–1911

1644–1911
民間大量印刷年畫
New Year pictures
printed in large quantities

1665
法國學術學報之始
First scholarly journal
published in France

1680
"殿版"之始
Imperial Editions
first issued

1698
水蒸氣抽水機
專利（英國）
T. Savery's
(Britain) patent for
the steam pump

序言

清代地方政府和機構的印書單位稱書局，刻書印刷最早的是康熙年間兩淮鹽政曹寅建立的揚州詩局，所刻有名的書是《全唐詩》。雍正年間，各省布政司也先後建立印刷機構。

清代地方政府印刷最活躍的是同治年間以後，不少地方政府相繼建立了官書局，其中比較著名的官書局有金陵書局、浙江書局、廣雅書局、崇文書局、思賢書局等，從而形成了我國歷史上前所未有的政府出版印刷網。書局本的主要印刷品有《十三經古注》、《經典釋文》、《國語》、《史記》、《百子全書》、《二十二子》、《九通》、《玉海》等。其中由幾個書局分工刻印的《二十四史》最負盛名。

清代印刷的一個重要方面是家刻本。所謂家刻本是由封建官僚或文人以私人一己之力刊刻的古籍或時人的詩文集，這種書不以盈利為目的，往往是紙墨優良、刊刻精雅、流傳無多，後世多目為善本。其中著名的有張氏澤存堂小學五種、林佶四寫以及黃氏士禮居、許氏古韻閣所刻各書。

清代的民間印刷業分布面很廣，以江浙為最繁榮，杭州、蘇州、常州等地，集中了一大批印刷作坊。湖廣等地的印刷業從清代中期也發展起來。北京的民間印刷業明代就很繁榮，從清初開始，在琉璃廠、隆福寺等處，集中了100多家作坊。

清代民間印刷業最突出的是年畫的印刷。明代開創的木版彩色套印技術，到清代用來大量印刷年畫。由於年畫走進千家萬戶，銷量很大，從而促進了印刷業的發展。最著名的有天津的楊柳青、濰坊的楊家埠、蘇州的桃花塢。河南朱仙鎮、陝西鳳翔、四川綿竹、山西臨汾、廣東佛山等地，都集中了一批年畫作坊。年畫的題材多為民間喜聞樂見的戲曲故事、門神、灶馬、仕女以及表示吉祥、豐收等內容的畫面。一直到本世紀20年代，由於現代印刷技術的興起，手工木版年畫業才逐漸被取代。

清代最著名的木版套印書籍為《芥子園畫傳》，這是一本系統介紹繪畫技法的書，共分四集18卷，由李漁、沈因伯主持，畫家王概（安節）作畫，開雕於康熙十八年（1679年），康熙四十一年（1702年）完成前三集。它完全繼承了《十竹齋畫譜》的刻印技術，是清代前期具有代表性的木刻印刷工程。

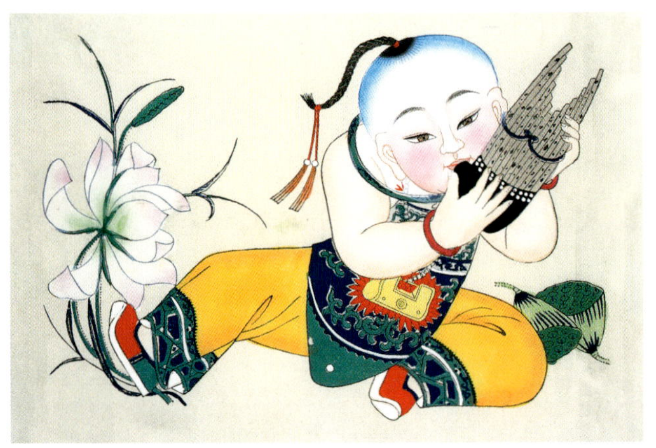

1700 | 1750

清 Qing
1644–1911

1708–1718
西洋銅版刻印
《皇輿全覽圖》（地圖）
Printing of an atlas of China using copper plate printing techniques borrowed from the West

1710–1716
《康熙字典》
The *Kangxi Dictionary*

c. 1719
四色印刷（銅版）
4-colour bronze plate printing

c. 1729
銅版刻印
Stereotype (bronze plates)

1709
最早版權法通過（英國）
Passing of the earliest copyright law (Britain)

c. 1733– c. 1880
西方工業革命
Industrial Revolution

Woodblock colour printing became ever more popular and its quality kept improving. Lunar New Year posters were a new commercial product that became popular. They gave rise to a big business, with millions of households being adorned by them, making the penetration of printing in society deeper than any dynasty before Qing. In this sense then, application of traditional technology of printing reached a pinnacle during the Qing Dynasty.

The official editing and printing organization of the Qing (1644–1911) government was located in the Hall of Military Eminence. During the Shunzhi years of the Qing Dynasty, the goverment relied mainly on the technical strength passed on from the official printing houses of the Ming Dynasty where lithographic printing was standard. In the latter part of the reign of Kangxi, bronze movable type was used. By the Yongzheng years, the typesetting and printing of the *Imperial Encyclopaedia* was completed. During the Qianlong years, the Hall of Military Eminence, under Jin Jian's management, engraved two sets of 250,000 jujube wooden movable types, one small and the other big, which were used in the printing of *A Collection of Rare Editions of the Hall of Military Eminence*. *Printing Manual for the Collection of Rare Editions of the Hall of Military Eminence*, an invaluable monograph on ancient printing techniques edited by Jin Jian, comprehensively introduced the craft and techniques of wooden type printing at the Hall of Military Eminence.

Printing workshops in local governments and organizations during the Qing were known as "bookstores or book bureaus." The Yangzhou Poetry Bureau set up by Cao Yin, the Liang-Huai Salt Administrator in the Kangxi years, was the first bookstore to print the famous collection *The Complete Poems of the Tang Dynasty*. During the Yongzheng years, governors of the various provinces also set up their printing offices.

Printing by regional governments was most active after the start of the Tongzhi era (1862–1874) when more and more government printers were established in the provinces. The renowned official book bureaux were Jinling, Zhejiang, Guangya, Chongwen, and Sixian. They formed an extensive network of government printers that was unprecedented in history. The following publications are examples of its noted output: *Ancient Exegeses of Thirteen Classics*, *Interpreted Text of Canonical Classics*, *Guoyu*, *Shi Ji*, *Compendium of Writings by One Hundred Masters*, *Twenty-two Masters*, *Nine Encyclopaedias*, and *Yü Hai*. The most famous publication was the *Twenty-four Histories* which was collaboratively printed by several bureaux.

An important development in printing during the Qing Dynasty is the popularisation of "private blockprints" of poems and essays written by feudal lords and literati of the day. As they did not print the books for profit, they commissioned private printers to issue them with fine paper and ink. The layout and the craftsmanship of the woodblocks were exquisite and elegant. Only a few of these rare books can be found today. The well-known titles are the Zecun Hall Series issued by the Zhang Family on philology (five series), works written by Lin Jisi, and those books by the Shili Residence of the Huang Family and by the Guyun Lodge of the Xu Family.

Private printing industry in the Qing Dynasty was scattered throughout different parts of China, but it was most prosperous in the Jiangsu and Zhejiang areas. Printing houses also concentrated in places like Hangzhou, Suzhou and Changzhou. Printing in the Hu-Guang region also began to pick up from the middle of the Qing Dynasty. Private printing in Beijing flourished during the Ming. From the early Qing more than a hundred presses began to concentrate in places such as Liulichang and Longfu Temple.

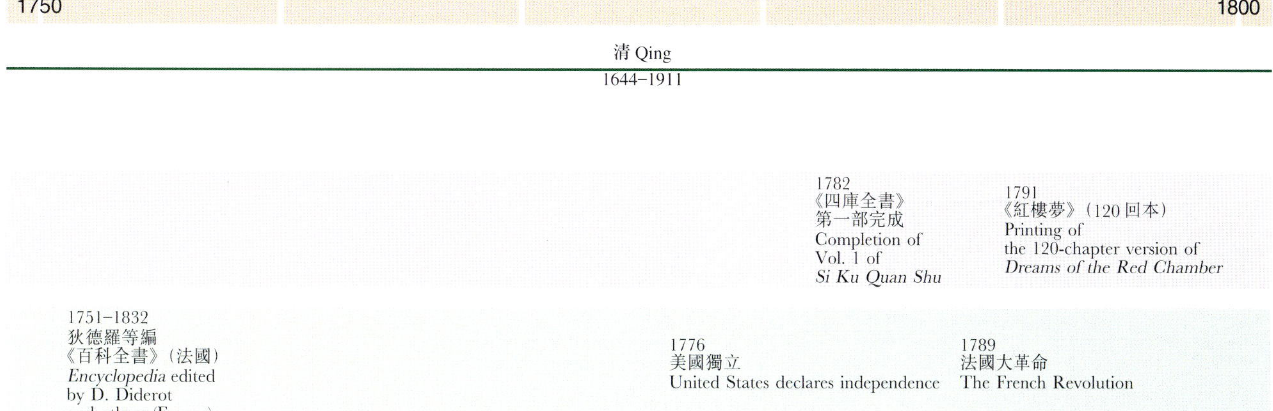

小結

以上簡要介紹，使我們概括地了解中國古代印刷技術的發展歷程。事實證明，中國不但發明了雕版印刷術、木活字和泥活字版，而且在使用木活字、金屬活字等方面都是世界最早的。從宋代開始，中國就出現雙色套印技術，到元代已正式用於印書，而且從雙色發展到三色、四色套印。明代首創的彩色套印，是世界上最早可以印出近似於原畫的，有漸變層次的印刷品。在印版材料方面，除木版印刷外，還有印墨方面的貢獻。從宋代起出現了銅版印刷，這說明早在宋代就已經解決了適於金屬版所用印墨的技術問題。總之，在印刷史上，中國的發明是多方面的，是逐步完善的，它對人類文明和社會進步的貢獻是巨大的。

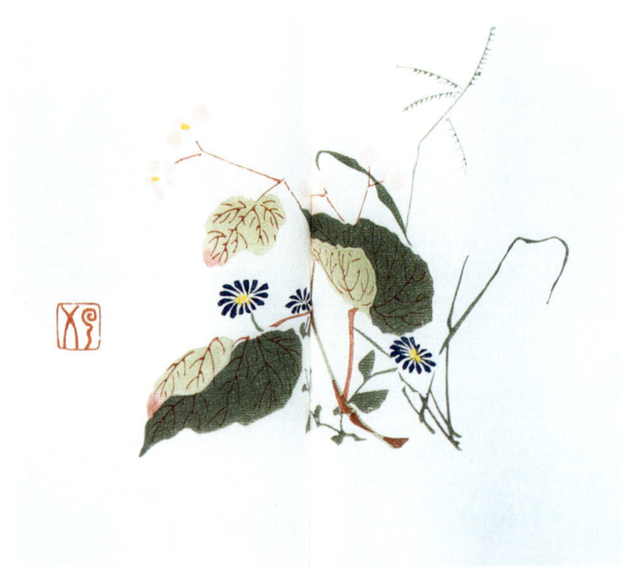

1800 — 1850

清 Qing
1644–1911

1798
自動製造紙廠出現（法國）取代手工造紙
Factory automatic production of paper rolls replaces manual workshops

1800
鐵版印刷出現
Printing with cast iron plates

1810
英國教士馬禮遜在廣州出版《使徒行傳》
British missionany Robert Morrison prints *The Apostles* in Canton

1818–1883
馬克思在世
Karl Marx

1823
照相術發明
Invention of photography

1825–1846
林春祺造銅字 40 萬個
Lin Chunqi manufactures a bronze typefont of 400,000 characters

1839
（英國）商用電報
First commercial telegraph system (Britain)

1844
翟金生製泥活字十萬個
Zhai Jinsheng manufactures 100,000 clay types

1847
輪轉印刷機出現（美國）
Rotary press (USA)

1848
共產黨宣言
The Communist Manifesto

The most outstanding publication of the Qing private presses was the printing of the New Year pictures. The woodblock colour printing method created during the Ming Dynasty was used for the mass production of New Year pictures. They were distributed to thousands of households and sold in great quantities, thus leading to the development of a New Year picture industry. The famous presses included Yangliuqing in Tianjin, Yangjiabu in Weifang, and Taohuawu in Suzhou. Printshops of New Year pictures also concentrated in places such as Zhuxianzhen in Henan, Fengxiang in Shaanxi, Mianzhu in Sichuan, Linfen in Shanxi and Foshan in Guangdong. The motifs of these pictures were mostly what common people liked to see and hear, such as stories from plays, door-gods, crickets (symbol of kitchen gods), beautiful ladies and contents symbolizing such things as good luck and bumper harvests. It was not until the 1920s, with the rise of modern offset printing techniques, that hand-made woodblock printing of New Year pictures was gradually replaced by the new methods.

The best-known woodblock registered books in the Qing Dynasty was *Painting Album of the Mustard-seed Garden*. This album, comprising 4 volumes and 18 chapters, systematically introduced painting techniques. It was edited by Li Yu and Shen Yinbo, and illustrated by Wang Gai (Wang Anjie). Carving began in the eighteenth year of the Kangxi period (1679) and the first three volumes were completed in the forty-first year of the same period (1702). This work, whose carving skills derived completely from *Painting Manual of the Ten-bamboo Studio*, was a representative example of woodblock printing in the early Qing Dynasty.

Summary

The above introduction provides us with a general picture of the development of printing techniques in ancient China. The facts and artefacts prove not only that China invented woodblock printing and clay movable type, but also that China was the first country in the world to use wooden movable type and metal movable type. The use of two-colour printing began in the Song Dynasty (960–1279). By the Yuan Dynasty (1271–1368), it was used to print books, and it further developed into three-colour and four-colour printing. The colour printing invented in the Ming Dynasty was the first in the world. The results produced could almost match the original and the printed products showed levels of gradual colourization.

With regard to the printing materials, China contributed to the use of ink in printing apart from the use of woodblocks. The fact that bronze plates were used since the Song Dynasty indicates that technical problems associated with printing ink suitable for metal plates had been solved by then. The above shows that in the history of printing, the inventions in China were multi-faceted and were perfected gradually. These inventions have contributed enormously to human civilization and social progress.

1850 1900

清 Qing
1644–1911

1850–1852
唐姓印工鑄成錫活字 20 萬個
Tin movable types (200,000 characters) cast by a worker surnamed Tang

1859
達爾文進化論
Origin of Species by Charles Darwin

1861–1865
美國南北戰爭
American Civil War

1872
愛迪生發明電動打字機
Thomas Edison patents an electric typewriter

1876
貝爾發明電話
A. Bell patents the telephone

1894
甲午之戰爆發
Sino-Japanese War breaks out

1898
嚴復《天演論》出版
Yan Fu's translation of T. H. Huxley's book on evolution

印刷術的起源

The Origins of Printing

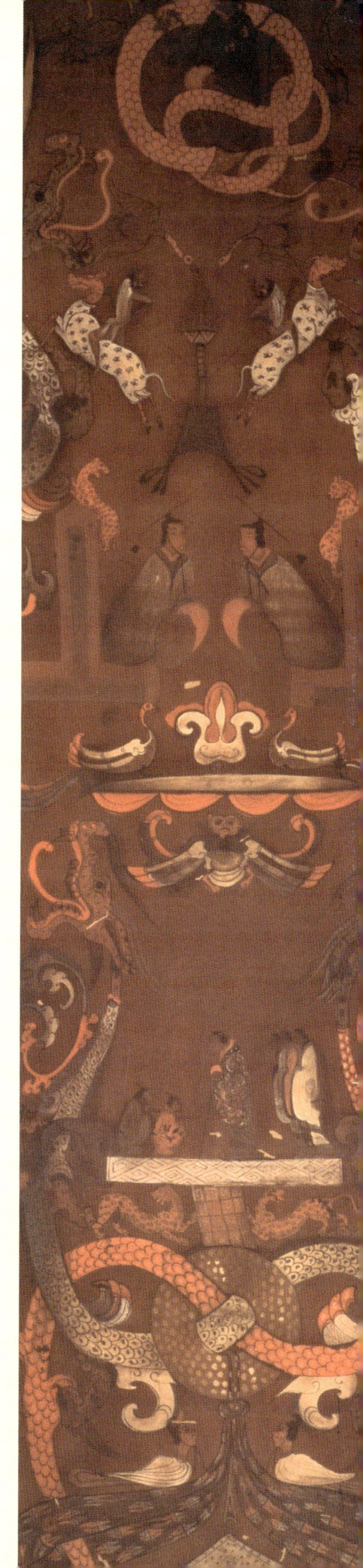

印刷術發明前的相關歷史

印刷術的發明，經歷了長期的歷史演變過程，在這個歷史的長河中，各種與印刷術發明相關的文化、技藝、物料等，都經歷了從萌芽、發展到成熟的演變過程，因而為印刷術的發明創造了必要的條件。

發明印刷術一般需要具備四個方面的條件：

一、 必須有成熟、定型、規範的文字

文字是印刷的主要對象，沒有文字的廣泛應用，就不具備發明印刷術的條件。中國的漢字已有五千年的歷史，早在新石器時代的彩陶上，就有一些記事符號，被認為是漢字的原始形態。公元前 14 世紀的殷商時代，人們將文字刻於龜甲和獸骨上，這就是甲骨文。經研究，甲骨文已有單字 4,600 個，目前可以識別約1,000多個，它可以記錄較完整的事件。繼甲骨文之後，漢字的書體經歷了大篆、小篆、隸書等演變過程，東漢末年出現楷書，從而完成了漢字書體的演變過程，為印刷術的應用創造了良好的條件。

二、 熟練的文字雕刻技藝

最早出現的印刷術為雕版印刷，文字反雕於木板上，再進行刷印。因此，文字雕刻技術是印刷術發明的重要技術條件。中國漢字的雕刻技術起源很早，甲骨文就是雕刻在龜甲獸骨上面的；商至西周的青銅器銘文，在鑄造之前需要刻製泥笵，也需要文字雕刻技術。文字的石刻技術也源遠流長，在上古時代就有岩壁的摩崖石刻，春秋時期的石鼓文，是大篆體的最早石刻。秦始皇時的刻石為小篆，東漢的《熹平石經》為隸書體，是歷史上最早的大規模文字石刻工程。它將儒家經典刻於 46 塊石碑上，約 20 萬字。此後歷代多次雕刻石經，使文字的雕刻技術更為成熟。與雕版印刷更密切的是文字的反刻技術。最具代表性的是印章，它不但是反刻文字，而且用於蓋印，更近似於印刷工藝。

三、 紙、筆、墨等印刷所必需的工具，材料

筆和墨起源都很早，甲骨文就是先寫後刻的，說明當時已有筆墨。簡帛時代，筆墨更是廣泛應用的工具和材料。現存最早的毛筆是從長沙市左家公山的戰國墓出土的戰國筆，它的製造工藝已十分精細。早期的墨是用天然色料調合而成的。春秋戰國時期，墨的質量已有很大改進，漢代已能用松煙製墨。

紙張是印刷的重要材料。據史料記載和實物發現，早在西漢初期，我國就開始使用紙張，東漢和帝元興元年（105 年），蔡倫改良了造紙工藝，用樹膚，敝布，魚網等原料，造出優質紙張，對造紙技術的發展作出重大貢獻。此後，紙張的應用不斷擴大，到公元四世紀時，已完全代替了簡帛，成為書寫的主要材料。

社會對文字和圖象複製品的大量需求，也是促成印刷術發明的社會條件。隨着社會文化的發展，讀書的人越來越多，傳統用手抄書籍的方式，已不能滿足社會的需要，人們就希望有一種更快速複製文字、圖像的方法。在這種社會條件下，印刷術就產生了。早在西漢初期，已能採用凸版和漏版在絲織品上印花。紙張出現後，為印刷提供了理想的承印材料。到東漢末年，發明印刷術的技術、物料等條件都已具備。

四、 與印刷相關的技術、工藝

印刷術發明前，已經出現了各種圖文複製方法。它們為印刷術的發明，在工藝、技術方面有一定的啟示作用。其中印章的捺印和石碑拓印文字，與印刷術的關係更密切。印章有着悠久的歷史。它起源於商代，秦漢時期最為興盛。印章的文字反刻和捺印，可稱為印刷之前奏。紙張廣泛應用後，人們開始將石刻文字拓印在紙張上，以便於保存和閱讀。這種工藝方法，更近似於印刷。

以上諸條件具備後，一旦社會對書籍及各種圖文複製品的需求量變得很大，印刷術就會誕生。

Developments Leading to the Invention of Printing

The foregoing description of the evolution of printing can be summarized in terms of four cultural, technical and material developments leading to the invention of printing.

1. Standardized Characters

Symbols on painted pottery can be dated back to the New Stone Age about five thousand years ago. These symbols are the prototypes of Chinese characters.

Oracle bone inscriptions appeared in the fourteenth century B.C. Of the 4,600 distinct inscriptions discovered so far, about 1,000 have been deciphered. They had been used to record events in considerable detail. Since then, Chinese characters evolved in several stages: The great-seal script, the small-seal script, the clerical script, and the regular script. By the Eastern Han era, about two thousand years ago, this factor of printing was in place.

2. Character-carving Skills

The skill of carving characters is the next technical condition for the invention of printing. The skill emerged very early. The oldest inscriptions were made on oracle bones like animal bones and shells. Inscriptions on bronze ware flourished from the Shang Dynasty to the Western Zhou Dynasty (1,500–771 B.C.). Chinese characters were inscribed in clay moulds before casting. Carving characters on stones came even earlier. Symbol-carving on surfaces of cliffs has been traced to extremely ancient times. The classics in great-seal script and small-seal script were all carved on stones. The *Xiping Stone Inscriptions* of the Eastern Han involved carving the Confucian classics in the clerical script onto 46 stone tablets, totalling around 200,000 characters.

The technique of reverse-character carving was an essential precursor to woodblock carving. Seals and signets not only used reverse-character carving but also stamping.

3. Paper, Writing Brush, and Ink

Oracle bone inscriptions were first written and then engraved. This indicates that brushes and ink had already existed. By the time of bamboo slips and silk books, brushes and ink had been in wide use for a long time. During the Spring and Autumn and Warring States periods (722–221 B.C.), the quality of ink greatly improved. In the Han Dynasty (206 B.C.–A.D. 220), pine-soot was first used in ink-making.

As to paper, historical records and unearthed artefacts provide evidence that the Chinese people began to use paper as early as the third century B.C., at the beginning of the Western Han. In A.D. 105, an Eastern Han man Cai Lun improved the paper-making techniques by using an assortment of materials such as tree bark, worn-out cloth and fishnets to produce a high quality paper. From then on, paper was used on an ever wider scale and, by about A.D. 300, had replaced bamboo slips and silk as the major material for writing books.

The great social demand for reproductions of words and illustrations created the social conditions for the invention of printing. So, paper became the ideal material for mass printing.

4. Associated Technologies and Skills

Methods to reproduce drawings had been devised well before printing appeared in history. Artistic and technical ideas of these methods must have contributed in significant ways to the invention of printing technology. We can see this point from the close relationship between printing and rubbing, stamping and inscription techniques. Seals can be dated back to the Shang Dynasty, 3,000 to 3,500 years ago; they were most popular during the Qin Dynasty (221–206 B.C.). The advent of paper enabled people to ink the tablets and then press paper over it to "print" words. This method came rather close to printing as we know it today.

Given the existence of the four factors listed above, the rise of social demand for reproducing drawings and written texts would inevitably give birth to the invention of printing.

印刷術起源圖

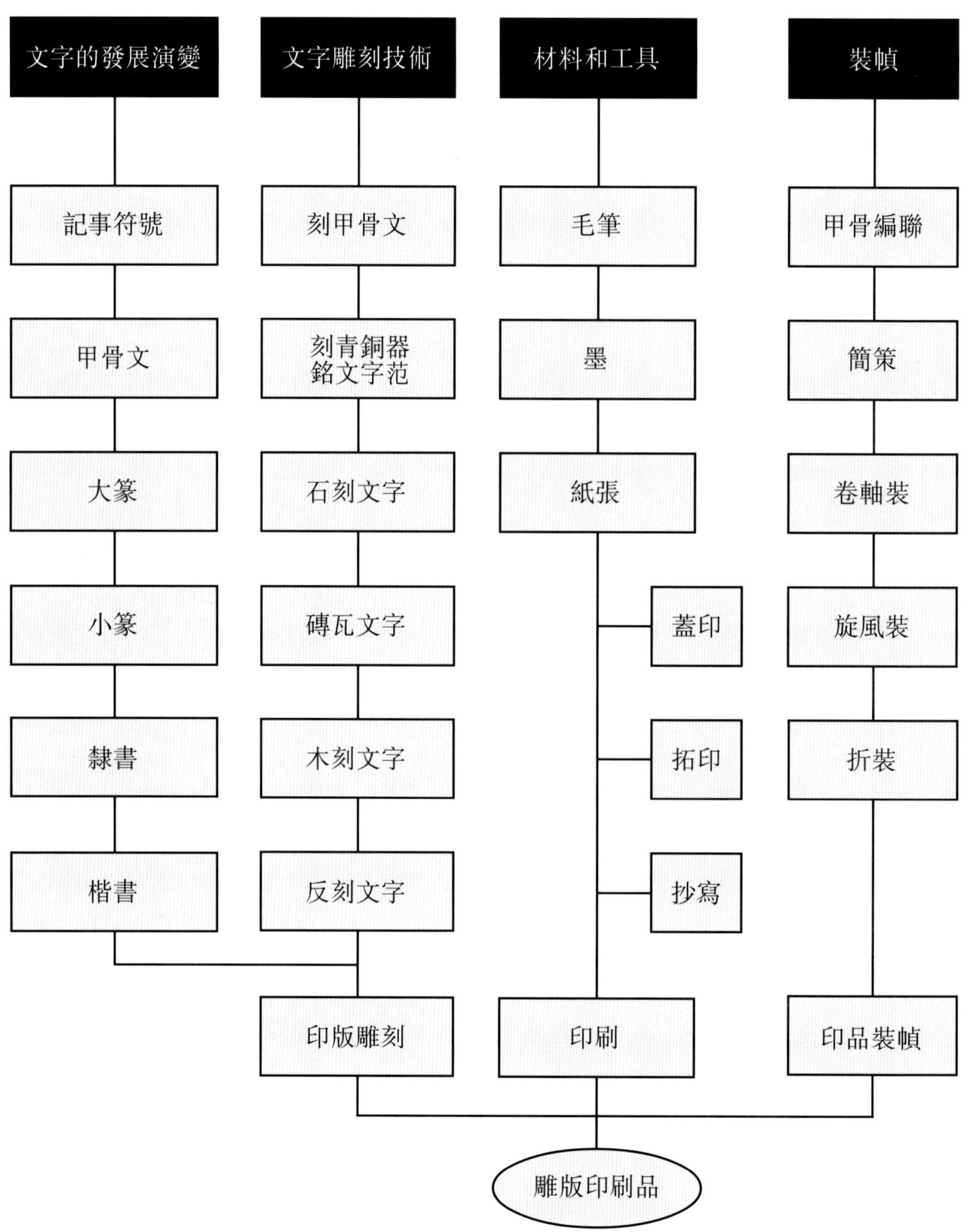

文字的發展演變
文字雕刻技術
材料和工具
裝幀
記事符號
刻甲骨文
毛筆
甲骨編聯
甲骨文
刻青銅器
銘文字范
墨
簡策
大篆
石刻文字
紙張
卷軸裝
小篆
磚瓦文字
蓋印
旋風裝
隸書
木刻文字
拓印
折裝
楷書
反刻文字
抄寫
印版雕刻
印刷
印品裝幀
雕版印刷品

The Origins of Printing Technology

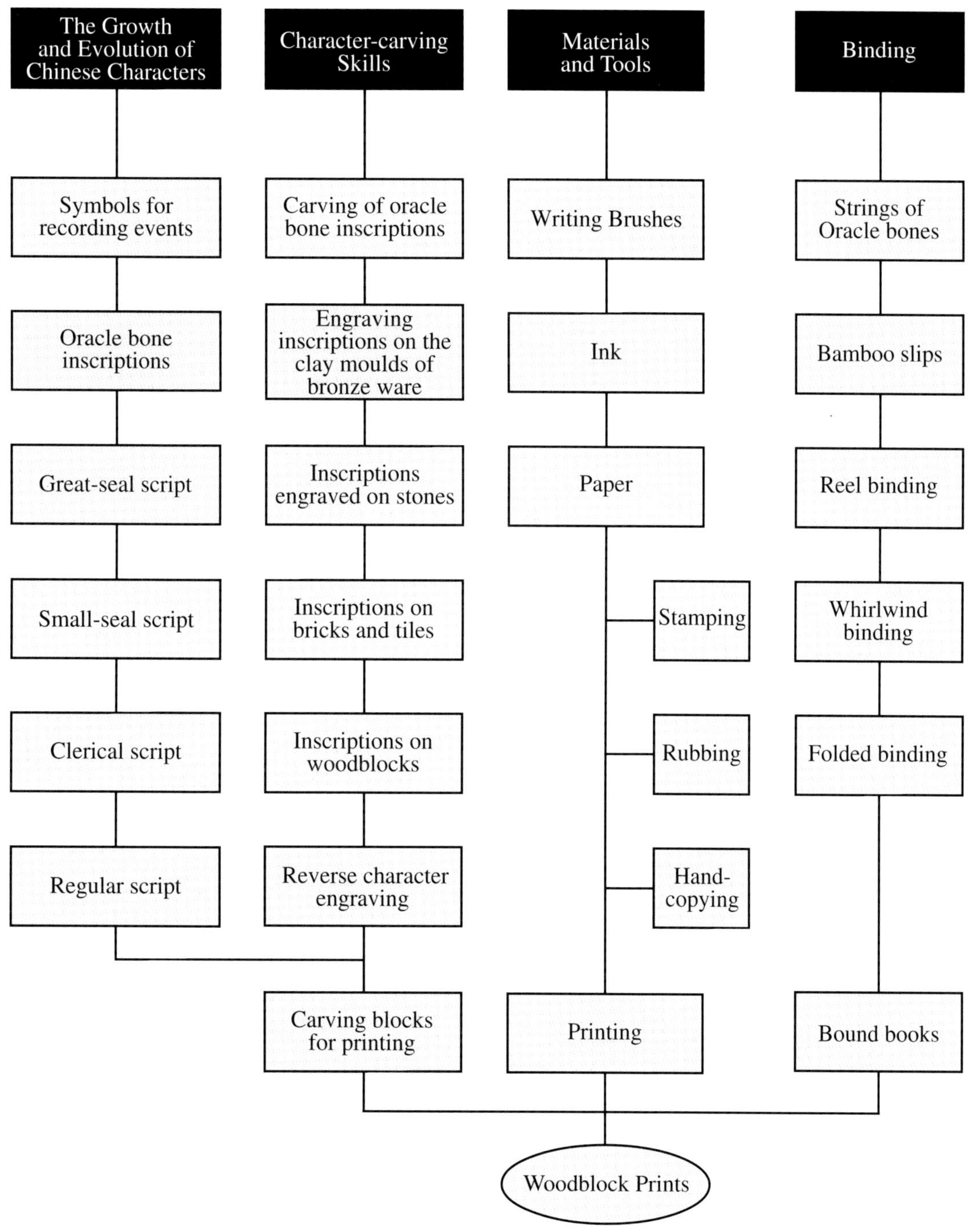

漢字的起源與演變

文字是印刷的主要對象，漢字約起源於新石器時代後期，商代的甲骨文，已是成熟的漢字。以後，漢字又經歷了大篆、小篆、隸書；東漢末年出現楷書。

文字的載體及雕刻技術

文字出現後，曾用各種載體進行記錄和傳播，雕刻是最常用的方法，從而使文字的雕刻技術更為熟練。為後世的雕版印刷提供了技術基礎。

甲骨文

公元前 13 世紀殷商時代，將文字刻於龜甲、獸骨之上，稱甲骨文，甲骨文是已成熟的漢字，它符合漢字傳統的造字理論“六書”的要求。

青銅器銘文（大篆）

鑄於青銅器上的文字稱金文，屬大篆系統。金文起源於商代，興盛於西周。銘文鑄造前，需刻製泥范。

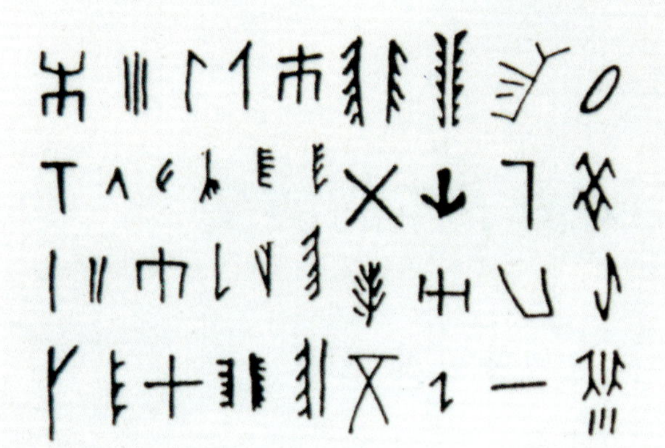

新石器時代陶器上的符號（約公元前四千年）
Written symbols on the painted pottery of the New Stone Age (c. 4000 BC).

甲骨文	商周金文	石鼓文小篆	隶书	正书
			魚	魚
			龍	龍 龙
			馬	馬 马
			象	象
			虎	虎
			鹿	鹿
			舟	舟
			車	車

漢字演變圖
A diagram showing the evolution of Chinese characters.

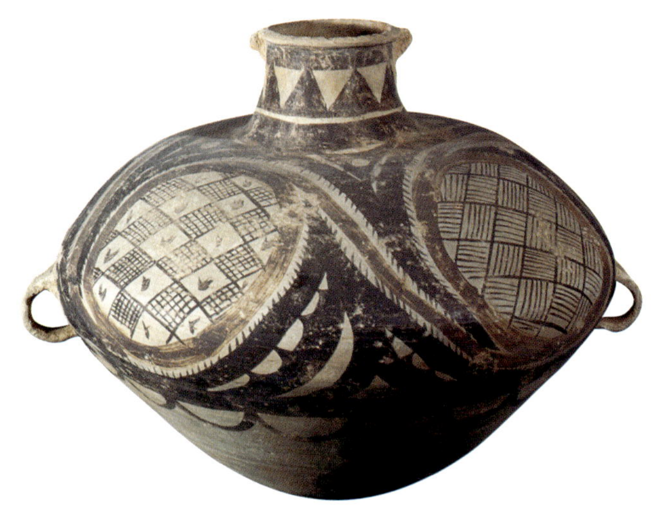

新石器時期的彩陶，上有花紋和記事符號，這些就是漢字的濫觴。
On the surface of the painted pottery of the New Stone Age there were floral designs and symbols recording events. The symbols are precursors of Chinese characters.

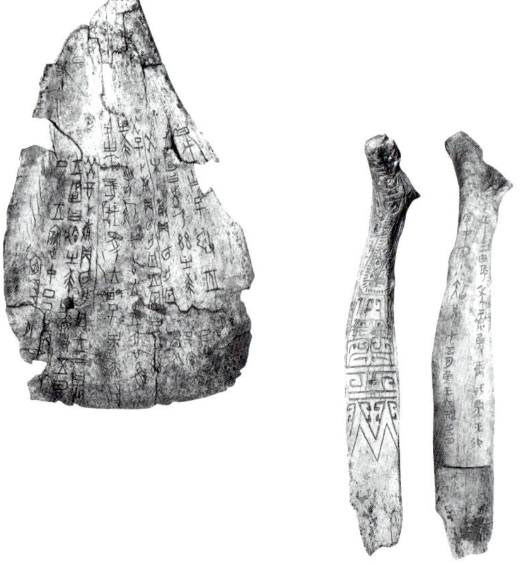

甲骨文
Inscribed oracle bones.

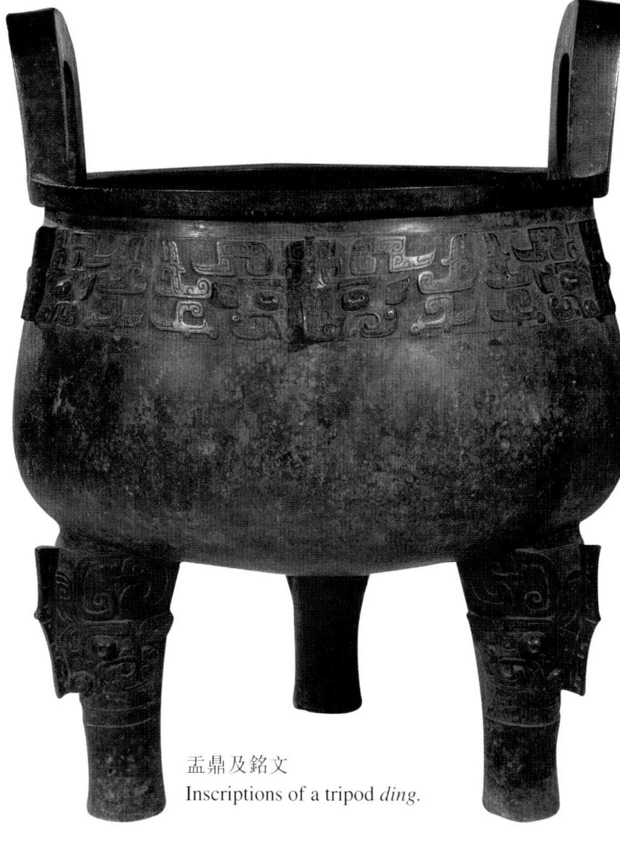
盂鼎及銘文
Inscriptions of a tripod *ding*.

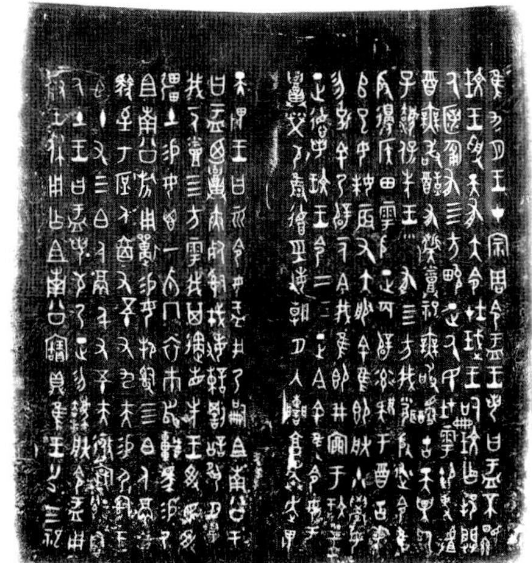

The Origin and Evolution of Chinese Characters

Characters are the main subject matter of printing. Chinese characters originated in the latter part of the New Stone Age. The oracle bone inscriptions of the Shang Dynasty (1600–1066 B.C.) were well-formed Chinese characters. From then on, Chinese characters evolved from *great-seal* script, *small-seal* script, and *clerical* script to *regular* script which appeared towards the end of the Eastern Han Dynasty (A.D. 25–220).

Characters and Woodblock Carving Techniques

After the emergence of characters, various media were used to record and disseminate events. As carving was the most common method, character-carving techniques became more refined. This in turn provided the skills for woodblock printing.

Oracle-bone Inscriptions

In the Shang Dynasty (13th century B.C.), characters were engraved on animal bones and tortoise shells known as oracle bone inscriptions. These were well-formed Chinese characters which met the conditions of the Six Principles of Chinese character formation.

Inscriptions on Bronze Ware (Great-seal Script)

Characters cast on bronze ware were known as "inscriptions on metal," which were written in the great-seal script. Originating in the Shang Dynasty, they became popular during the Western Zhou (1066–771 B.C.). Before the bronze was cast, the inscriptions were engraved on the clay moulds.

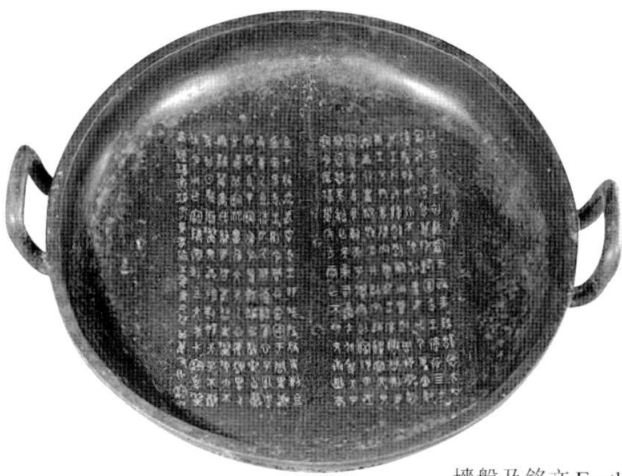
墻盤及銘文 Earthen tray and inscriptions

石刻文字

石鼓文，戰國秦國之物，是現存最早的石刻文字，大篆。

Characters Inscribed on Stone

Stone-drum inscriptions dated from the Warring States and the Qin periods. These are the earliest extant stone inscriptions written in the *great-seal* script.

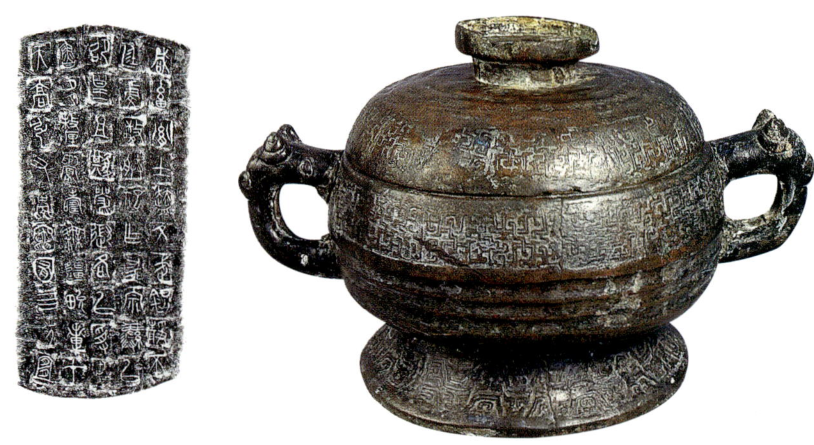

《秦公簋》銘文是用單個泥字范拼成

Inscriptions on a *gui* bronze vessel of Qin, made by welding together individual sections cast from clay moulds inscribed with characters.

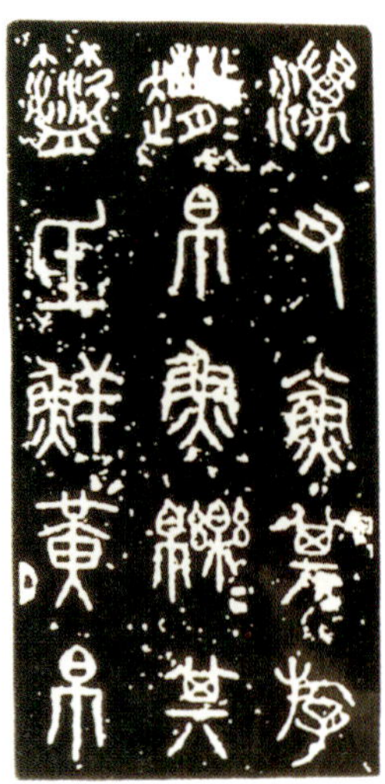

石鼓文，戰國
(403 B.C.–221 B.C.) 大篆
Stone-drum inscriptions from the Warring States Period. (403 B.C.–221 B.C.).

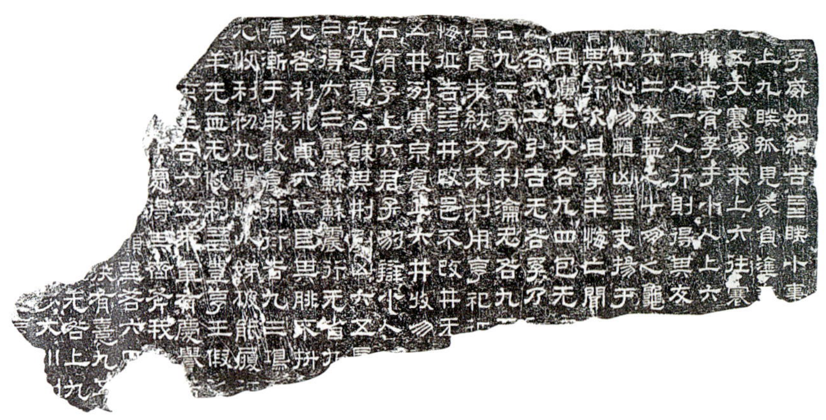

《熹平石經》東漢熹平四年（175年）至光和六年（183年），刻碑46塊，20餘萬字，載儒家七經、隸書。

The Xiping Stone Classics were inscribed between the fourth year of the Xiping period (A.D. 175) and the sixth year of the Guanghe period (A.D. 183) during the Eastern Han Dyansty. Seven Confucian classics in the *clerical* script were inscribed on 46 stones, totalling more than 200,000 characters.

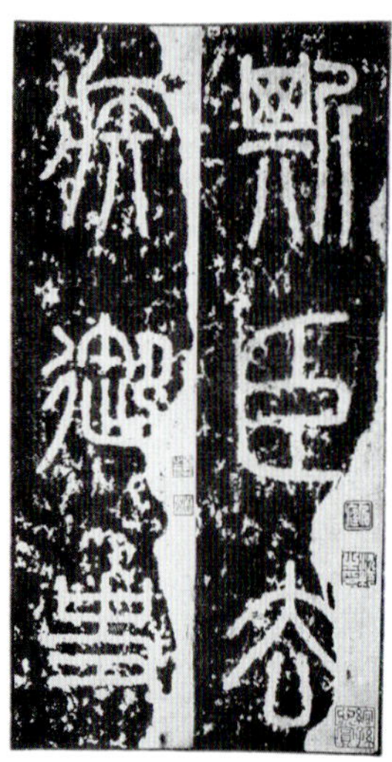

秦瑯玡刻石，小篆
Stone inscriptions on Langye of the Qin period, written in the *small-seal* script.

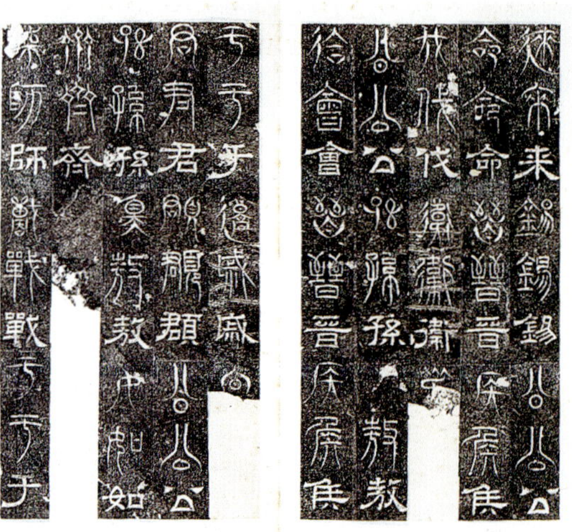

《三體石經》（三國）用大篆、小篆、隸書三體刻成

Stone Inscriptions in Three Scripts (The Three Kingdoms) were inscribed in the *great-seal* script, *small-seal* script and *regular* script.

龍門石刻中的正體凸字
Relief characters on *Stone Inscriptions at Longmen.*

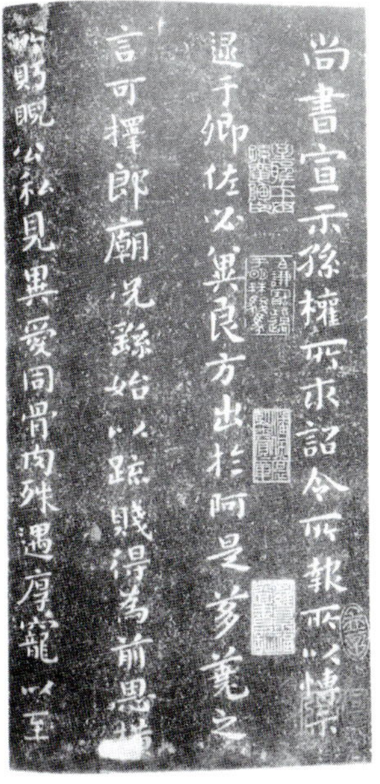

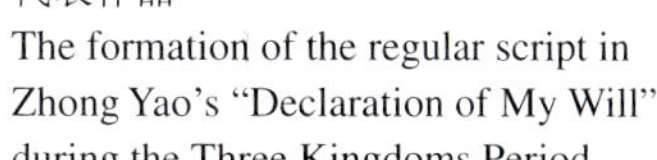

三國鍾繇《宣示表》楷書形成初期的代表作品
The formation of the regular script in Zhong Yao's "Declaration of My Will" during the Three Kingdoms Period.

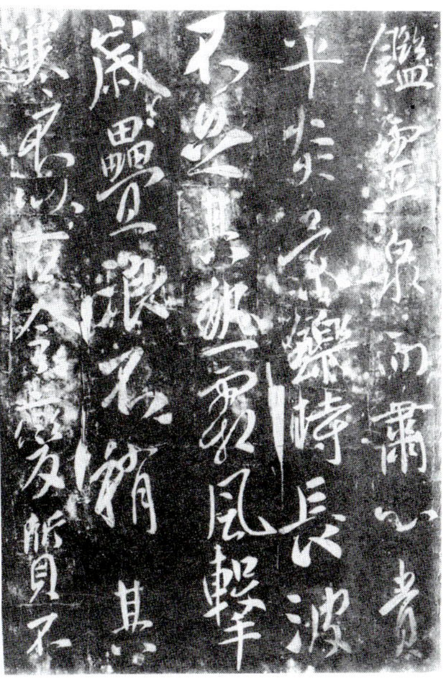

《温泉銘》唐太宗書體
On Hot Springs, written in the calligraphic style of Emperor Taizong of the Tang Dynasty.

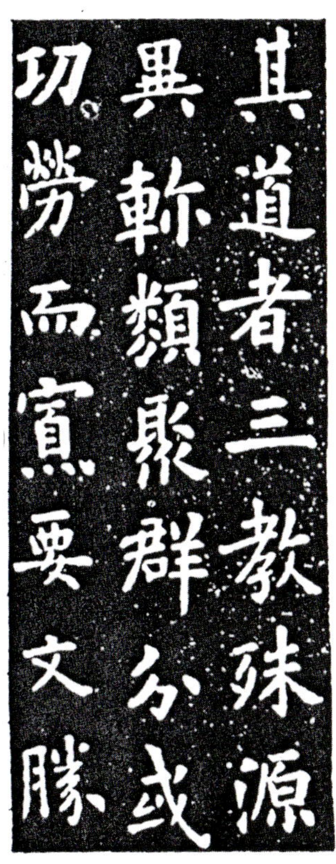

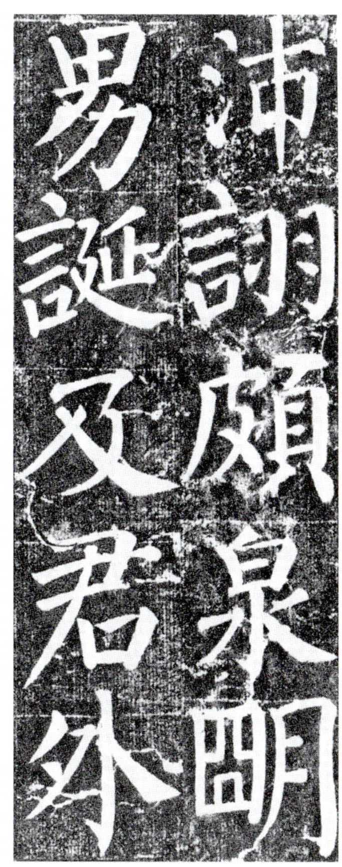

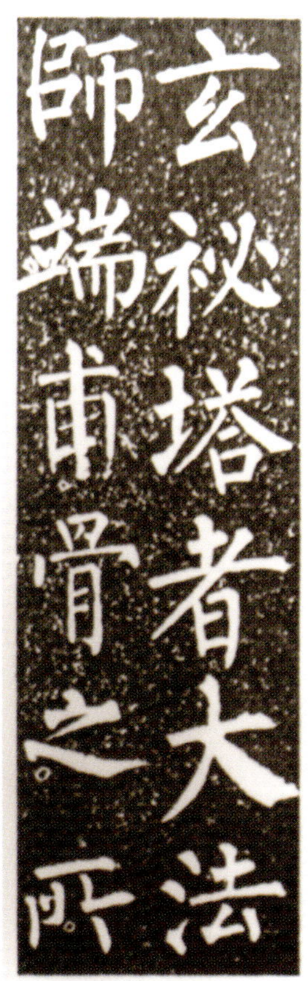

（左起） 歐陽詢、顏真卿及柳公權書體
唐代有代表性書體，為早期雕版所常用的字體
(From left) The calligraphy of Ouyang Xun, Yan Zhenqing and Liu Gongquan.
Representative calligraphic styles of the Tang Dynasty were the typefaces commonly used in woodblock printing.

印章、封泥

印章起源於商代，刻於銅、石及木等材料上 。有反體陰字及陽字，印章的反刻文字及蓋印，與印刷十分近似。這些都為刻版提供了技術和經驗。

Stamping-seals and Sealing-clay

Stamping-seals originated in the Shang Dynasty. They were engraved on such materials as bronze, stone and wood, in relief or intaglio. The reverse-character engraving and the stamping seal were similar to printing. These techniques contributed to the development of printing.

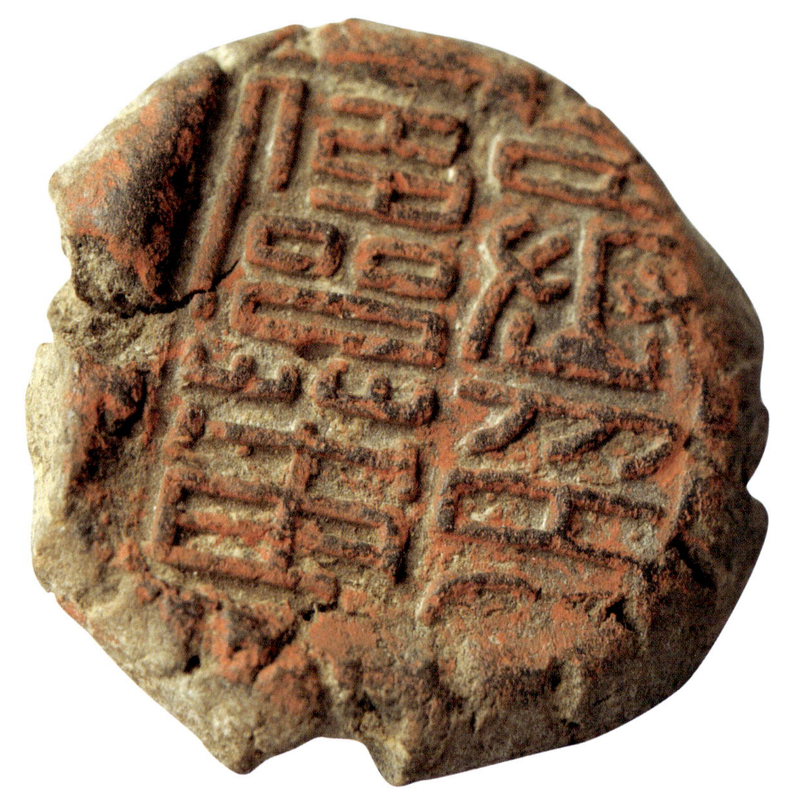

漢軑侯家丞封泥　長沙馬王堆出土
Sealing-clay of the Han Dynasty, unearthed in Changsha, Hunan.

漢及漢以前印章
Pre-Han and Han stamping-seals

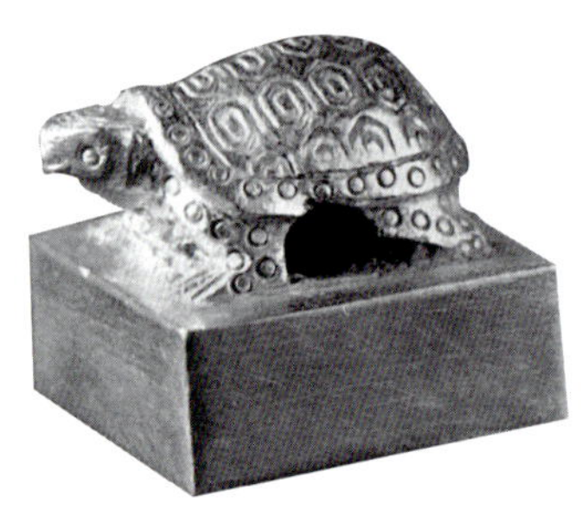

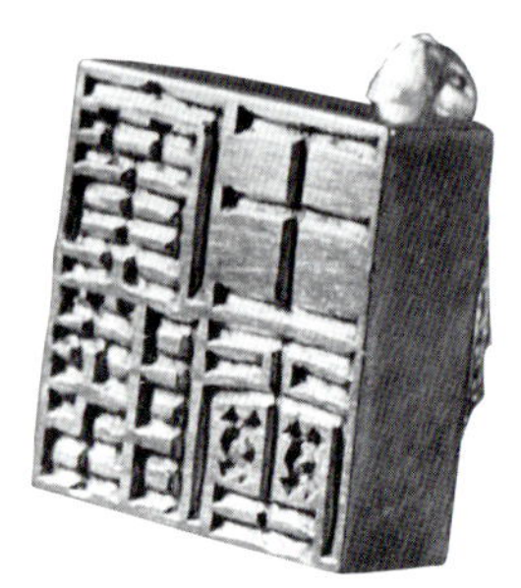

秦磚漢瓦

秦漢之間，將文字、圖案製於磚瓦及陶器上，有的文字是直接刻的，有的先刻製模具。

Bricks of Qin and Tiles of Han

Between the Qin and the Han periods, characters and designs were engraved on bricks, tiles and pottery. Some characters were directly engraved, while others were first written on the moulds.

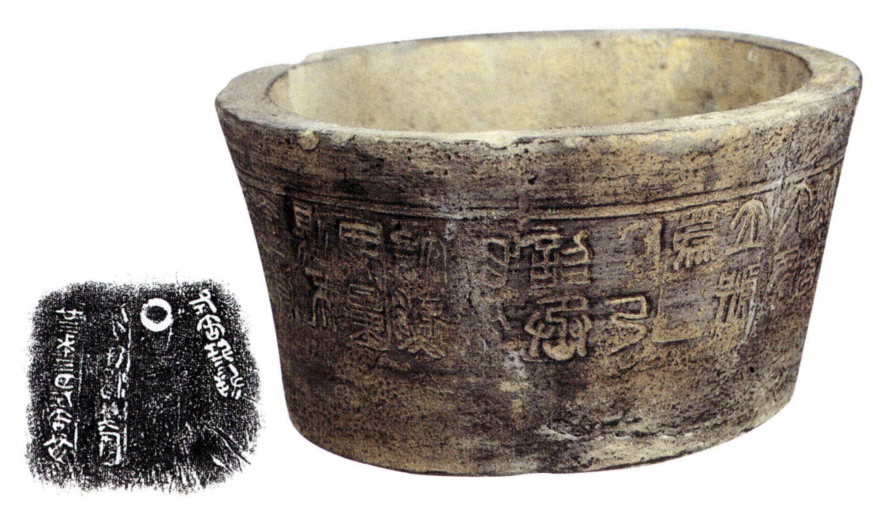

秦始皇二十六年陶量及銘文 (221 B.C.)
A pottery measuring vessel with words inscribed in the twenty-sixth year of the First Emperor of Qin and inscriptions on a vessel.

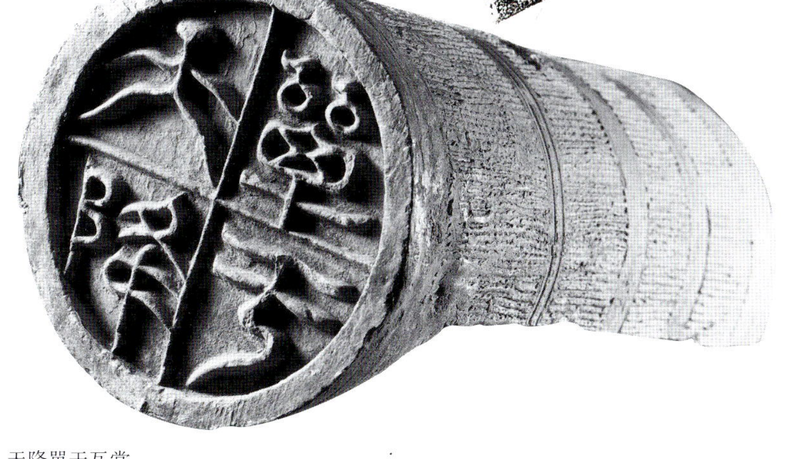

天降單于瓦當
A roof-end tile with an inscription that reads: "Heaven will subdue the Mongolian Chief Shan Yü."

漢十二字磚范
A brick mould with twelve characters.

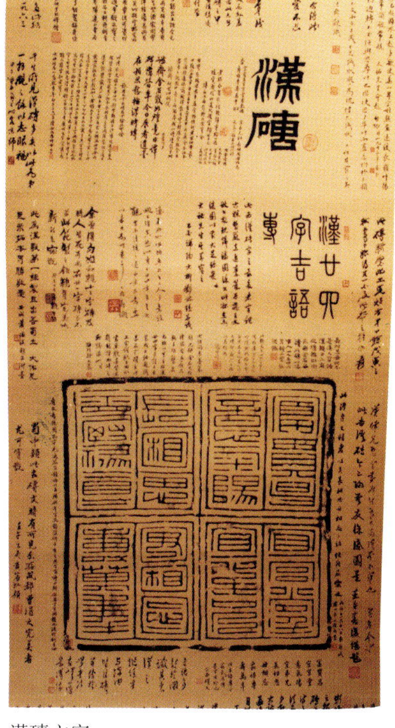

漢磚文字
Characters on bricks of the Han Dynasty.

筆墨的發明和應用

筆墨是書寫和印刷不可缺少的工具和材料。筆墨起源於商代（公元前1600–1066 年），現存最早的筆是戰國（公元前 403–221 年）筆。漢代（公元前 206 年－公元 220 年）已用松煙製墨。

The Invention of the Writing Brush and Ink and Their Application

Writing brushes and ink are the indispensable tools for writing and printing. Brushes and ink originated in the Shang Dynasty (1600–1066 B.C.). The earliest extant brush dates from the Warring States Period (403–221 B.C.). In the Han Dynasty (206 B.C.–A.D. 220), pine soot was used in the making of ink.

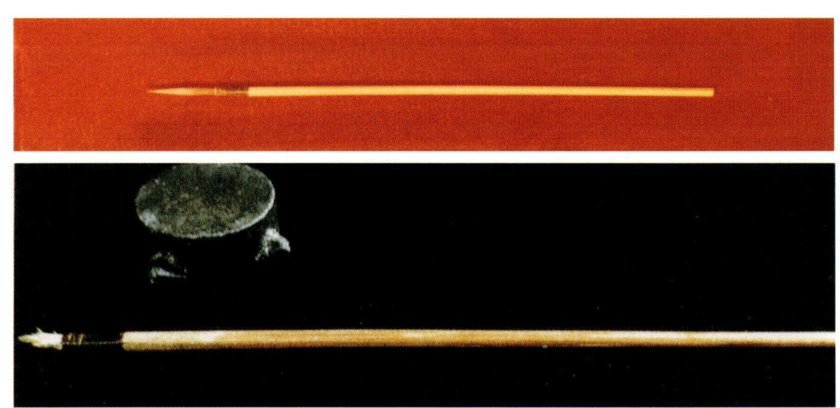

現存古代的筆。從上至下為戰國筆、漢代筆、東晉筆
Brushes dating from ancient times.
From top to bottom: Warring States brush, Han brush, and Eastern Jin brush.

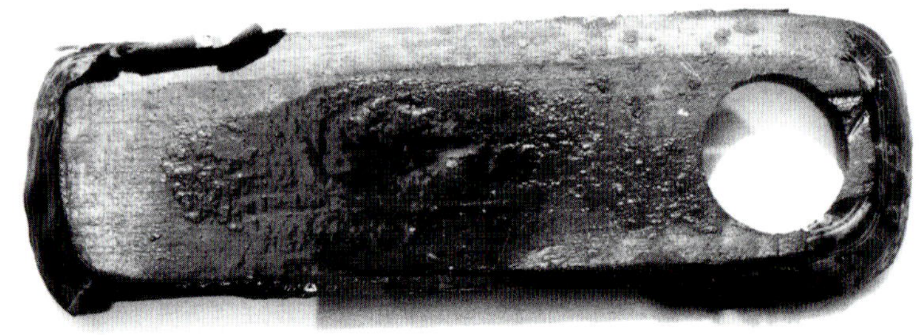

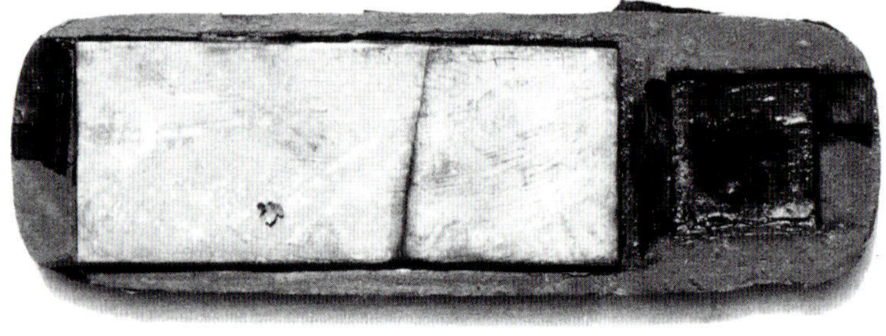

漢代漆盒（上）
漢代石硯（下）
Lacquer box *(top)* containing inkstone *(bottom)*, Han Dynasty.

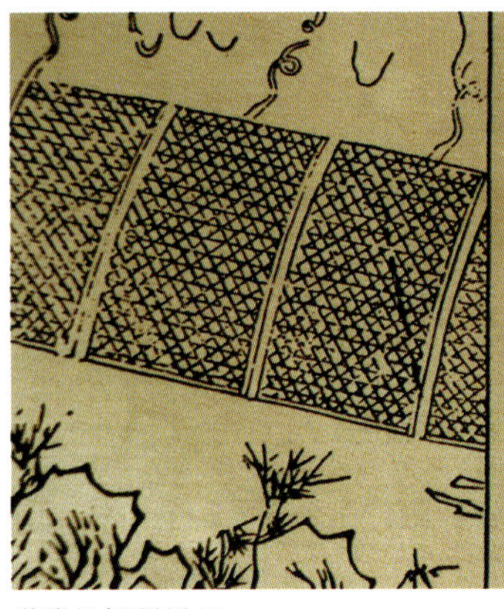

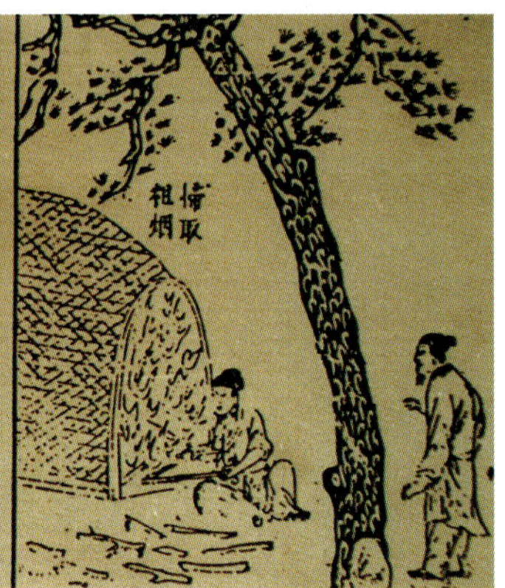

漢代松煙製墨圖
Making ink from pine soot, Han Dynasty.

簡牘和帛書——最早的書籍

紙發明前，人們用竹片，木片及絲織品作為書寫繪畫的載體，用以傳播文化，這就是書的早期形態，也可視為最早的書籍。

Books on Bamboo Slips and Books on Silk — The Earliest Books

Before the invention of paper, people used bamboo slips, wooden slips and silk fabrics as media for writing and painting. These were the earliest books used to disseminate knowledge.

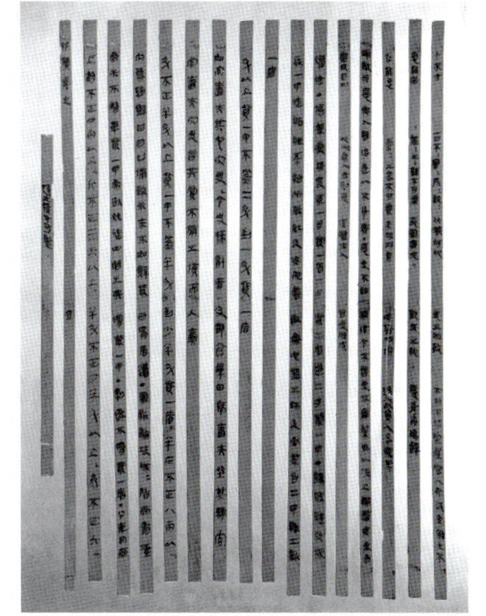

秦簡
Bamboo slips from the Qin Dynasty.

湖南長沙
馬王堆漢代竹簡
Han bamboo slips found at Mawangdui, Changsha, Hunan.

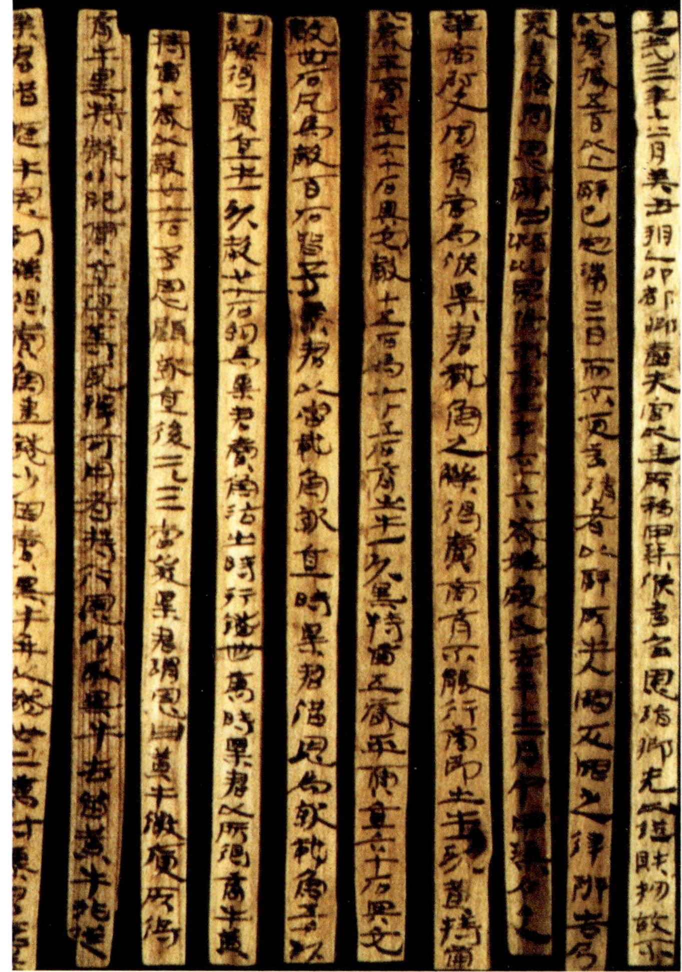

甘肅地區出土的漢代木簡
Wooden strips unearthed in Gansu Province.

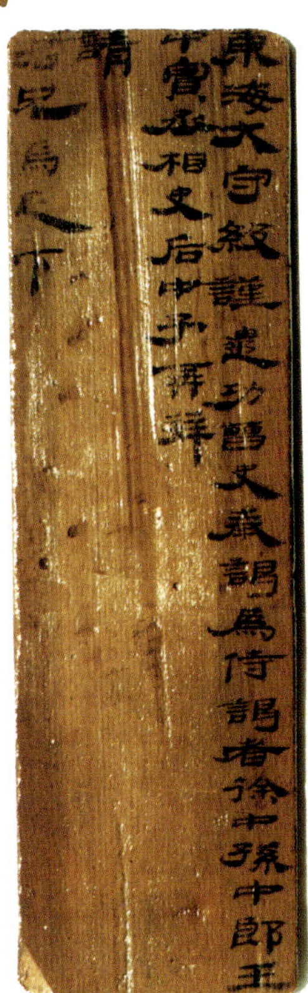

木牘
Inscribed wooden tablets.

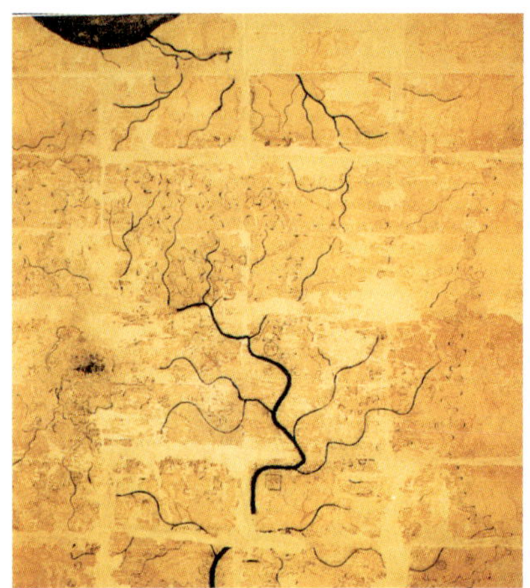

畫於絲織品上的地圖（西漢）
A map painted on silk fabric.

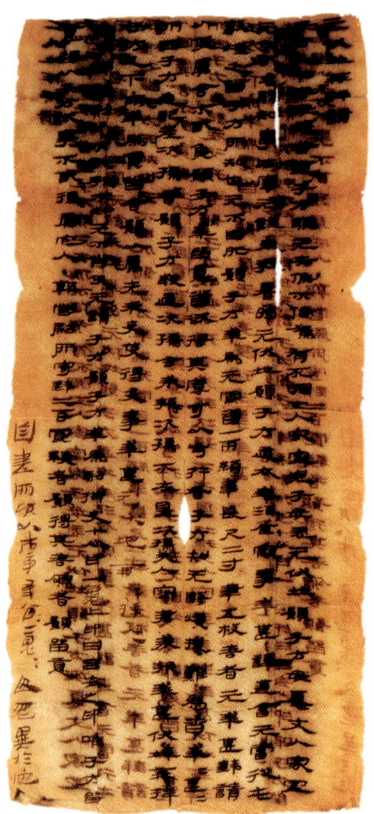

帛書（西漢） 1990 年甘肅敦煌出土
Writing on silk, Western Han, unearthed in Dunhuang in 1990.

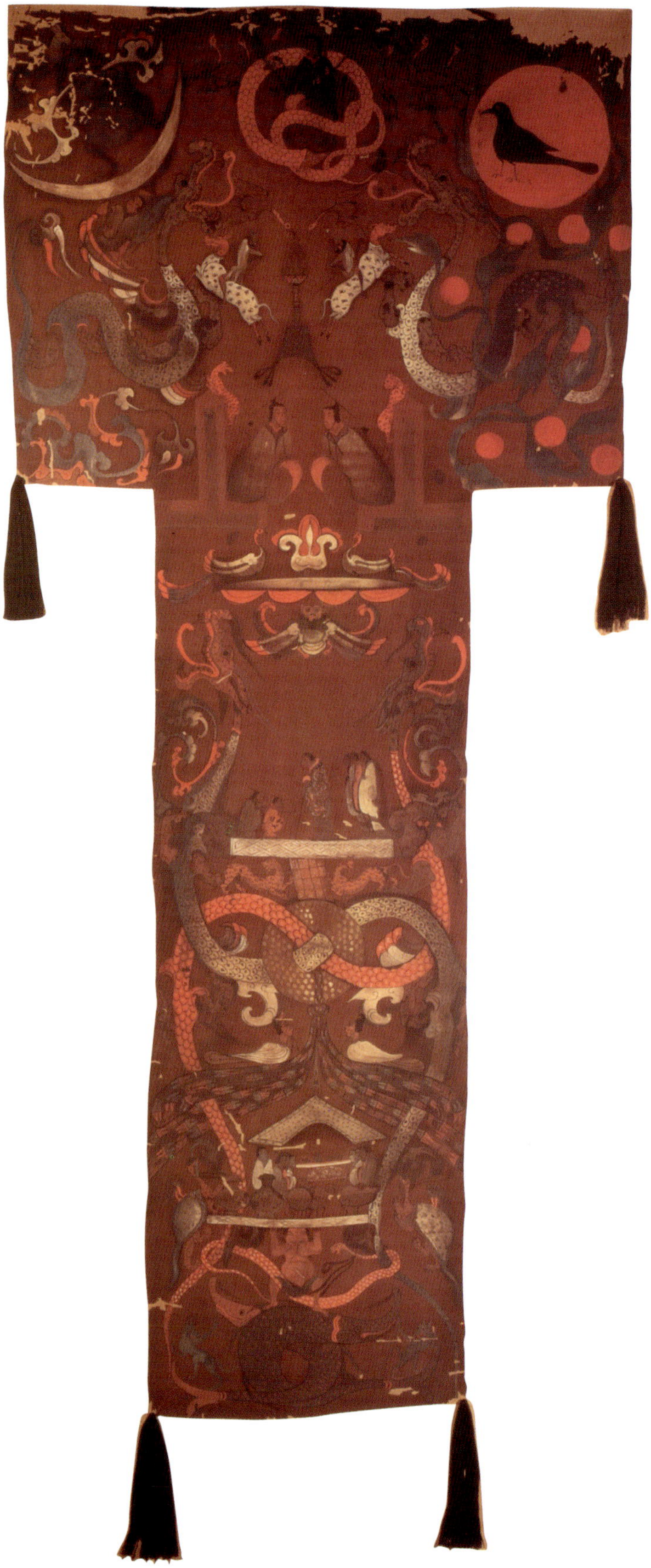

帛畫（馬王堆西漢墓出土）
Painting on silk, unearthed from the Western Han Tombs at Mawangdui, Changsha, Hunan.

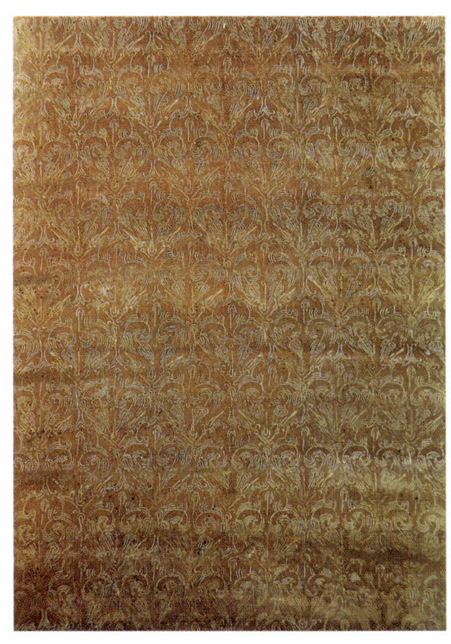

凸印套色的金銀火焰印花紗
（馬王堆西漢墓出土）
Relief-coloured printed gauze with a golden flame design (Unearthed from the Western Han Tombs at Mawangdui, Changsha).

早期的織物印花技術

在長沙馬王堆西漢墓中出土了一批絲絹印花紗。其中有用凸版套印的金銀火焰印花紗，和用漏印方法加手工着色的印花敷彩紗。這是否就是最早的印刷術呢？還需要進一步研究。但它確與印刷的原理完全相同。

Early Fabric Printing Technique

A number of examples of painted gauze were unearthed from the Western Han Tombs at Mawangdui, Changsha, Hunan Province. One example was painted with flames in gold and silver using relief register and another was coloured gauze painted by hand and with leak-plates. Whether this was the earliest printing method needs to be studied further. Nevertheless, the principle was entirely the same as that of printing.

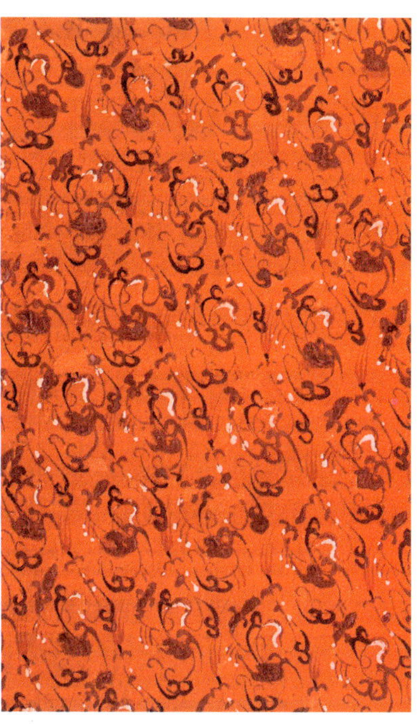

印花敷彩紗（馬王堆西漢墓出土）
Printed coloured gauze with leak-plates (Unearthed from the Western Han Tombs at Mawangdui, Changsha).

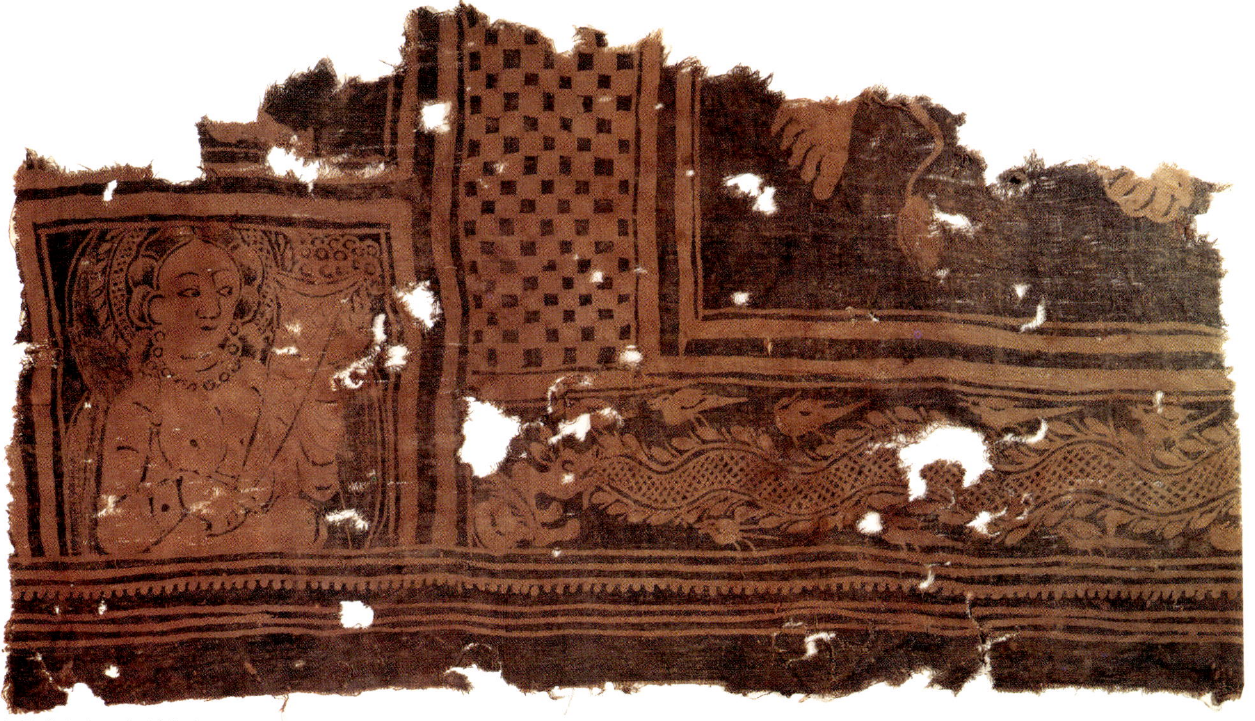

東漢藍印布，新疆出土
Cloth printed in blue in the Eastern Han, unearthed in Xinjiang.

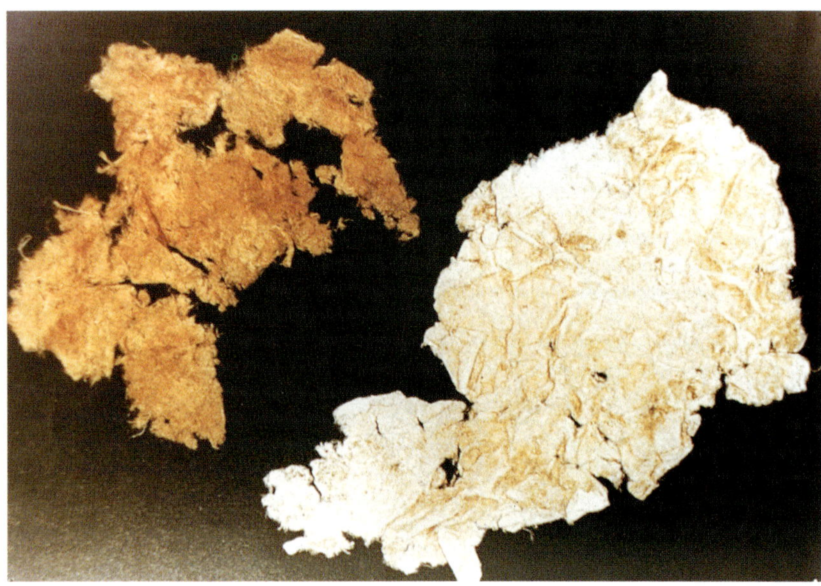

（左） 居延金關紙（西漢）1973 年出土
（右） 敦煌馬圈灣紙（西漢）1979 年出土
(Left) The Jinguan Paper of Juyan (Western Han), unearthed in 1973.
(Right) The Maquanwan Paper of Dunhuang (Western Han), unearthed in 1979.

紙的發明和應用

紙是中國古代四大發明之一，它的發明和應用，給人類提供了一種最理想的書寫材料。也為印刷提供了優質承印材料。根據文獻記載和實物出土，紙的使用約始於西漢中期。

The Invention and Use of Paper

Paper was one of the four great inventions of China. Its invention and use provided the most ideal writing material for mankind. It also provided a good-quality, durable material for printing. According to records in literature and unearthed objects, the use of paper began around the middle of the Western Han Dynasty.

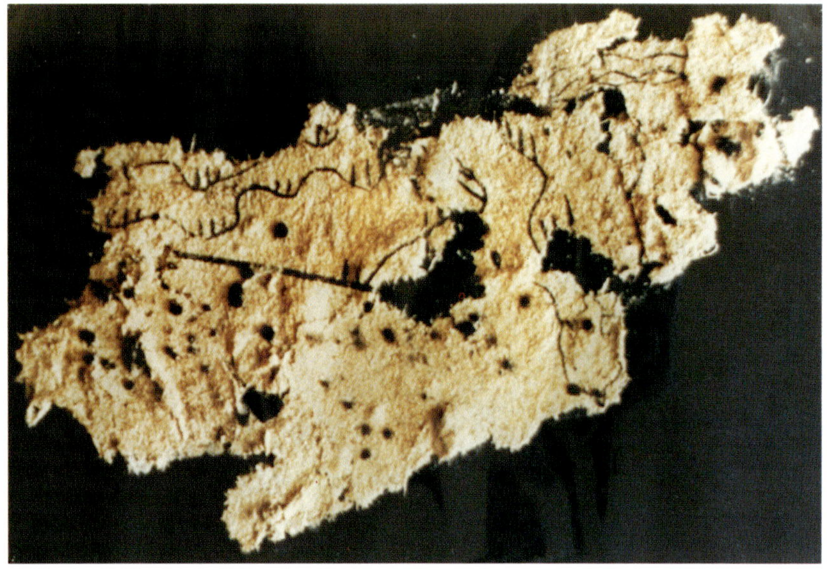

畫有地圖的西漢紙
1986 年甘肅放馬灘出土
Western Han paper painted with a map, unearthed at Fangmatan, Gansu in 1986.

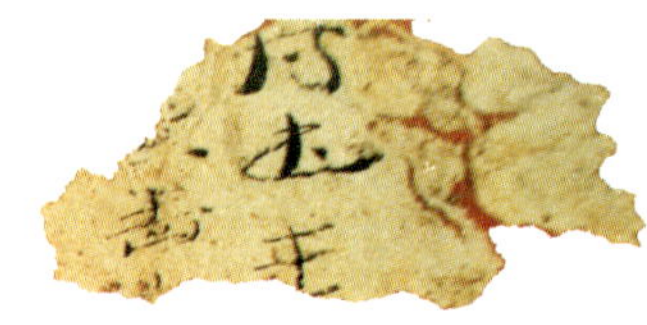

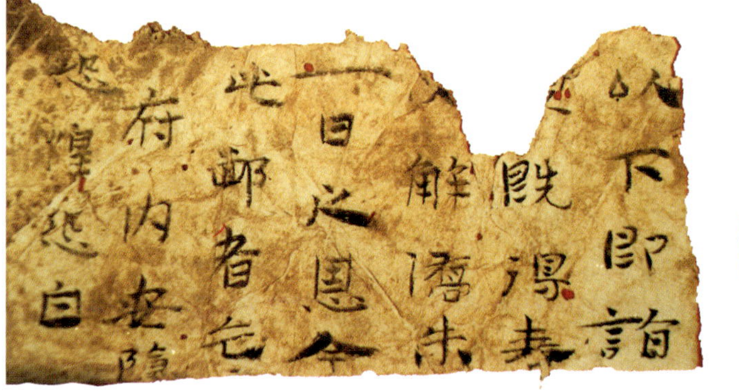

寫有文字的紙（東漢）1990 年甘肅敦煌懸泉出土
Characters on paper (Eastern Han)(AD 25–AD 220), unearthed at Xuanquan, Dunhuang in Gansu in 1990.

蔡倫與造紙術

據《後漢書》記載，宦官蔡倫於東漢元興元年（105）用樹膚、麻頭、敝布、魚網等材料造出優質紙張。蔡倫對造紙技術的發展做出了重要貢獻。

東漢以後，紙的使用不斷擴大，到南北朝時，紙已完全代替了簡帛。

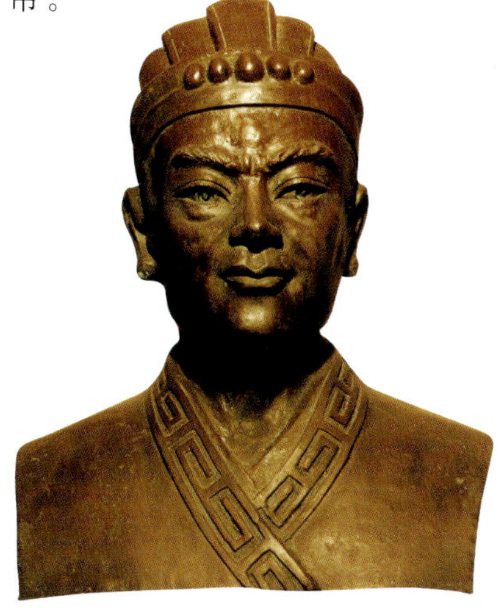

Cai Lun and the Art of Papermaking

According to *The History of the Later Han Dynasty*, Cai Lun, a eunuch, used materials such as tree bark, shreds of hemp, fragments of worn-out cloth and fishnets to produce a high quality paper in A.D. 105. He made a great contribution to the development of papermaking techniques.

From the Eastern Han onwards, the use of paper increased rapidly. By the Southern and Northern Dynasties (420–581), paper entirely replaced bamboo and silk.

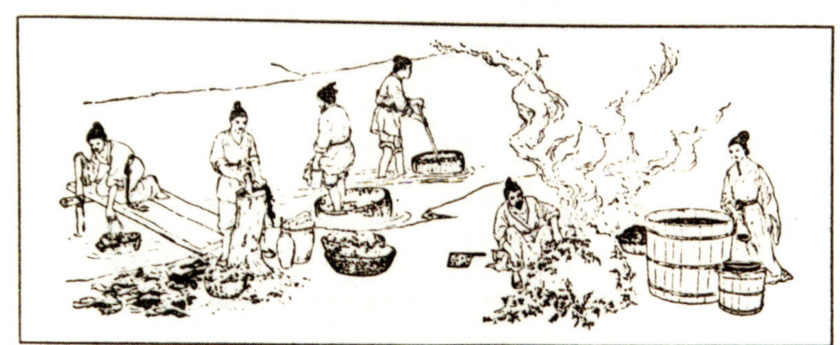

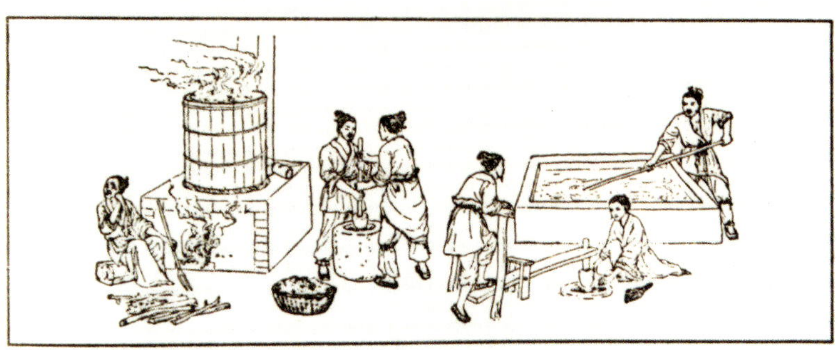

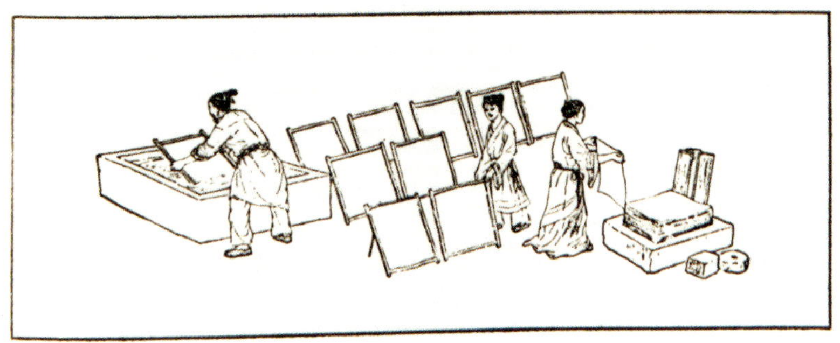

東漢造紙工藝圖

A picture showing the technique of papermaking in the Eastern Han Dynasty (AD 25–220).

我今於中夜 當入於涅槃 汝一心精進 當離於放逸
諸佛甚難值 億劫時一遇 世尊諸子等 聞佛入涅槃
各各懷悲惱 佛滅一何速 聖主法之王 安慰无量衆
我若滅度時 汝等勿憂怖 是德藏菩薩 於无漏實相
心已得通達 其次當作佛 号曰為淨身 亦度无量衆
佛此夜滅度 如薪盡火滅 分布諸舍利 而起无量塔
比丘比丘尼 其數如恒沙 倍復加精進 以求无上道
是妙光法師 奉持佛法藏 八十小劫中 廣宣法華經
是諸八王子 妙光所開化 堅固无上道 當見无數佛
供養諸佛已 隨順行大道 相繼得成佛 轉次而授記
最後天中天 号曰燃燈佛 諸仙之導師 度脫无量衆
是妙光法師 時有一弟子 心常懷懈怠 貪著於名利
求名利无猒 多遊族姓家 棄捨所習誦 廢忘不通利
以是因緣故 号之為求名 亦行衆善業 得見无數佛
供養於諸佛 隨順行大道 具六波羅蜜 今見釋師子
其後當作佛 号名曰彌勒 廣度諸衆生 其數无有量
彼佛滅度後 懈怠者汝是 妙光法師者 今則我身是
我見燈明佛 本光瑞如此 以是知今佛 欲說法華經
今相如本瑞 是諸佛方便 今佛放光明 助發實相義
諸人今當知 合掌一心待 佛當雨法雨 充足求道者
諸求三乘人 若有疑悔者 佛當為除斷 令盡无有餘

《唐人寫經》唐代抄寫在紙上的佛經

Buddhist scritpures on paper from the Tang Dynasty.

雕版印刷術的發明及唐五代印刷

The Invention of Woodblock Printing and Printing in the Tang and the Five Dynasties

618–960

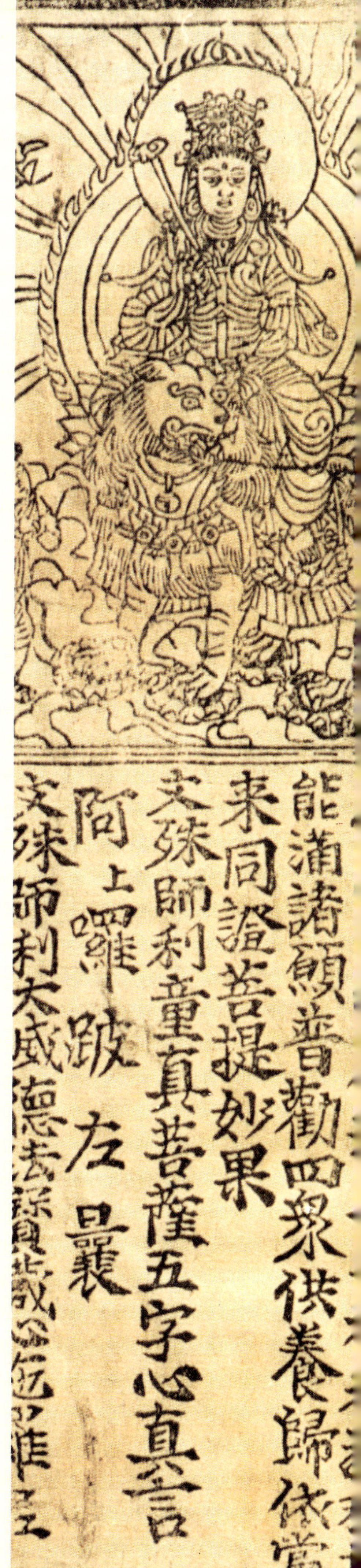

雕版印刷術的發明及唐、五代印刷

印刷術是中國古代偉大發明之一。據文獻記載，隋末唐初（公元七世紀初）就開始使用雕版印刷術。它的發明、應用和傳播，對人類文明和社會進步，做出了巨大貢獻。

文字的定型和廣泛應用，熟練的圖文雕刻技藝，筆墨紙張的精良，再加上社會文化發展的需要，是發明印刷術的基本條件。

The Invention of Woodblock Carving and Printing in the Tang and Five Dynasties

Printing was one of the great inventions in ancient China. According to documentary records, the use of woodblock printing began in the late Sui and early Tang period (early seventh century). Its invention, use and dissemination contributed enormously to human civilization and social progress.

The basic conditions for the invention of printing are: the standardization and wide application of characters, the proficiency in the skills of engraving text and images, advances in brushes, ink and paper, and the need for social and cultural development.

雕版印刷工藝
Technology of woodblock printing.

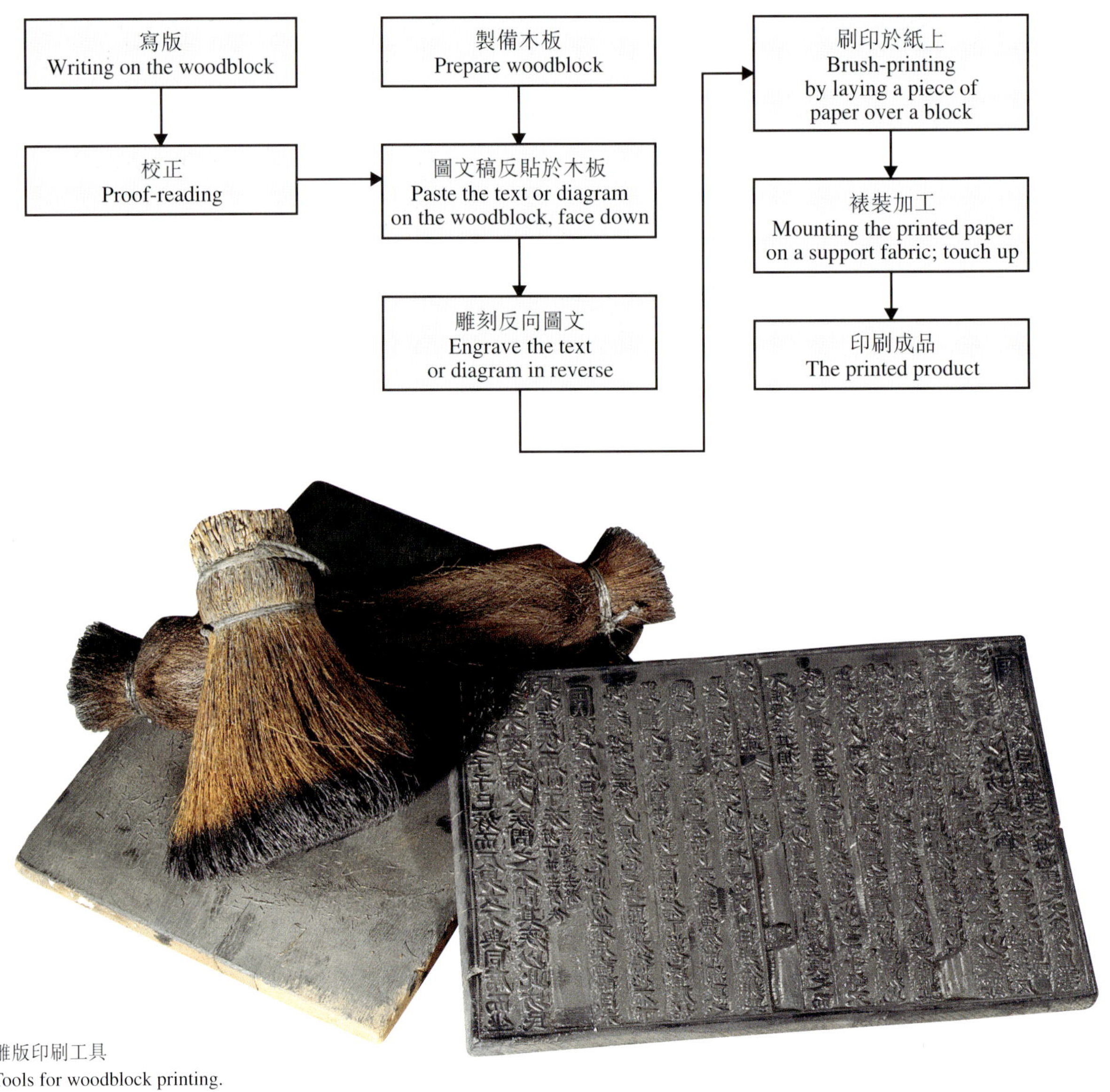

雕版印刷工具
Tools for woodblock printing.

現存早期的印刷品實物

由於歷史久遠，早期的印刷品實物流傳至今者十分稀少。

The earliest extant printing

Owing to its long history, early examples of printing are extremely rare.

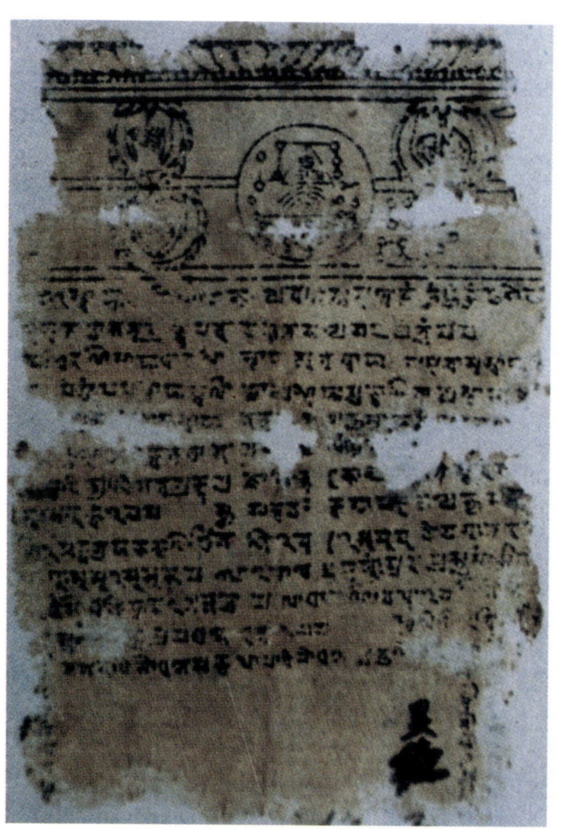

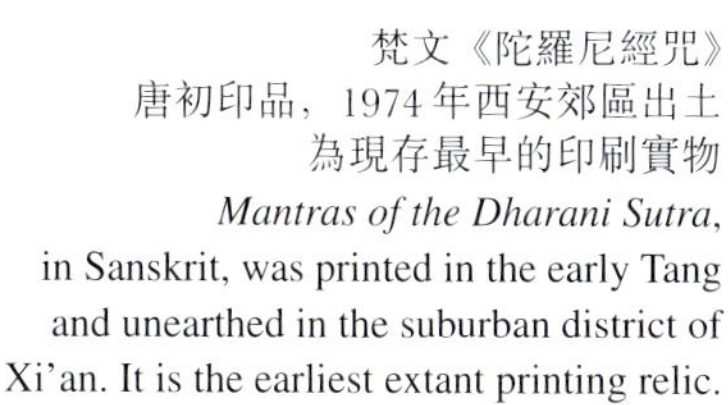

梵文《陀羅尼經咒》
唐初印品，1974 年西安郊區出土
為現存最早的印刷實物

Mantras of the Dharani Sutra, in Sanskrit, was printed in the early Tang and unearthed in the suburban district of Xi'an. It is the earliest extant printing relic.

1906 年在中國新疆吐魯番發現的雕版印刷品《妙法蓮華經》卷五《如來佛壽品第十六》殘卷及《分別功德品第十七》全卷（原件現藏日本"書道博物館"）經專家認定為武周時期 (690–705) 的刻印本。

In 1906, a corrupted version of Chapter 5, entitled "Tathagata Powers and Eternity," and a full version of Chapter 17 entitled "Discrimination of Merits" from *The Sutra of the Lotus Flower of the Wonderful Law* (the original is now in Japan) were found in Turpan in Xinjiang, China. According to experts, the sutra was engraved and printed during the reign of Empress Wu Zetian of the Wu-Zhou Dynasty (690–705).

1966 年於韓國慶州佛國寺釋迦塔內發現一印本《無垢淨光大陀羅尼經》，經文為漢字，且有武周制字，經中外學者考證，為武周後期（690–705）中國洛陽刻印。

In 1966, a copy of the *Dharani Sutra of Spotless Pure Light* was recovered from the Sokka Pagoda in Pulguk-sa Monastery in Kyongju, Korea. This sutra was written in Chinese and some of the characters were of the Wu-Zhou Dynasty. Chinese and foreign scholars have determined that it was engraved and printed in Luoyang, China, during the latter part of the reign of Empress Wu Zetian (690–705).

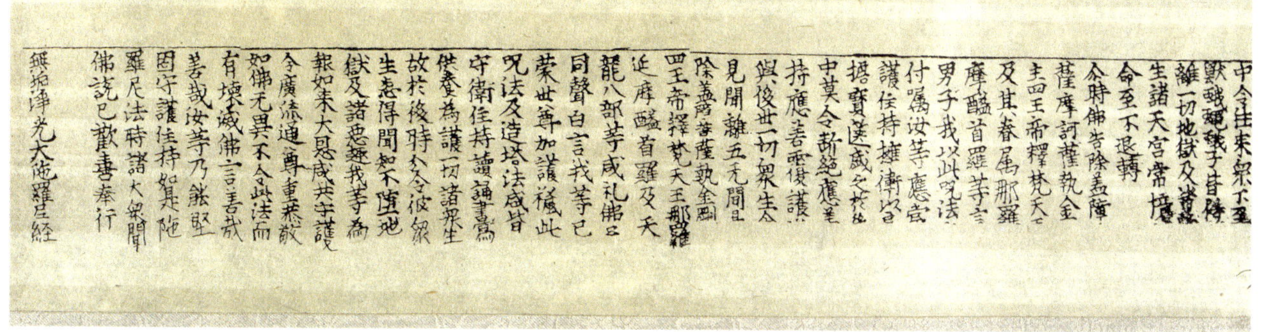

雕版印刷的第一次高潮——唐中後期

公元 9 世紀的近百年中，出現了雕版印刷的第一次高潮。當時的印刷活動分布於長安、洛陽、成都、淮南、敦煌等地。除佛經、佛像印刷外，民間廣泛印刷曆日，相宅，陰陽，字書，韻書等。流傳至今的印刷品也較多。

The First High Tide of Woodblock Printing — The Middle and Late Tang Dynasty

The ninth century B.C. gave rise to the first high tide in woodblock printing. During that period, printing was active in places such as Chang'an, Luoyang, Chengdu, Huainan and Dunhuang. Apart from the printing of Buddhist scriptures and Buddha portraits, private printing of almanacs, books on geomancy and fortune telling, glossaries and rhyming dictionaries were widespread. A considerable amount of printed material dating from this period has survived to the present day.

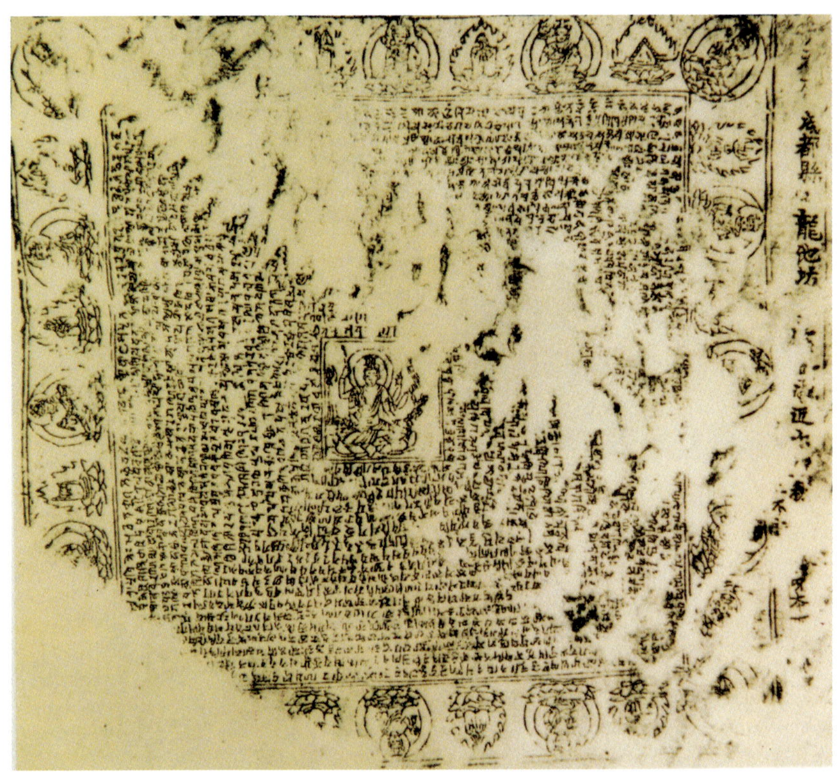

梵文《陀羅尼經》1944 年發現於四川成都唐墓，為 8 世紀印品。
紙薄而堅牢，可能為麻、楮、青檀樹皮等製成。

The Dharani Sutra in Sanskrit. In 1944, this sutra was found in a Tang tomb in Chengdu, Sichuan. The sutra was printed in the 8th century. Its paper was thin but strong, possibly made from hemp, paper mulberry, and wingceltis bark.

1900 年發現於敦煌藏經洞的雕版印刷品《金剛波羅蜜經》，為卷軸裝，刻印精良，印品完整，並有“咸通九年（868 年）四月十五日王玠為二親敬造普施”字樣。為雕版印刷術成熟之作。

In 1900, a woodblock printing of *The Diamond Sutra* was found in Scripture Storage Cave in Dunhuang. It was rolled and the engraving and printing were excellent.
The scripture was in perfect condition and was engraved with the following words:
"Made on the 15th day of the 4th lunar month in the 9th year of the Xiantong period (868) by Wang Jie for my parents and for wide distribution for the sake of charity."
The woodblock printing techniques were fully developed.

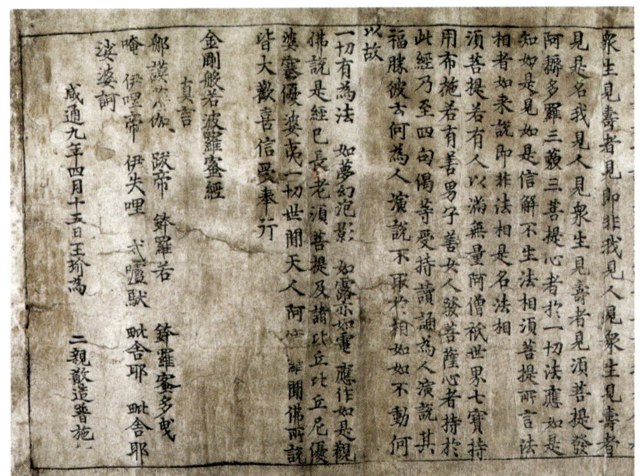

衆生見壽者見即非我見人見衆生見壽者
見是名我見人見衆生見壽者見須菩提發
阿耨多羅三藐三菩提心者於一切法應如是
知如是見如是信解不生法相須菩提所言法
相者如來說即非法相是名法相
須菩提若有人以滿無量阿僧祇世界七寶持
用布施若有善男子善女人發菩薩心者持於
此經乃至四句偈等受持讀誦為人演說其
福勝彼云何為人演說不取於相如如不動何
以故
一切有為法　如夢幻泡影　如露亦如電　應作如是觀
佛說是經已長老須菩提及諸比丘比丘尼優
婆塞優婆夷一切世間天人阿修羅聞佛所說
皆大歡喜信受奉行
金剛般若波羅蜜經
真言
那謨薄伽　跋帝　鉢羅若　鉢羅蜜多曳
唵　伊哩帝　伊失哩　戍嚧馱　毗舍耶　毗舍耶
莎婆訶
咸通九年四月十五日王玠為　二親敬造普施

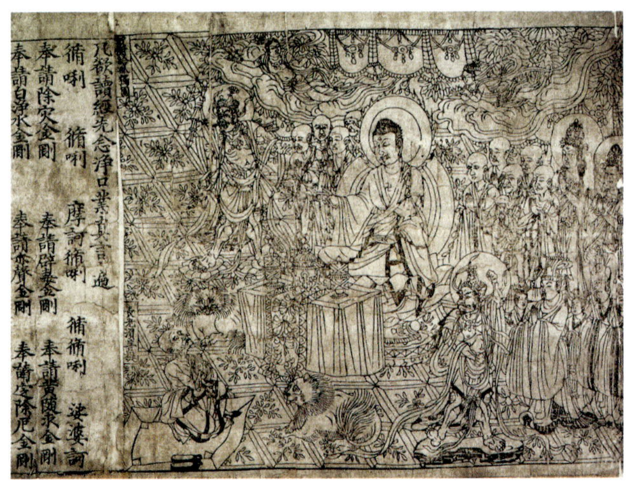

唐代曆書印刷

唐代中後期，四川、淮南一帶民間大量刻印曆書，在市場上出售。唐文宗（827–840 年）依據馮宿的奏章，下令"敕禁斷印曆日版。劍南兩川及淮南道，皆以版印曆日鬻於市。每歲司天台未奏頒下新曆，其印曆已滿天下，有乖敬授之道。故命禁之。"但此後，民間刻印歷書仍綿延不絕。

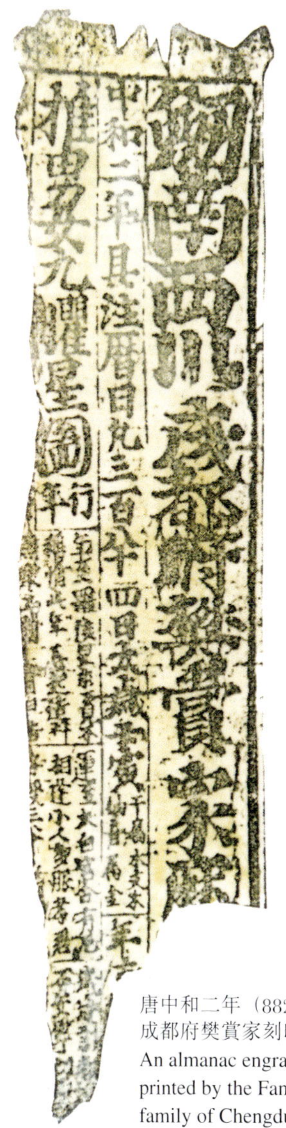

唐中和二年（882 年）成都府樊賞家刻印的曆書

An almanac engraved and printed by the Fan Shang family of Chengdu in the second year of the Zhonghe period of the Tang Dynasty (882).

The Printing of Almanacs in the Tang Dynasty

In the middle and latter part of the Tang Dynasty, around the areas of Sichuan and Huainan, people printed a large number of almanacs and sold them in the market. The Tang Emperor Wenzong, based on the recommendation made in Feng Su's memorials, ordered that "the printing of almanacs must be prohibited. The Jiannan, Liang Chuan and Huainan districts all printed almanacs and sold them in the market. Every year, before the head of the observatory made public the new calender, almanacs were sold everywhere, and this runs contrary to the principle of reverently working out the almanacs for distribution to the people." And yet this did not stop the people from printing almanacs.

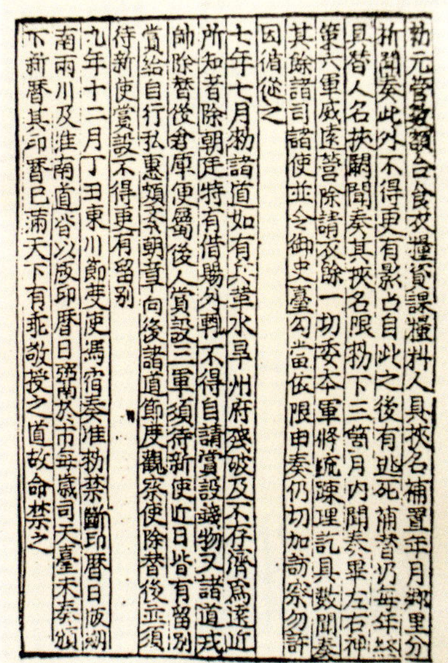

勑元管額令食衣糧資課糧料人具姓名補置年月鄉里分
析聞奏此外不得更有影占自此之後有逃死補替仍每年終
具替人名挾闕聞奏其挾名限勑下三箇月內聞奏畢左右神
策六軍威遠營除請衣糧一切委本軍將疏理訖具數聞奏
其餘諸司諸使並令御史臺勾當依限申奏仍切加勘察勿許
因循從之
七年七月勑諸道如有兵革水旱州府殘破及不存濟爲遠近
所知者除朝廷特有借賜外輒不得自請賞設錢物又諸道戎
帥除替後倉庫便爲後人賞設三軍須待新使近日皆有留別
賞給自行私惠頗紊朝章向後諸道節度觀察使除替後並須
待新使賞設不得更有留別
九年十二月丁丑東川節度使馮宿奏准勑禁斷印曆日版劍
南兩川及淮南道皆以版印曆日鬻於市每歲司天臺未奏頒
下新曆其印曆已滿天下有乖敬授之道故命禁之

《舊唐書》中關於唐文宗（827–840 年）下令禁止民間刻印曆書的記載

A passage in the *History of the Former Tang Dynasty* recording Emperor Wenzong's prohibition of engraving and printing almanacs by the public (827–840).

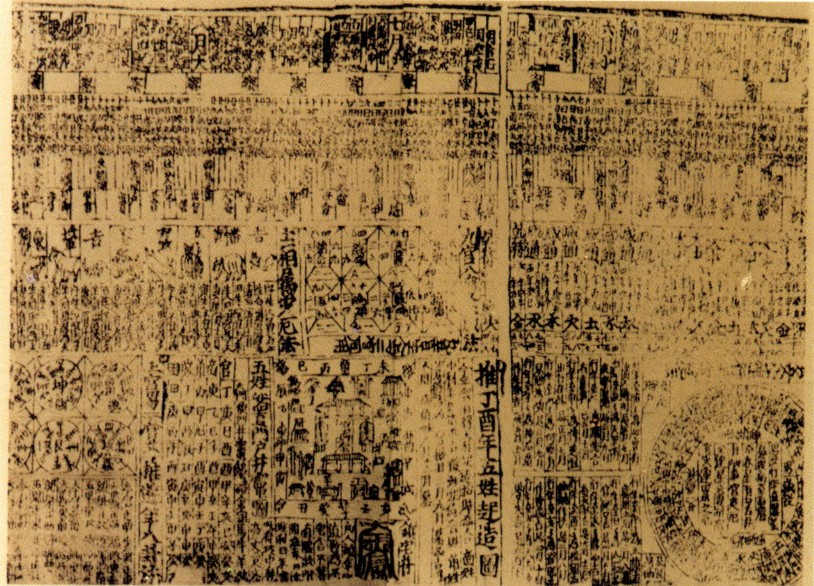

唐僖宗乾符四年（877 年）刻印的曆書

An almanac engraved and printed in the fourth year of Qianfu (877) in the reign of Emperor Xizong of the Tang Dynasty.

五代十國的印刷 (907–960 年)

五代是個割據和朝代更替頻繁的時代，但印刷業仍在發展，而且有新的突破。最主要的標誌是政府對印刷的重視。唐、晉、漢、周四朝連續不斷組織刻印了歷史上第一部儒家經典總集《九經》，使印刷術的應用領域更為擴大。由於佛教仍受到統治者的重視，佛經、佛像的印刷也更為興盛。

在當時統治者的倡導下，在馮道、田敏等人的親自主持下，雇請了大批刻版工匠，歷時22年（932–953年），刻印了整套儒家經典《九經》，這是官方大量應用印刷術的開始。

Printing in the Five Dynasties and the Ten Kingdoms (907–960)

The Five Dynasties was a period of disunity and frequent dynastic changes. But the printing industry still thrived and even broke new ground. The most important indication of this was the emphasis that governments placed on printing. There was the first organized engraving and printing of the collection of Confucian classics under the title of *The Nine Classics,* which enlarged the scope of printing's application. As the rulers placed a great deal of importance on Buddhism, the printing of Buddhist scriptures and Buddha portraits thrived.

Under the auspices of the rulers and the direct management of people like Feng Dao and Tian Min, a large number of engravers and printers were hired. They spent 22 years (932–953) engraving and printing the entire set of the Confucian classics *The Nine Classics* and this was the beginning of the wide application of printing by the government.

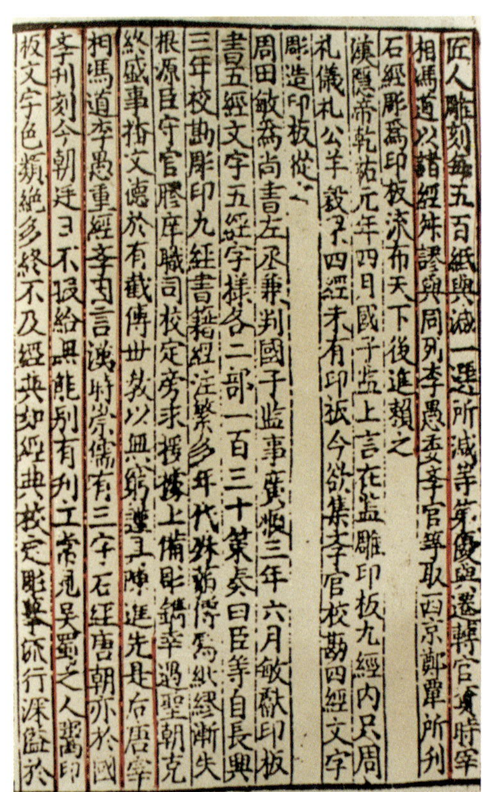

匠人雕刻每五百紙與減一選所減等第優與遷轉官資時宰
相馮道以諸經舛謬與同列李愚委學官田敏取西京鄭覃所刊
石經雕爲印板流布天下後進賴之
漢隱帝乾祐元年四月國子監上言在監雕印板九經內只周
禮儀禮公羊穀梁四經未有印板今欲集學官校勘四經文字
雕造印板從之
周田敏爲尚書左丞兼判國子監事廣順三年六月敏獻印板
書五經文字九經字樣各二部一百三十策奏曰臣等自長興
三年校勘雕印九經書籍經注繁多年代殊邈傳寫紕繆漸失
根源臣守官膠庠職司校定旁求援據上備雕鐫幸遇聖朝克
終盛事播文德於有截傳世教以無窮謹具陳進先是官學
相馮道李愚重經學因言漢時崇儒有三字石經唐朝亦於國
學刊刻今朝廷日不暇給無能別有刊立嘗見吳蜀之人鬻印
板文字色類絕多終不及經典如經典校定雕摹流行深益於

《冊府元龜》中有關於馮道組織刻印《九經》的記載
In A Collection of Information on the Lives of Emperors and Ministers, mention was made on the engraving and printing of *The Nine Classics* organized by Feng Dao.

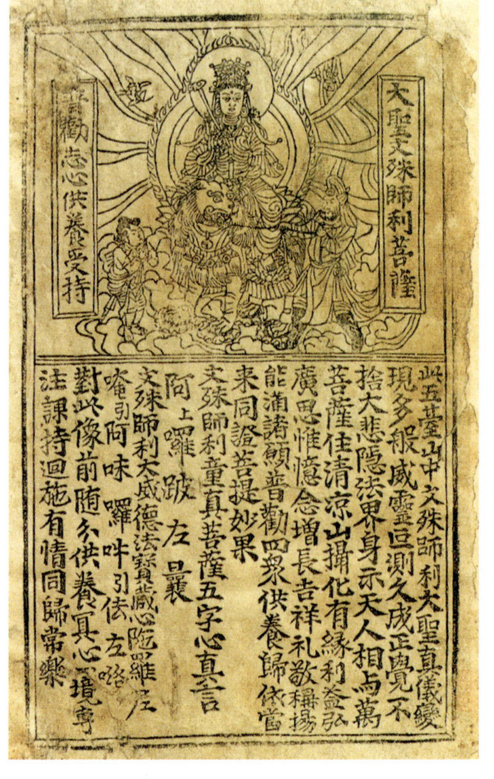

文殊師利菩薩像（五代刻印）
A portrait of Manjusri, the Bodhisattva of Supreme Wisdom.

五代十國的佛教印刷

五代十國，佛教很興盛，當時有寺院 2,964 所，僧尼 61,200 人。在一些寺院內，多數都進行佛經佛像的印刷。

五代後晉時任瓜沙州節度使的曹元忠崇尚佛教，他於開運四年（947 年）組織刻印了一批佛像，大量散發。其版面特點都是上圖下文。

五代十國時的吳越國統治者錢繆，錢弘俶十分崇尚佛教，不但大建寺院，而且刻印不少佛經。

Buddhist Printing in the Five Dynasties and Ten Kingdoms Period

Buddhism was very popular during the Five Dynasties and Ten Kingdoms period (907–939). There were 2,964 temples and 61,200 monks and nuns. The printing of Buddhist scriptures and Buddha portraits was conducted in some temples.

Cao Yuanzong, Governor the Guasha Region in the Later Jin Dynasty of the Five Dynasties, was a Buddhist. In the fourth year of the Kaiyun period (947), he organized the engraving and printing of a large number of Buddha portraits. He distributed them widely. The layout was characterized by printing the drawing in the upper part of the page and the text in the lower part.

Qian Miao and Qian Hongshu, rulers of the states of Wu and Yue in the Five Dynasties and Ten Kingdoms period, were worshippers of Buddhism. They not only built many temples, but also printed many Buddhist scriptures.

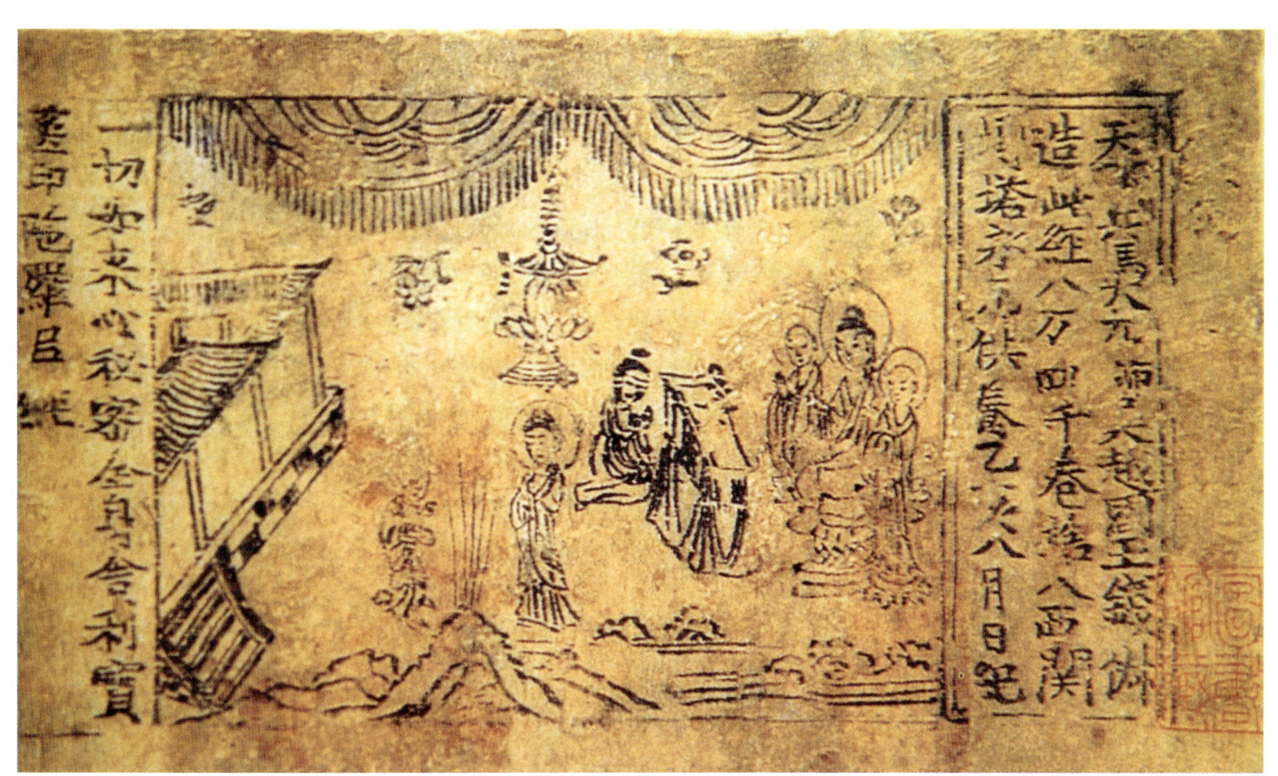

1924 年杭州雷峯塔發現的《寶篋印經》，高 7 厘米，長 2 米，為吳越國所刻印，但當時已是宋開寶八年 (975 年)。
In 1924, *Printed Sutras in a Stupa* was found in the Leifeng Pagoda in Hangzhou. It was 7 centimeters high, 2 meters long, engraved and printed in the kingdom of Wuyue in the eighth year of the Kaibao period (975) in the Song Dynasty.

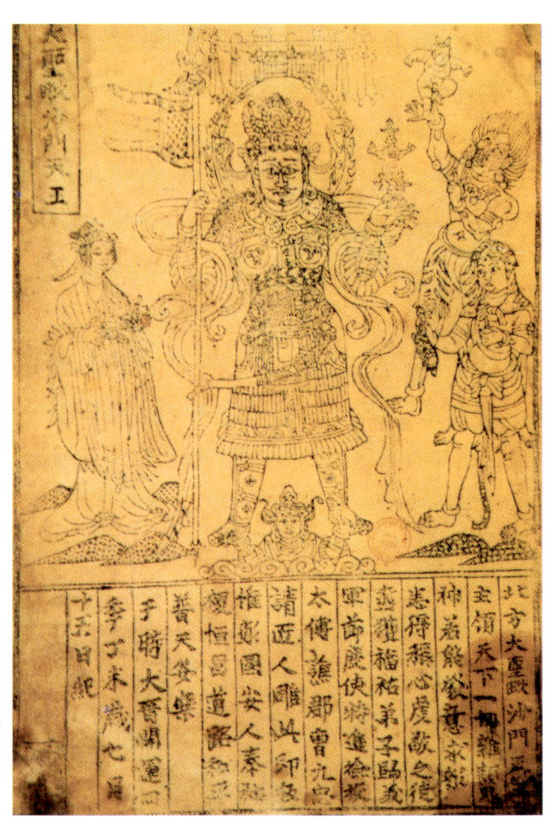

大聖毗沙門天王像
（五代刻印）
A portrait of the great diety Vaishravana. (Printed in the Five Dynasties).

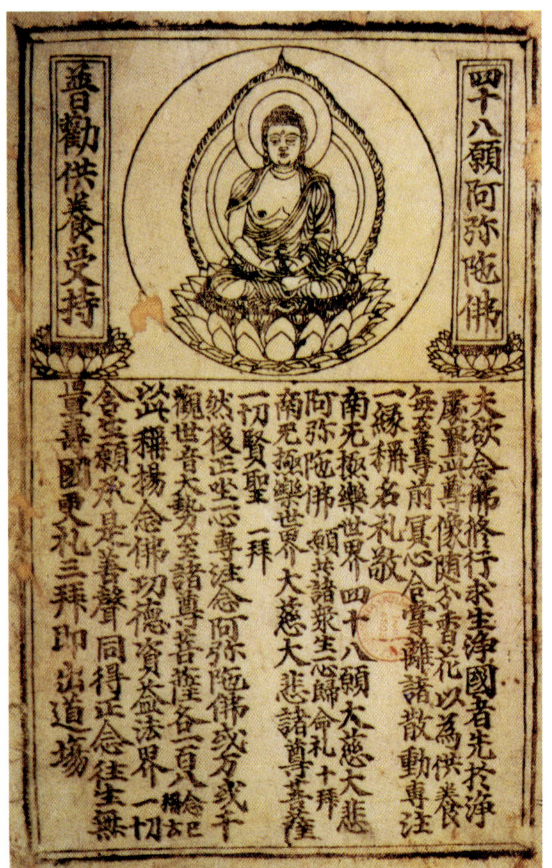

四十八願阿彌陀佛
Guide to chanting "48-Wishes Buddha".

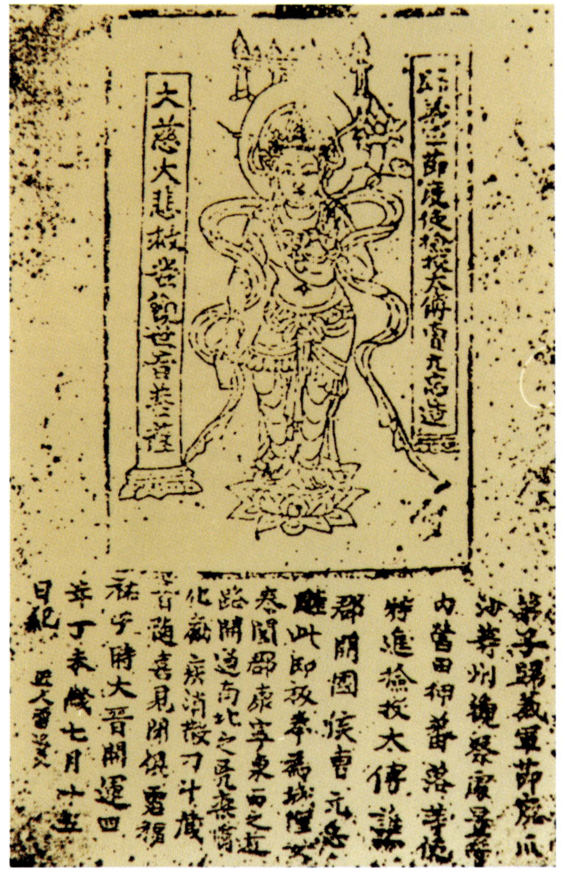

觀世音菩薩像　（五代瓜沙州刻印）
載有刻版工匠雷延美的名字
A portrait of the Goddess of Mercy, with the signature of the engraver Lei Yanmei. (Five Dynasties in the Guasha Region)

宋代印刷

Printing in the Song Dynasty

960–1279

版印書籍唐人尚未盛為之自馮瀛王始印
五經已後典籍皆為版本慶曆中有布衣
畢昇又為活版其法用膠泥刻字薄如錢
脣每字為一印火燒令堅先設一鐵版其

宋代印刷
(960–1279 年)

宋代是我國古代雕版印刷的鼎盛時期，其主要特點是：一、政府對印刷非常重視，從中央到地方的各級機構大都從事印刷活動。二、由於政府對印刷業的開放政策，民間印刷業十分活躍，形成了汴京、杭州、建陽、四川、江西等幾個印刷業集中地。三、印刷數量增加，印刷品種齊全，歷史上流傳的各種著作及當代的著作幾乎都有印刷。四、印刷品質量更為精良，刻印技藝更為精湛，書籍版式逐漸規範化。成為後世雕版印刷的楷模。

宋代政府印刷

宋代中央主管印刷的機構是國子監，在建國後的四十多年間，國子監已存印版十餘萬，包括經、史、子、集諸書。到北宋中期，日印刷量達到一萬張，可見生產規模之大。

宋代的各級地方政府，大都從事印刷活動。所刻書不但數量很大，而且質量很高。

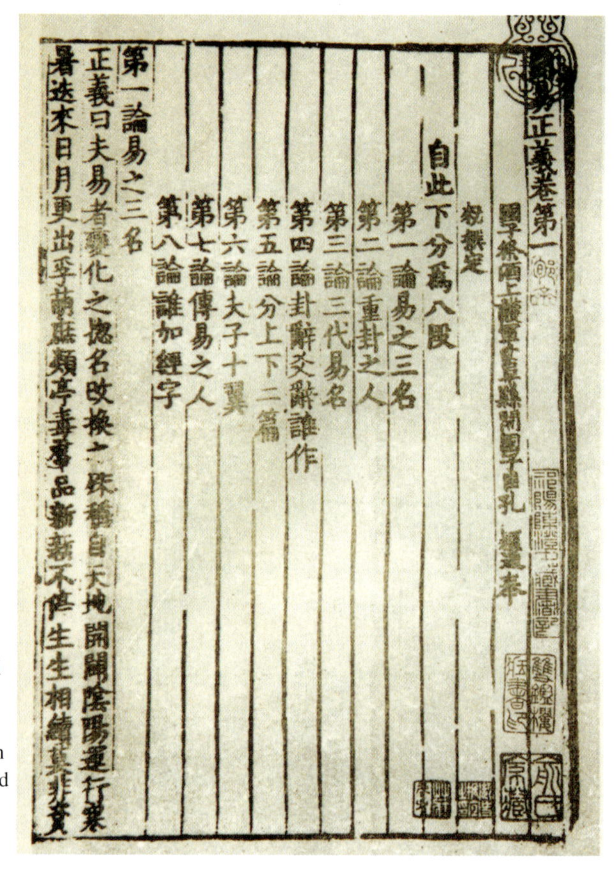
周易正義卷第一
國子祭酒上護軍曲阜縣開國子臣孔穎達奉
敕撰定
自此下分爲八段
第一論易之三名
第二論重卦之人
第三論三代易名
第四論卦辭爻辭誰作
第五論分上下二篇
第六論夫子十翼
第七論傳易之人
第八論誰加經字
第一論易之三名
正義曰夫易者變化之總名改換之殊稱自天地開闢陰陽運行寒
暑迭來日月更出孚萌庶類亭毒群品新新不停生生相續莫非資

《周易正義》
南宋國子監本
約紹興十五年（1145 年）
原版 23.3 × 15.7 厘米
Correct Meanings of the Book of Changes, a copy kept at the National Academy in the Southern Song Dynasty in approximately the fifteenth year of the Shaoxing period (1145). The original measures 23.3 × 15.7 cm.

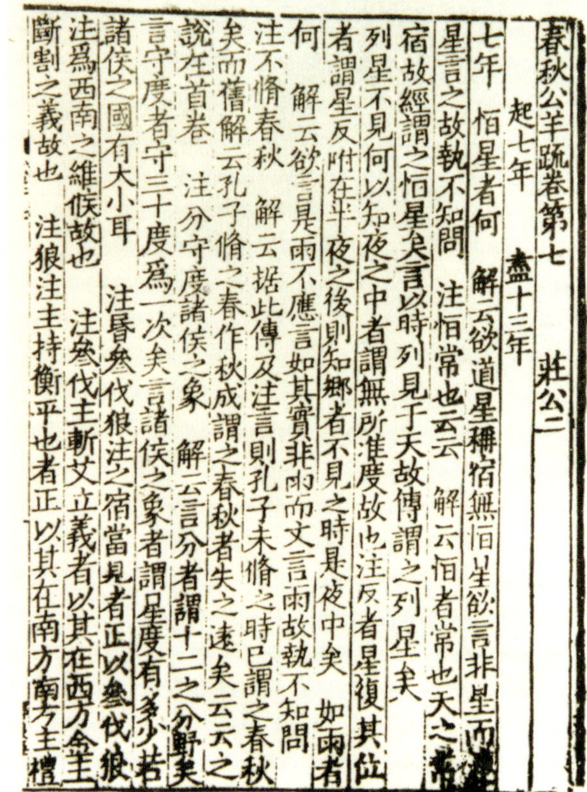
春秋公羊疏卷第七　起七年　盡十三年　莊公二
七年　恒星者何　解云欲道星稱宿無恒星欲言非星而經
星言之故執不知問　注恒常也云云　解云恒者常也天之常
宿故經謂之恒星矣言以時列見于天故傳謂之列星矣
列星不見何以知夜之中者謂無所准度故也注反者星復其位
者謂星反附在半夜之後則知鄉者不見之時是夜中矣　如雨者
何　解云欲言是雨不應言如其實非雨而文言雨故執不知問
注不脩春秋　解云据此傳及注言則孔子未脩之時已謂之春秋
矣而舊解云孔子脩之春作秋成謂之春秋者失之遠矣云云之
說在首卷　注分守度諸侯之象　解云言分者謂十二之分野矣
言守度者守三十度爲一次矣言諸侯之象者謂星度有多少若
諸侯之國有大小耳　注昏參伐狼注之宿當見者正以參伐狼
注爲西南之維候故也　注參伐主斬艾立義者以其在西方金主
斷割之義故也　注狼注主持衡平也者正以其在南方南方主禮

《春秋公羊疏》
南宋國子監本
原版 22 × 15.8 厘米
The Gong-Yang Commentary on the Spring and Autumn Annals, a copy kept at the National Academy in the Southern Song Dynasty. The original measures 22 × 15.8 cm.

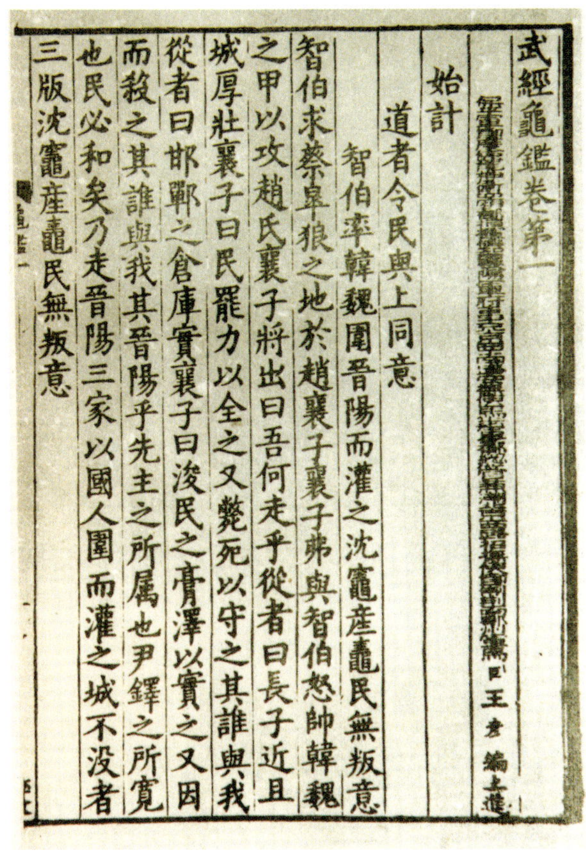

武經龜鑑卷第一

王彥編上進

始計

道者令民與上同意

智伯率韓魏圍晉陽而灌之沈竈產鼃民無叛意

智伯求蔡皋狼之地於趙襄子襄子弗與智伯怒帥韓魏之甲以攻趙氏襄子將出曰吾何走乎從者曰長子近且城厚壯襄子曰民罷力以全之又斃死以守之其誰與我從者曰邯鄲之倉庫實襄子曰浚民之膏澤以實之又因而殺之其誰與我其晉陽乎先主之所屬也尹鐸之所寬也民必和矣乃走晉陽三家以國人圍而灌之城不沒者三版沈竈產鼃民無叛意

《武經龜鑒》
南宋初杭州政府官刻本
約隆興二年(1164 年) 後
原版 24.2 × 17.1 厘米
The Magic Mirror for Military Techniques, engraved by the Hangzhou government in the early Southern Song period after the second year of the Longxing period (1164). The original measures 24.2 × 17.1 cm.

《事類賦注》
兩浙東路茶鹽司刻本
紹興十六年（1146 年）
原版 21.8 × 14.9 厘米
刻工：丁珪、毛諒、王珍、朱瑣等
Commentaries on Classified Affairs, a copy kept at the East Route Office of Tea and Salt of the Liang-Zhe region in the sixteenth year of the Shaoxing period (1146). The original measures 21.8 × 14.9 cm. The engravers included Ding Gui, Mao Liang, Wang Zhen, Zhu Suo and others.

Printing in the Song Dynasty (960–1279)

The Song Dynasty was the prime period of woodblock printing in ancient China. Printing in Song has several characteristics. Firstly, the government attached great importance to printing. Most of the officials in the central and local governments were involved in printing activities. Secondly, the government's open policy on printing resulted in the formation of printing centres in such places as Bianjing, Hangzhou, Jianyang, Sichuan and Jiangxi where private printing was extremely popular. Thirdly, there was a great increase in the quantity and variety of texts, and popular works through the ages and contemporary works were printed. Fourthly, the quality and quantity became considerably better, the printing techniques were more advanced and the layout became standardized.

Government Printing

In the Song Dynasty, the central organization in charge of printing was the National Academy. During the forty years after the founding of the dynasty, the National Academy accumulated over 100,000 printing plates, including classics, histories, philology and collected works. By the middle part of the Northern Song Dynasty, the daily printing volume reached more than 10,000 sheets. From this, we can see the magnitude of production in those days.

Most local governments at various levels in the Song Dynasty engaged in printing. The number of books engraved was large and the quality was also superior.

政府印刷

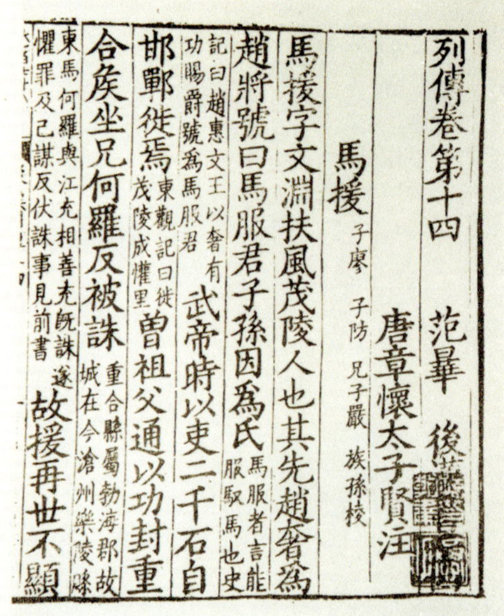

列傳卷第十四　范曄　後漢書　唐章懷太子賢注

馬援　子廖　子防　兄子嚴　族孫棱

馬援字文淵扶風茂陵人也其先趙奢爲趙將號曰馬服君子孫因爲氏 馬服者言能服馭馬也史記曰趙惠文王以奢有功賜爵號爲馬服君 武帝時以吏二千石自邯鄲徙焉 東觀記曰徙茂陵成懽里 曾祖父通以功封重合侯 重合縣屬勃海郡故城在今滄州樂陵縣東 坐兄何羅反被誅 馬何羅與江充相善充既誅懼罪及己謀反伏誅事見前書 故援再世不顯

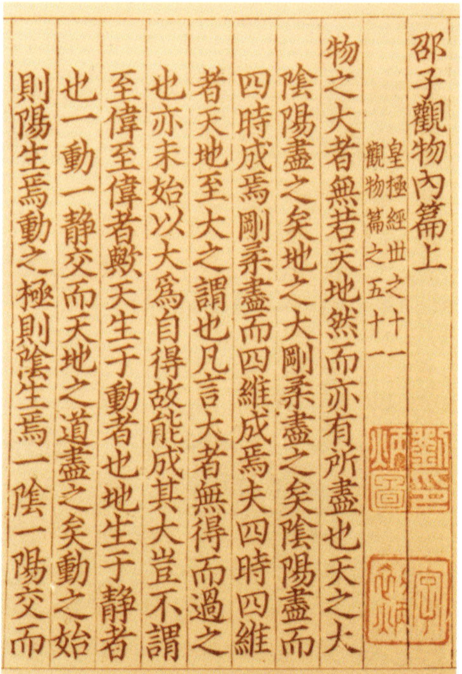

邵子觀物內篇上

皇極經世之十一　觀物篇之五十一

物之大者無若天地然而亦有所盡也天之大陰陽盡之矣地之大剛柔盡之矣陰陽盡而四時成焉剛柔盡而四維成焉夫四時四維者天地至大之謂也凡言大者無得而過之也亦未始以大爲自得故能成其大豈不謂至偉至偉者歟天生于動者也地生于靜者也一動一靜交而天地之道盡之矣動之始則陽生焉動之極則陰生焉一陰一陽交而

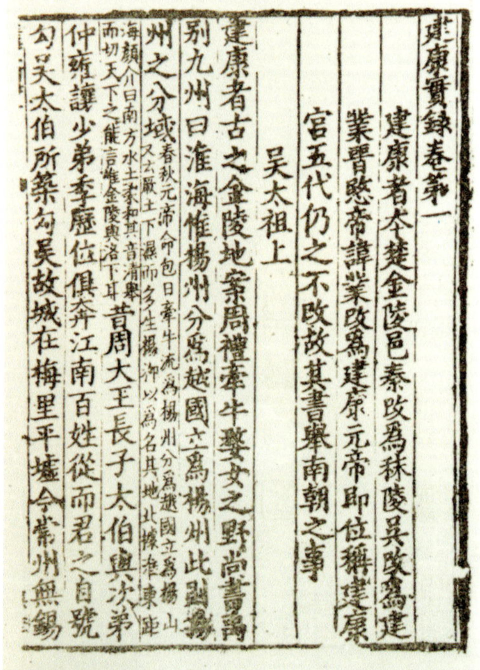

建康實錄卷第一

建康者本楚金陵邑秦改爲秣陵吳改爲建業晉愍帝諱業改爲建康元帝即位稱建康宮五代仍之不改故其書舉南朝之事

吳太祖上

建康者古之金陵地案周禮牽牛婺女之野尚書禹別九州曰淮海惟揚州分爲越國立爲揚州此亂揚州之分域 春秋元命包曰牽牛流爲揚州分爲越國立爲揚山又云厥土下濕而多生楊柳以爲名其地北據淮東距海顏介曰南方水土柔和其音清舉而切天下之能言惟金陵與洛下耳 昔周大王長子太伯與次弟仲雍讓少弟季歷位俱奔江南百姓從而君之自號句吳太伯所築句吳故城在梅里平墟今常州無錫

(上)　《史記集解》　南宋淮南路轉運司刻本　南宋初期
原版：22.3 × 17.7 厘米

(Top)　*Commentaries on Records of the Grand Historian,* a copy kept at the Grain Transport Office of Huainan Circuit at the beginning of the Southern Song Dynasty. The original measures 22.3 × 17.7 cm.

(下)　《邵子觀物內篇》
南宋福建漕治刻印本

(Bottom) *The Inner Chapters of Viewing Things* by Shao Yong, engraved and printed at Caozhi, Fujian in the Southern Song.

(上)　《後漢書注》　南宋江南東路轉運司刻本
原版：21.4 × 17.1 厘米　刻工：陳震、丘甸、章日文等

(Top)　*Commentaries on the History of Later Han,* a printed copy kept at Transport Office of Jiangnan Eastern Route in the Southern Song Dynasty. The original measures 21.4 × 17.1 cm. The engravers included Chen Zhen, Qiu Dian, and Zhang Riwen.

(下)　《建康實錄》　荊湖北路安撫使司刻本（江陵）
宋紹興十八年（1148年）　原版：22.7 × 15.8 厘米

(Bottom) *Veritable Records of Emperor Jiankang,* a copy kept at the Imperial Commission of the Northern Route of Jinghu in the eigthteenth year of the Shaoxing period in the Song Dynasty (1148). The original measures 22.7 × 15.8 cm.

Samples of Government Printing

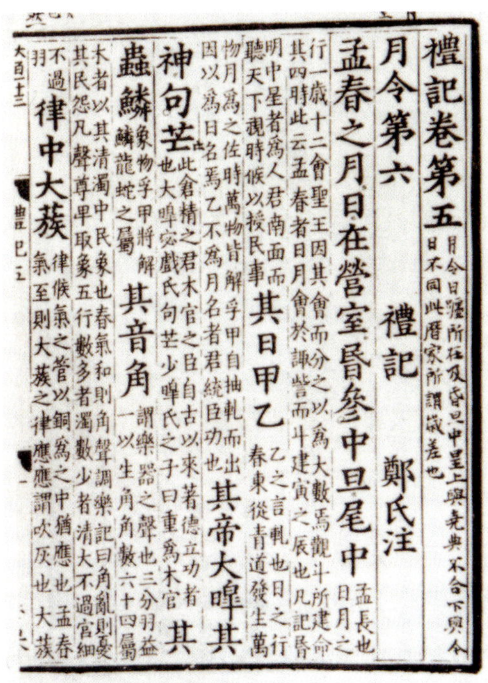

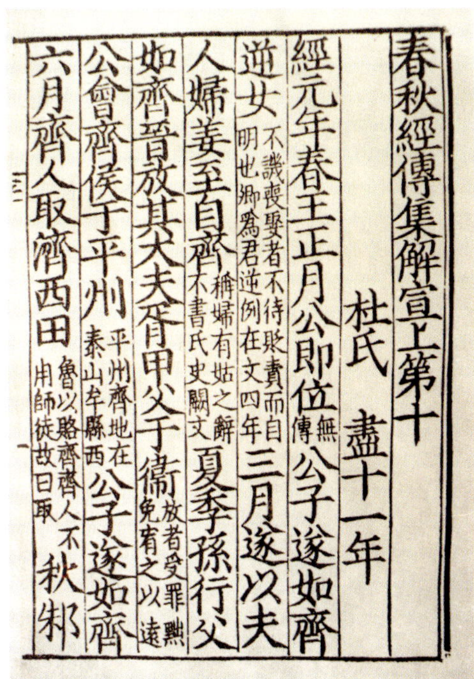

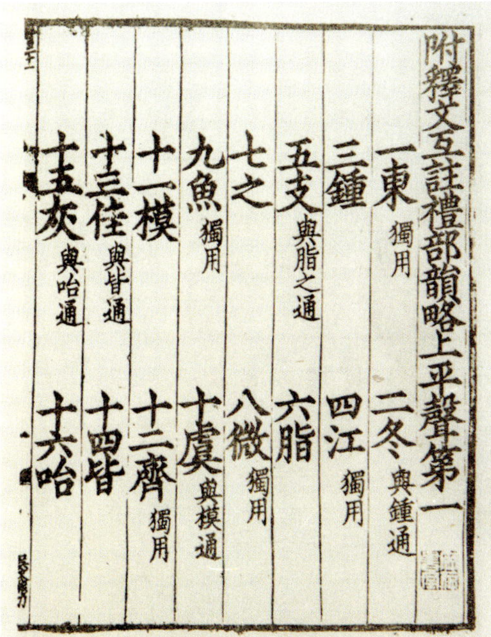

附釋文互註禮部韻略上平聲第一

一東 獨用　二冬 與鍾通

三鍾　四江 獨用

五支 與脂之通　六脂

七之　八微 獨用

九魚 獨用　十虞 與模通

十一模　十二齊 獨用

十三佳 與皆通　十四皆

十五灰 與咍通　十六咍

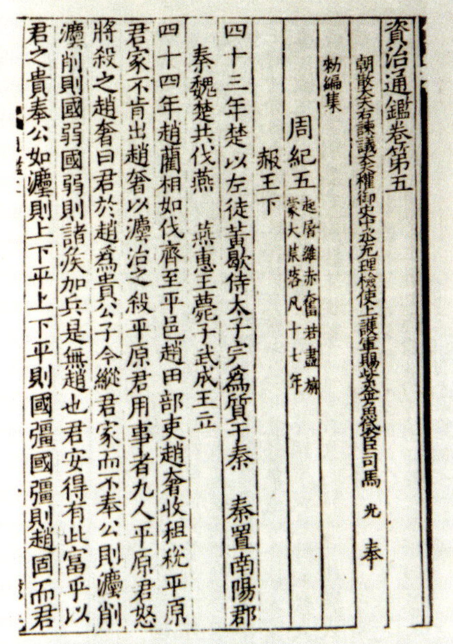

（上）《禮記注》撫州公使庫刻本
南宋淳熙四年（1177年）原版：20.2 × 14.7 厘米

(Top) *Commentaries on the Book of Rites*, an officially printed copy at Fuzhou in the fourth year of the Chunxi period of the Song Dynasty (1177).
The original measures 20.2 × 14.7 cm.

（下）《附釋文互注禮部韻略》南宋廣東漕司刻本

(Bottom) *Explanations and Commentaries on of the Book of Rites According to Rhyming Order*, engraved by the Guangdong Grain Transport Office in the Southern Song.

（上）《春秋經傳集解》宋成都官刻本

(Top) *Glosses on Commentaries on the Spring and Autumn Annals*, officially engraved by the government of Chengdu in the Song Dynasty.

（下）《資治通鑑》兩浙東路公使庫刻本
南宋紹興三年（1133年）
原版：21 × 14.1 厘米

(Bottom) *Comprehensive Mirror to Aid in Government*, an officially printed book by the Eastern Route Office in the Liang-Zhe region in the third year of the Shaoxing period of the Southern Song Dynasty (1133). The original measures 21 × 14.1 cm.

宋代學校印刷

宋代教育發達，不少書院、州、縣學都從事印刷事業，刻印了大量古今書籍。

School Printing in the Song Dynasty

Education in the Song Dynasty was popular. Many academies and schools in provinces and counties were involved in the printing of books.

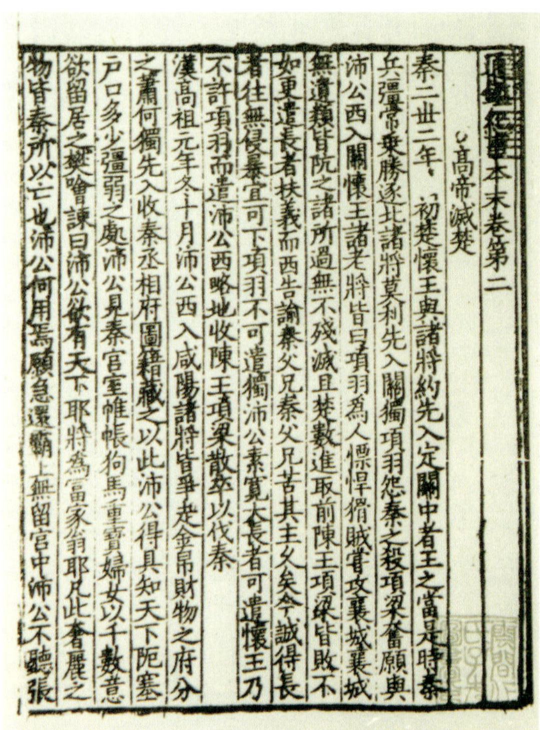

通鑑紀事本末卷第二

高帝滅楚

秦二世三年，初楚懷王與諸將約先入定關中者王之當是時秦兵彊常乘勝逐北諸將莫利先入關獨項羽怨秦之殺項梁奮願與沛公西入關懷王諸老將皆曰項羽爲人慓悍猾賊嘗攻襄城襄城無遺類皆阬之諸所過無不殘滅且楚數進取前陳王項梁皆敗不如更遣長者扶義而西告諭秦父兄秦父兄苦其主久矣今誠得長者往無侵暴宜可下項羽不可遣獨沛公素寬大長者可遣懷王乃不許項羽而遣沛公西略地收陳王項梁散卒以伐秦

漢高祖元年冬十月沛公西入咸陽諸將皆爭走金帛財物之府分之蕭何獨先入收秦丞相府圖籍藏之以此沛公得具知天下阨塞戶口多少彊弱之處沛公見秦宮室帷帳狗馬重寶婦女以千數意欲留居之樊噲諫曰沛公欲有天下耶將爲富家翁耶凡此奢麗之物皆秦所以亡也沛公何用焉願急還霸上無留宮中沛公不聽張

《通鑑紀事本末》
廣陵郡庠刻本　南宋淳熙二年（1175 年）
原版：19.2 × 15.4 厘米
"Chronicles of Events" in *Comprehensive Mirror to Aid in Government*, printed by the Guangling Commandery in the second year of the Chunxi period of the Southern Song Dynasty (1175).
The original measures 19.2 × 15.4 cm.

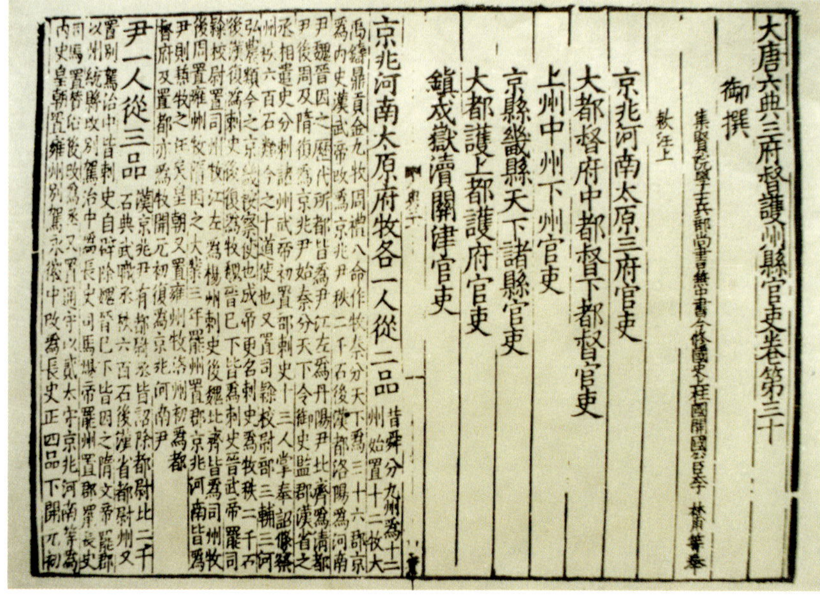

大唐六典三府督護州縣官吏卷第三十

御撰

京兆河南太原三府官吏

大都督府中都督下都督官吏

上州中州下州官吏

京縣畿縣天下諸縣官吏

大都護上都護府官吏

鎮戍嶽瀆關津官吏

京兆河南太原府牧各一人從二品

尹一人從三品

《大唐六典注》溫州州學刻本
南宋紹興四年（1134 年）
原版：20.8 × 13.7 厘米
Explanations of the Six Tang Administrative Codes, engraved by the Provincial School of Wenzhou in the fourth year of the Shaoxing period of the Song Dynasty (1134).
The original measures 20.8 × 13.7 cm.

宋代佛經印刷

佛經的印刷在印刷術發明初期，就已出現。而宋代佛經印刷的規模之大，是前代無法比擬的。宋至少刻印了六種版本的《大藏經》，即971–983 年印於益州（成都）的《開寶藏》；1080–1103 年印於福州的《崇寧藏》；1112–1172 年印於福州的《毗盧藏》；1132 年印於湖州的《圓覺藏》；1175 年印於安吉的《資福藏》；1231–1321 年印於平江（蘇州）的《磧砂藏》。每種在 5,000–7,000 卷，可見規模之大。

Buddhist Printing in the Song Dynasty

The printing of Buddhist sutras was carried out soon after printing was invented. The scale of printing Buddhist scriptures in the Song was far greater than that of the previous dynasties. At least six editions of the *Tripitaka* were printed. They were: *The Kaibao Tripitaka,* printed in Yizhou (Chengdu) between 971 and 983; *The Congning Tripitaka* printed in Fuzhou between 1080 and 1103; *The Vairocana Tripitaka* printed in Fuzhou between 1112 and 1172; *The Tripitaka of Complete Enlightenment* printed in Huzhou in 1132; *The Zilu Tripitaka* printed in Anji in 1175; and The *Zisha Tripitaka* printed in Pingjiang between 1231 and 1321. Each of these *Tripitakas* consisted of between 5,000 and 7,000 chapters, indicating that printing was undertaken on a great scale.

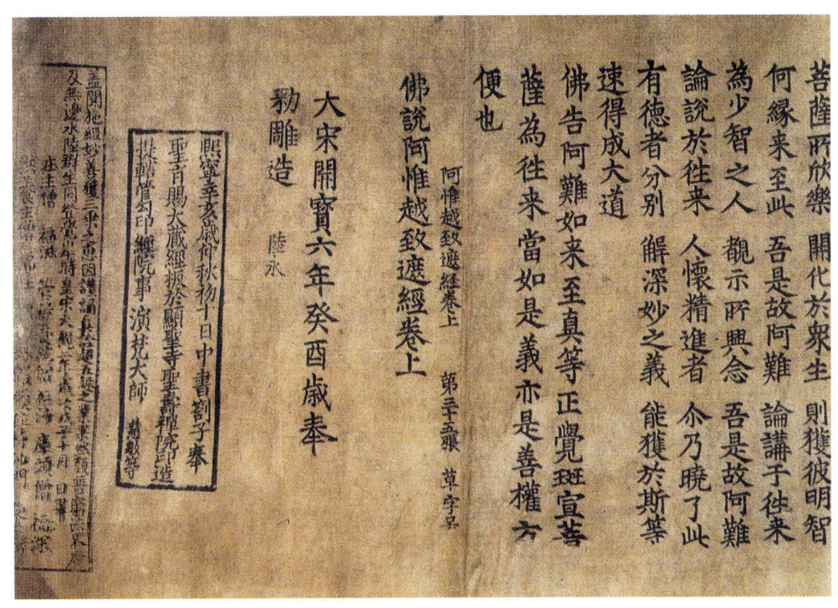

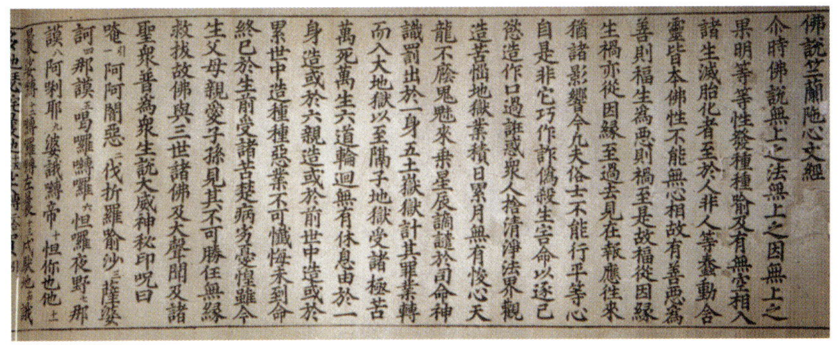

（上）《開寶藏》
北宋開寶四年（971 年）起，政府刻印於成都，歷時 12 年，雕版 13 萬塊。

(Top) The *Kaibao Tripitaka*
The printing of this Tripitaka began in 971. It took 12 years to print the entire publication and 130,000 plates were used.

（下）《佛說竺蘭陀心文經》北宋元豐六年（1083 年）

(Bottom) A Buddist sutra printed in the sixth year of the Yuanfeng period of the Song Dynasty (1083).

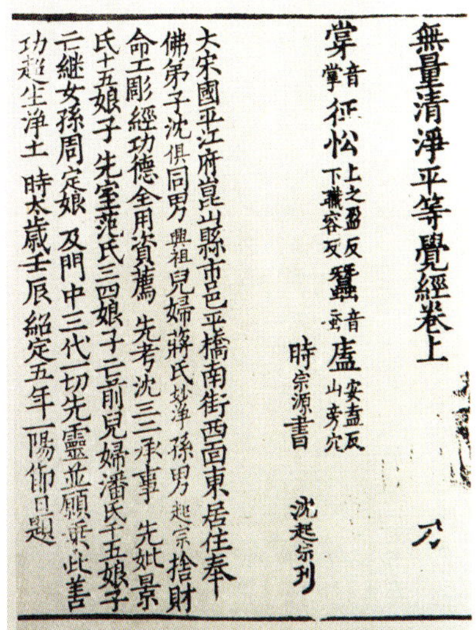

《磧砂藏》江蘇吳縣磧沙延聖院於南宋紹定四年（1231 年）設立經坊，雇工刻印，共 6,312 卷，按千字文排序，經折裝。

The Zisha Edition of the Buddhist *Tripitaka.* A workshop was set up at the Yansheng Academy in the fourth year of Shaoting in the Song Dynasty (1231) in Zhisha in the Wu County of Jiangsu. Engravers and printers were employed to print the *Tripitaka* in 6,312 chapters. It was printed and bound according to the order in *The Thousand-character Classics.*

宋代民間印刷

宋代民間印刷業十分發達，主要分布在福建、浙江、江西、江蘇、四川等地。

福建是宋代印刷業發達的地區之一，而印刷業最集中的是建陽和建安兩縣，尤以建陽的麻沙、崇化最為著名。到南宋，這裏印刷業已達全盛。有書坊三十三家。朱熹說："建陽書籍，上自六經，下及訓傳，行四方者，無遠不至。"就是說這裏印的書，不但品種齊全，而且遠銷全國各地。

Private Printing in the Song Dynasty

Private printing flourished in the Song with major centres at Fujian, Zhejiang, Jiangxi, Jiangsu, Sichuan and elsewhere.

Fujian was one of the areas during the Song where printing was well developed. Printing was concentrated in the two counties of Jianyang and Jian'an, with the two best known centres at Masha and Chonghua in Jianyang. By the Southern Song, printing in Jianyang reached its peak with 33 printshops. Zhu Xi once made the remark that "books printed in Jianyang ranged from the six classics to instructions and biographies. They were distributed to all places and no place was too far to be reached." This means that the books printed there covered a wide range of subjects and were distributed to places throughout the country.

《史記集解索隱》，南宋乾道七年（1171年），建陽蔡夢弼書坊刻印

Index to the Collected Commentaries on Records of the Grand Historian was printed by Cai Mengbai Bookstore in the seventh year of the Qiandao period (1171) of the Southern Song Dynasty.

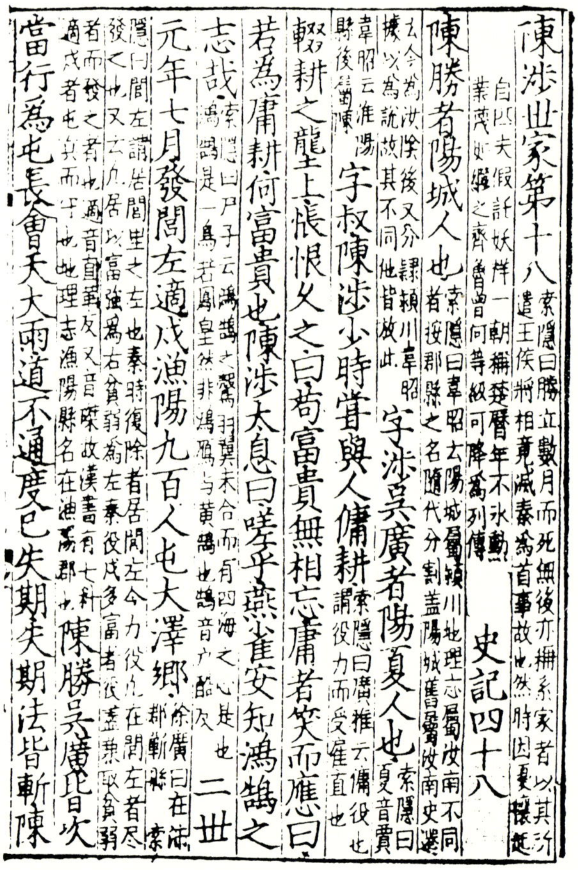

《陰騭文圖注》一書中有洛陽人程一德家雇工刻印書籍的情況，畫中有刻版、印刷、裝訂幾個工序。

In the book *Explanations of a Picture Showing Good Deeds Contributing to the Doer's Credit in the Future Life*, there is a picture showing engravers and printers working in the family of Cheng Yide, a native of Luoyang.The processes of engraving, printing and binding are all shown in the picture.

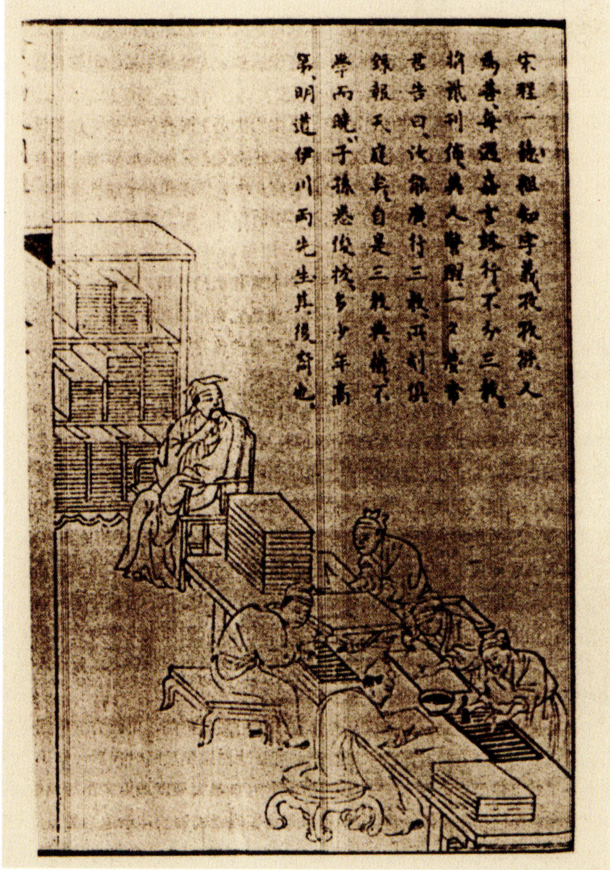

杭州印刷業起源於五代，以刻印精良而著名。

Printing in Hangzhou goes back to the Five Dynasties and the place was known for the high quality of printing.

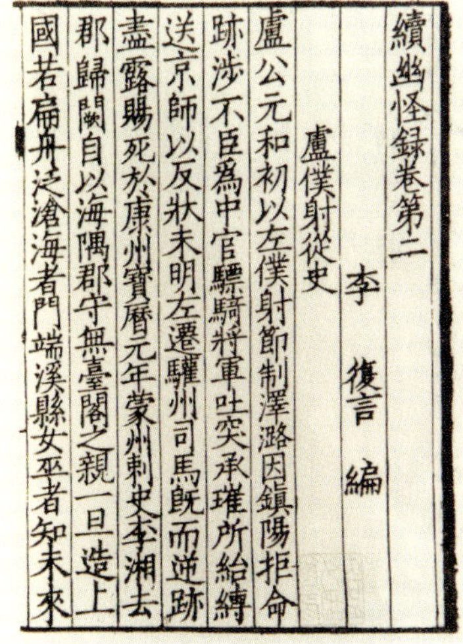
續幽怪錄卷第二　李復言 編
盧僕射從史
盧公元和初以左僕射節制澤潞因鎮陽拒命
跡涉不臣為中官驃騎將軍吐突承璀所給縛
送京師以反狀未明左遷驩州司馬既而逆跡
盡露賜死於康州寶曆元年蒙州刺史李湘去
郡歸闕自以海隅郡守無臺閣之親一旦造上
國若扁舟泛滄海者門端溪縣安平者知未來

《續幽怪錄》
南宋臨安府尹家書籍鋪刻印
A Sequel to a Collection of Ghost Stories and Weird Events, printed by Yin's Bookstone in Lin'an during the Southern Song.

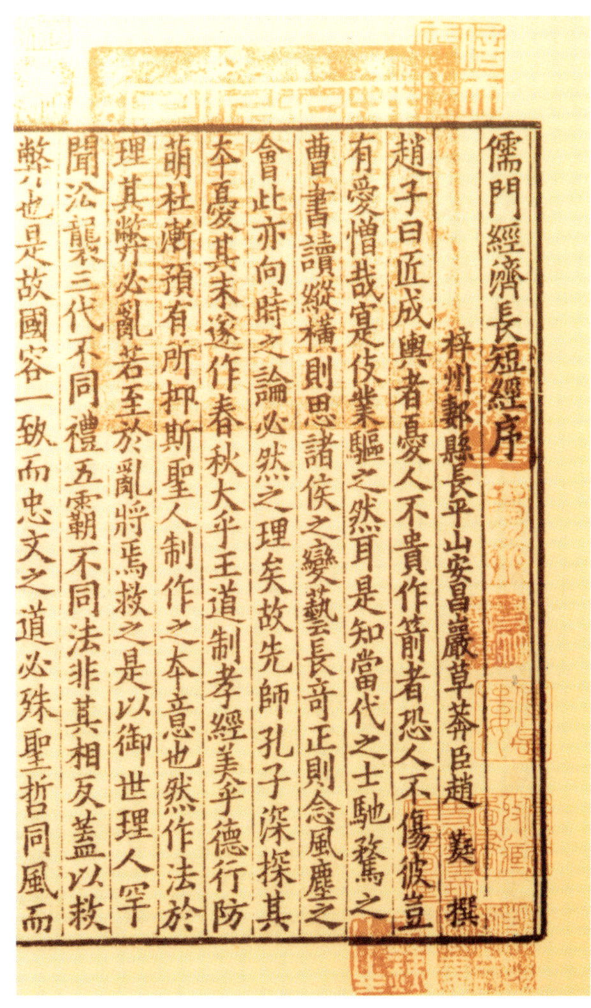
儒門經濟長短經序
梓州郪縣長平山安昌巖草莽臣趙蕤 撰
趙子曰匠成輿者憂人不貴作箭者恐人不傷彼豈
有愛憎哉寔伎業驅之然耳是知當代之士馳騖之
曹書讀縱橫則思諸侯之變藝長奇正則念風塵之
會此亦向時之論必然之理矣故先師孔子深探其
本憂其末遂作春秋大乎王道制孝經美乎德行防
萌杜漸預有所抑斯聖人制作之本意也然作法於
理其弊必亂若至於亂將焉救之是以御世理人罕
聞沿襲三代不同禮五霸不同法非其相反蓋以救
弊也是故國容一致而忠文之道必殊聖哲同風而

《唐女郎魚玄機詩集》
南宋杭州陳宅書籍鋪刻印
Collected Poems of Madam Yu Xuanji of Tang, printed by Chen's Bookstore in Hangzhou during the Southern Song.

《儒門經濟長短經》
南宋初杭州刻印
Essays on Confucian Economy, printed in Hangzhou in the early years of the Southern Song.

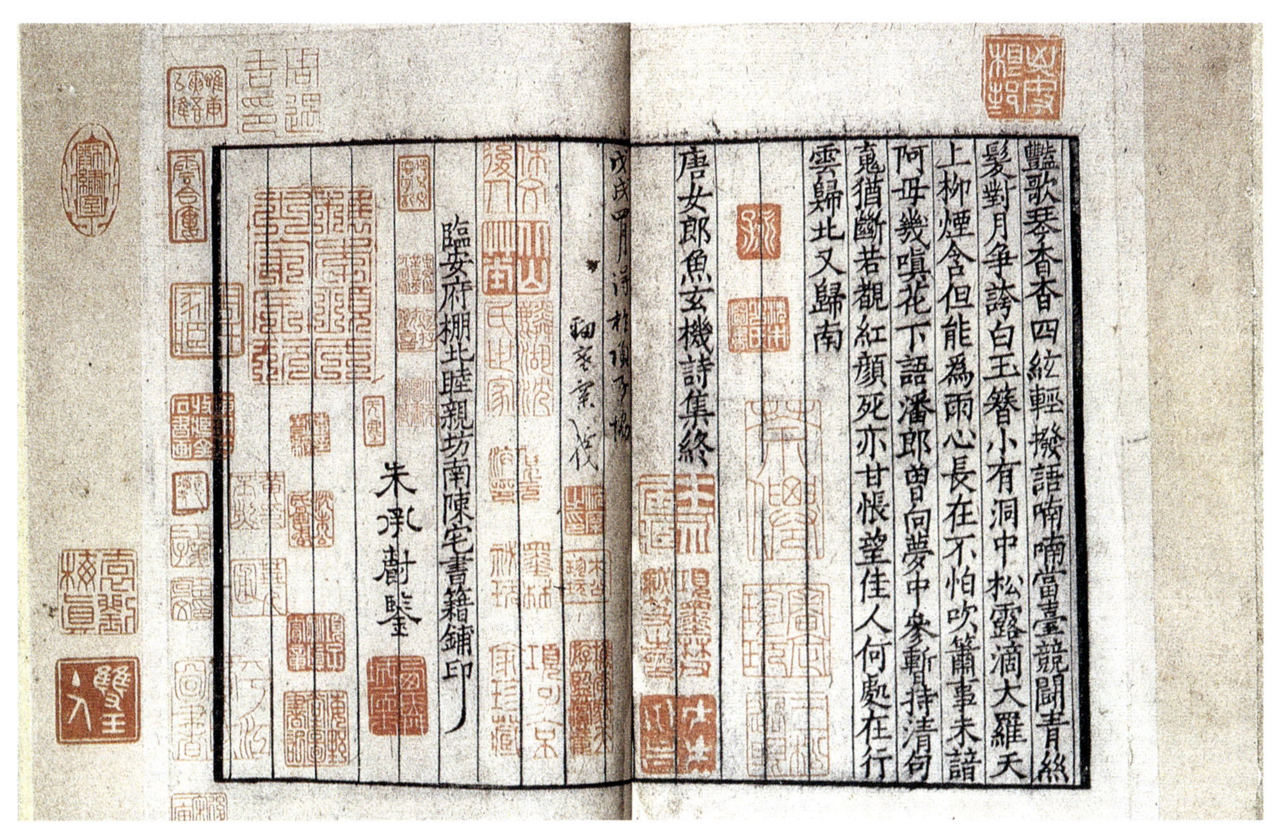
豔歌琴杳杳四絃輕撥語喃喃當臺競鬬青絲
鬢對月爭誇白玉簪小有洞中松露滴大羅天
上柳煙含但能為雨心長在不怕吹簫事未諳
阿母幾嗔花下語潘郎曾向夢中參暫持清句
魂猶斷若覩紅顏死亦甘悵望佳人何處在行
雲歸北又歸南
唐女郎魚玄機詩集終

臨安府棚北睦親坊南陳宅書籍鋪印

四川成都是印刷術發源較早地區之一。早在唐代中期，這裏的民間印刷業就已興起，宋初政府在此刻印《開寶藏》，説明此地有雄厚的技術力量。除建安、杭州、眉山外，民間印刷遍及各地。

Chengdu in Sichuan was one of the areas where printing was introduced relatively early. As early as the mid-Tang, private printing existed in Chengdu. That the Song government decided to print the *Kaibao Tripitaka* in Chengdu shows the technological sophistication found there. Besides Jian'an, Hangzhou and Meishan, private printing existed in virtually every district in the country.

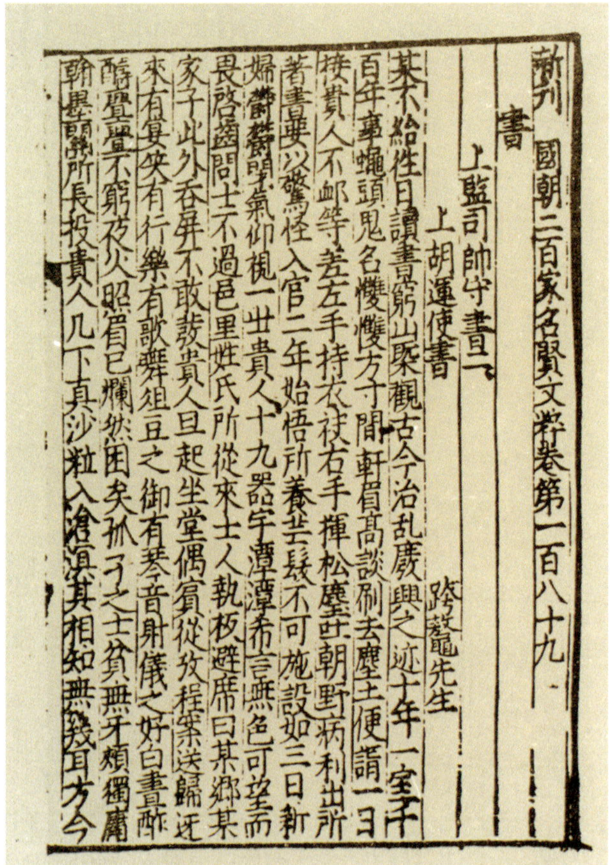
新刊國朝二百家名賢文粹卷第一百八十九
書
上監司帥守書
上胡運使書　跨鼇先生
某不佞生日讀書窮山聚觀古今治亂廢興之迹十年一室千
百年事蠅頭鬼名㦬㦬方寸間軒眉高談刷去塵土便謂一日
接貴人不卹等差左手持衣袂右手揮松麈出朝野病利出所
著書要以驚怪入官二年始悟所養芸穎不可施設如三日新
婦…頭氣仰視一世貴人十九器宇潭潭希言無色可望而
畏啓齒問士不過邑里姓氏所從來士人執板避席曰某鄉某
家子此外吞舌不敢發貴人旦起坐堂偶賓從效程案送歸…
來有宴笑有行樂有歌舞俎豆之御有琴音射儀之好白晝…
…疊疊不窮夜分昭宵已爛然困矣孤子之士貧無牙頰獨庸
…頭…所長投貴人几下真沙粒入滄溟其相知無幾日方今

《新刊國朝二百家名賢文粹》
南宋慶元三年（1197 年）
眉山書隱齋刻印
A New Anthology of Works by 200 Eminent Figures, printed by Shuyin Studio in Meishan in the third year of the Qingyuan period (1197) of the Song Dynasty.

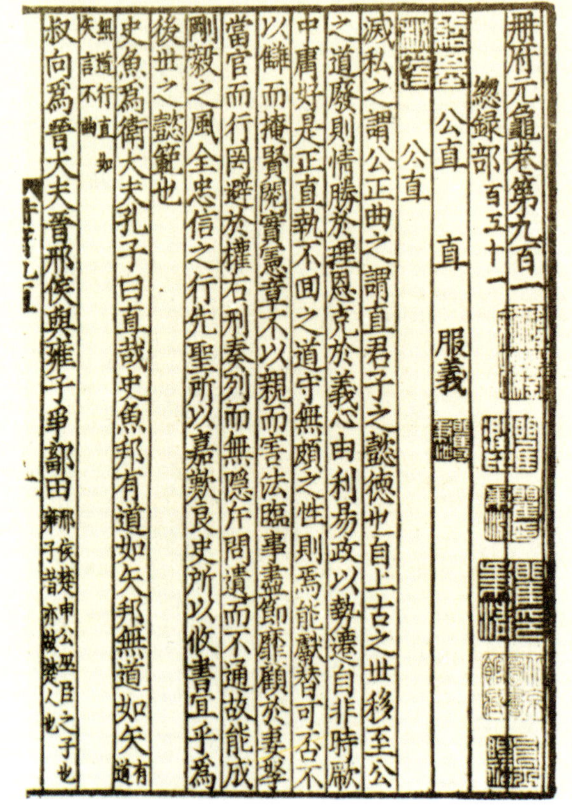
冊府元龜卷第九百一
總錄部　百五十一
公直　直　服義
公直
滅私之謂公正曲之謂直君子之懿德也自上古之世移至公
之道廢則情勝於理恩克於義心由利易政以勢遷自非時歟
中庸好是正直執不回之道守無頗之性則焉能獻替可否不
以讎而擁賢閼實憲章不以親而害法臨事盡節靡顧於妻孥
當官而行罔避於權右刑奏列而無隱斥問遺而不通故能成
剛毅之風全忠信之行先聖所以嘉歎良史所以攸書宜乎為
後世之懿範也
史魚為衛大夫孔子曰直哉史魚邦有道如矢邦無道如矢
叔向為晉大夫晉邢侯與雍子爭鄐田

《冊府元龜》南宋中期眉山書坊刻印
A Collection of Information on the Lives of Emperors and Ministers, engraved and printed by bookstores in Meishan in the middle part of the Southern Song.

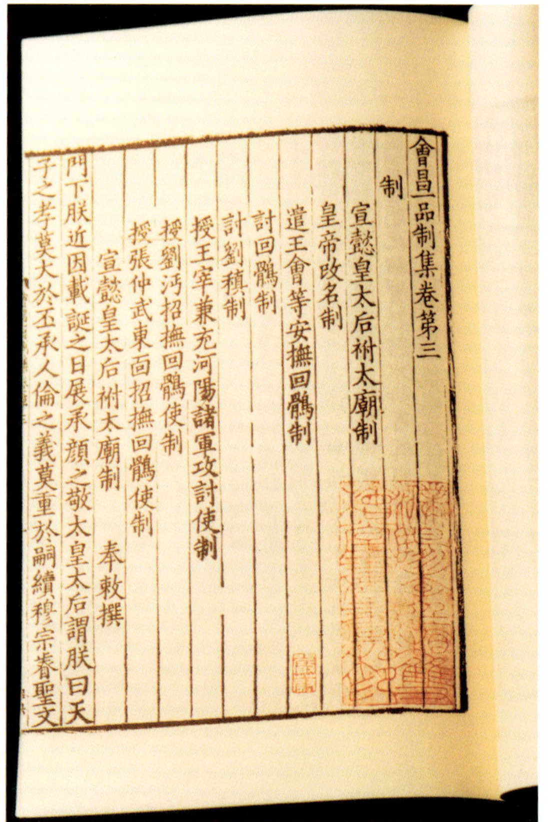
會昌一品制集卷第三
制
宣懿皇太后祔太廟制
皇帝改名制
遣王會等安撫回鶻制
討回鶻制
討劉稹制
授王宰兼充河陽諸軍攻討使制
授劉沔招撫回鶻使制
授張仲武東面招撫回鶻使制
宣懿皇太后祔太廟制　奉敕撰
門下朕近因載誕之日展承顏之敬太皇太后謂朕曰天
子之孝莫大於丕承人倫之義莫重於嗣續穆宗睿聖文

《會昌一品制集》南宋淳熙間浙江刻本
Collected Works of Li Deyu, printed in Zhejiang during the Chunxi period of the Southern Song Dynasty.

宋代印刷及相關技術

宋代圖版刻印達到很高水平。書籍插圖和字體亦開始受重視。

Printing in the Song Dynasty and Its Related Techniques

The engraving of printing plates reached a high level in the Song Dynasty. Attention was also paid to illustrations and typefaces.

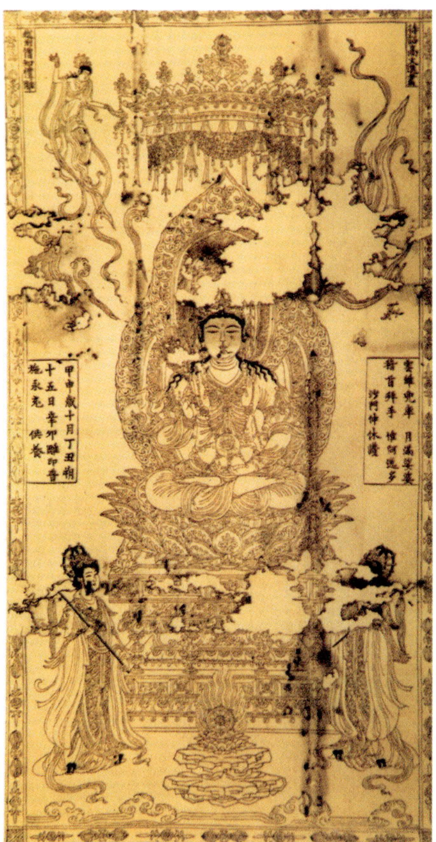

《彌勒菩薩》北宋雍熙元年（984 年）刻印
Maitreya Buddha, printed in the first year of the Yongxi period of the Northern Song Dynasty (984).

宋代繪畫中的書坊圖
Printing workshops in a Song painting.

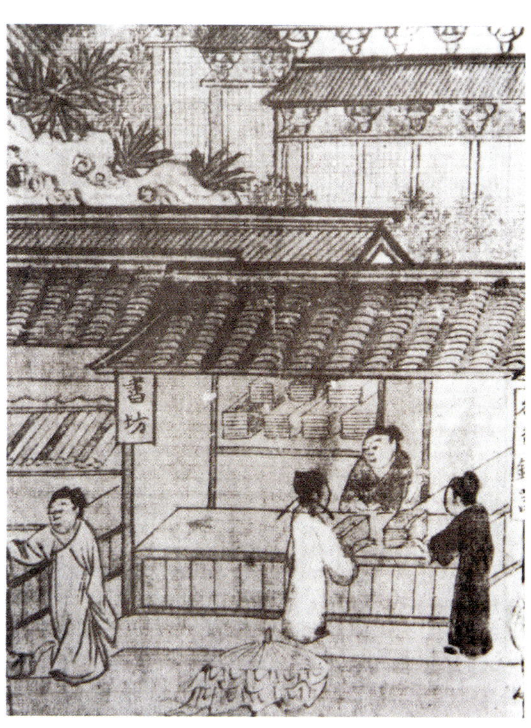

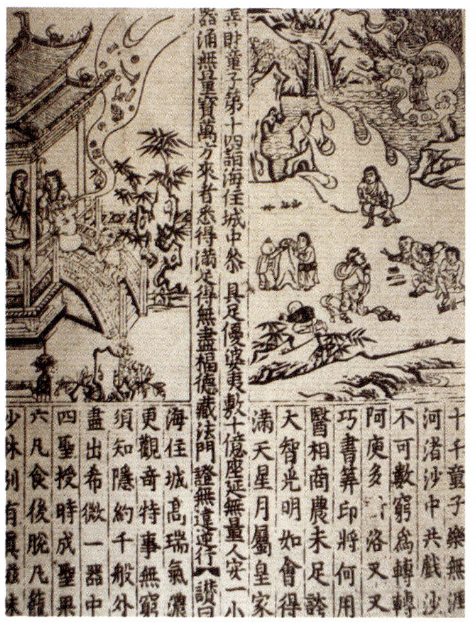

宋刻本《佛國禪師文殊指南》是一種圖文並茂的書籍形式
A Guide to the Chan Master Manjusri, engraved in Song, was a type of book in which the text was illustrated with pictures.

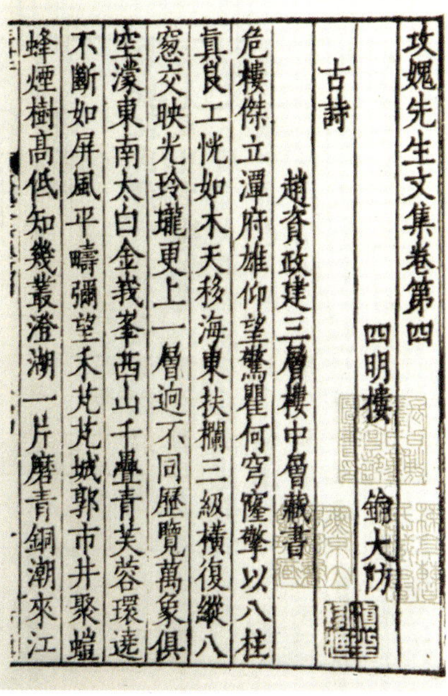

攻媿先生文集卷第四
四明樓 鑰大防
古詩
趙資政建三層樓中層藏書
危樓傑立潭府雄仰望驚瞿何穹窿擎以八柱
眞良工恍如木天移海東扶欄三級橫復縱八
窻交映光玲瓏更上一層迥不同歷覽萬象俱
空濛東南太白金峩峯西山千疊青芙蓉環遶
不斷如屏風平疇彌望禾芃芃城郭市井聚螘
蜂煙樹高低知幾叢滄湖一片磨青銅潮來江

宋體字的萌芽
The emergence of Song typeface.

遼、西夏、金印刷

Printing in the Liao, Western Xia and Jin Dynasties

907–1234

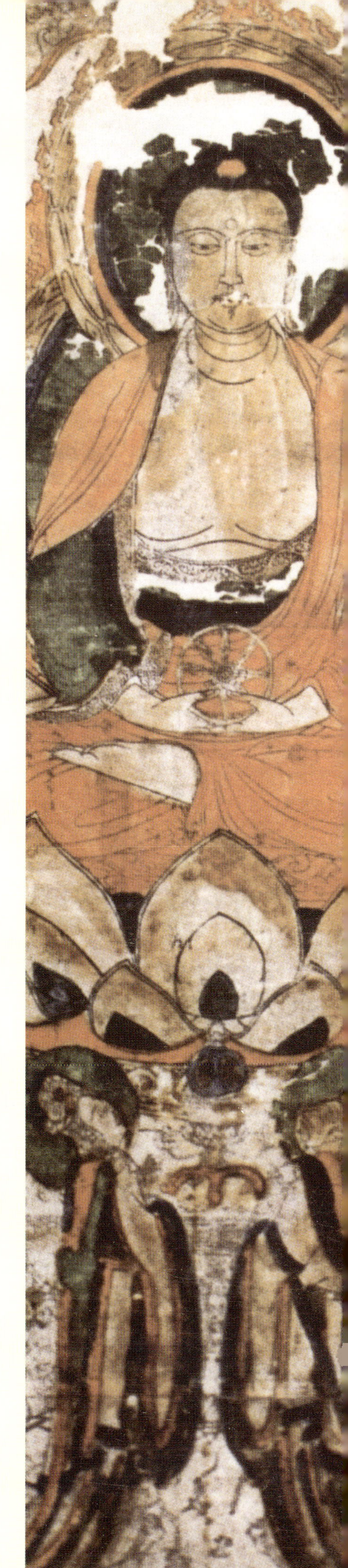

遼代印刷 (907–1115 年)

遼代的印刷品過去流傳很少，近年在山西應縣木塔內發現一批遼代印刷品，證明當時的印刷水平與北宋相當。

Printing in the Liao Dynasty (907–1115)

Very few actual printing specimens survive from the Liao Dynasty. In recent years, a selection of printed items from the Liao period were found in a wooden pagoda in the Ying County, Shanxi, proving that the standard of printing of that period was comparable to that of the Northern Song.

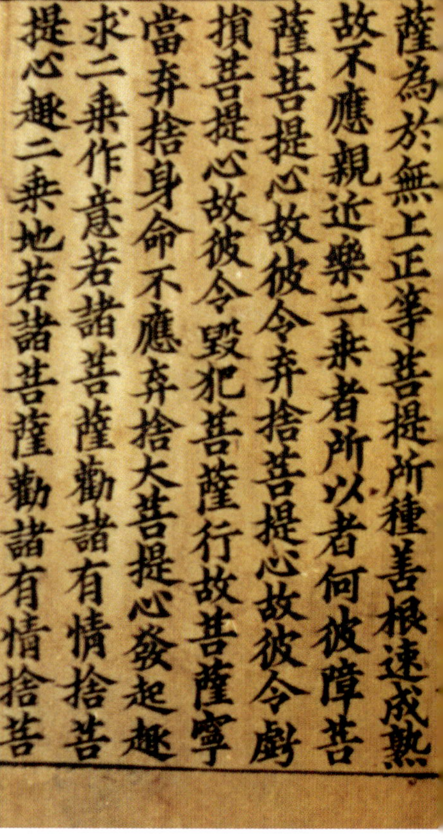

薩為於無上正等菩提所種善根速成熟
故不應親近樂二乘者所以者何彼障菩
薩菩提心故彼令弃捨菩提心故彼令虧
損菩提心故彼令毀犯菩薩行故菩薩寧
當弃捨身命不應弃捨大菩提心發起趣
求二乘作意若諸菩薩勸諸有情捨菩
提心趣二乘地若諸菩薩勸諸有情捨菩

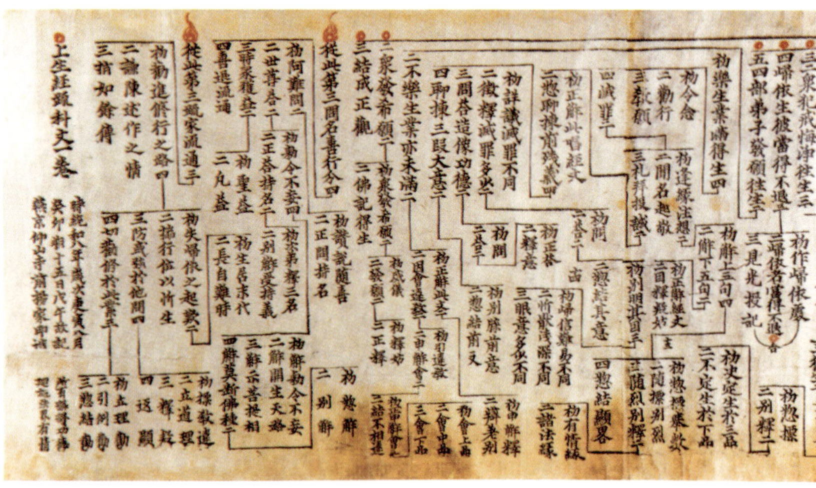

《上生經疏科文》（應縣木塔發現）
遼代北京最早的印刷品（約 990 年）
Items of Classics and Glosses (found in the wooden pagoda in the Ying County), was the earliest printed specimen found in the Liao period.

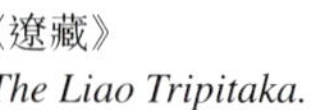

《遼藏》
The Liao Tripitaka.

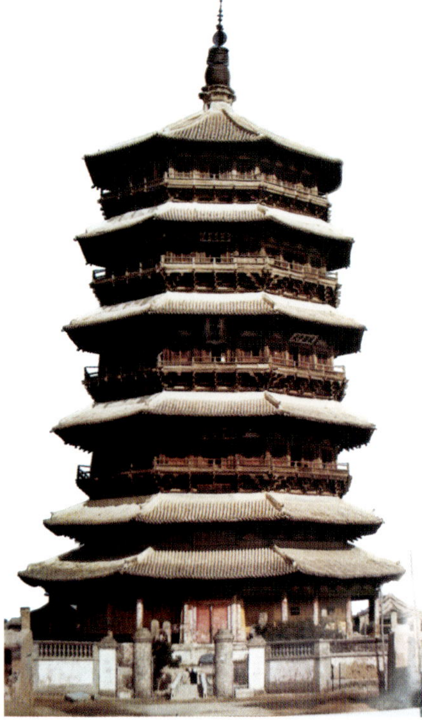

應縣木塔
The Wooden Pagoda in the Ying County.

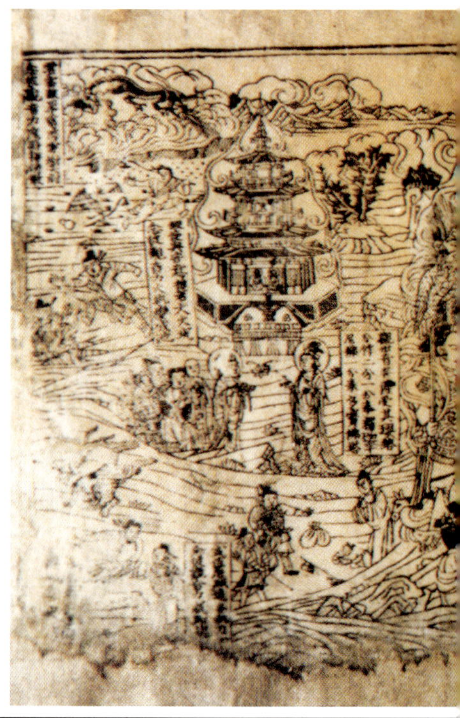

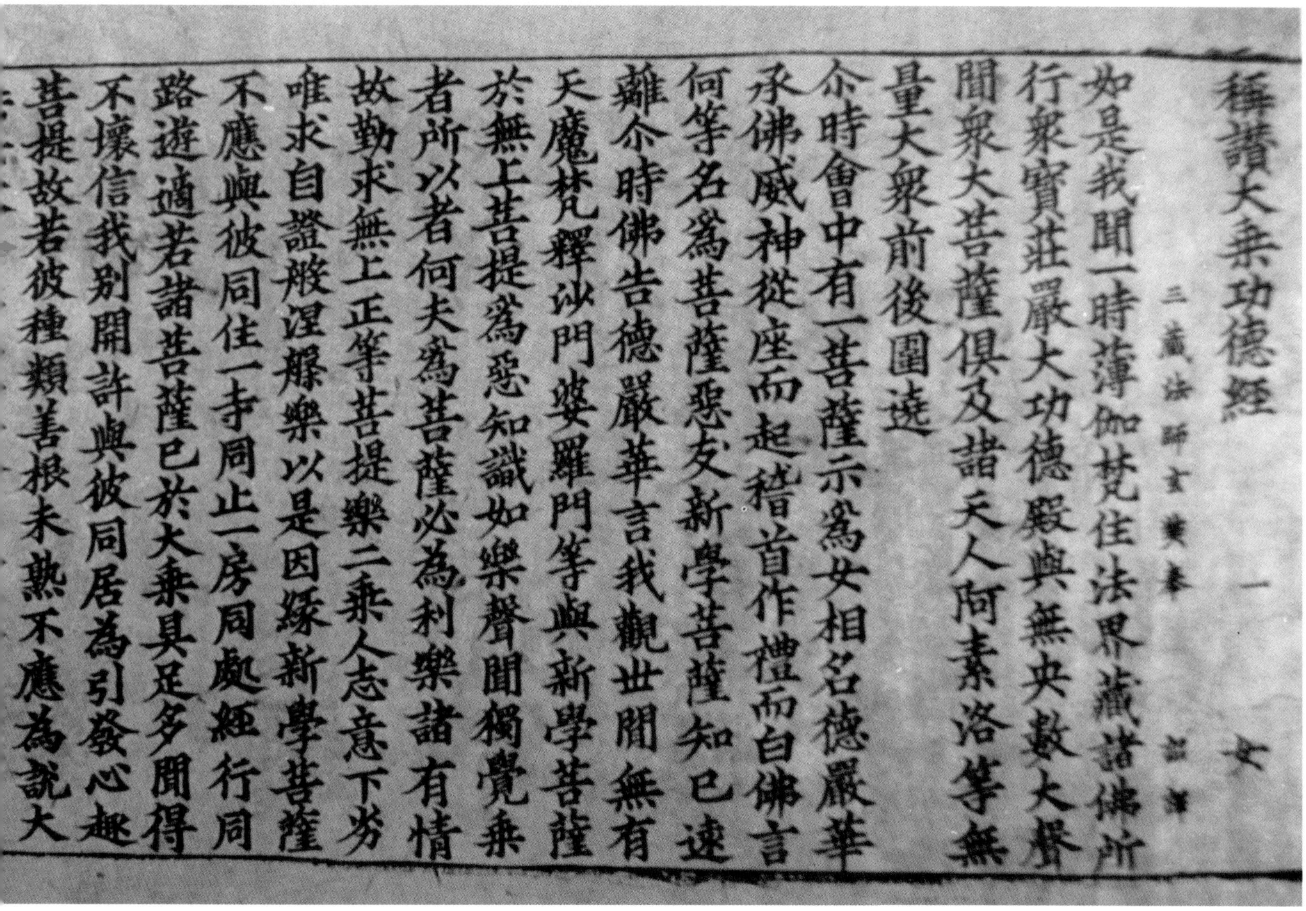

稱讚大乘功德經 一 女

三藏法師玄奘奉 詔譯

如是我聞一時薄伽梵住法界藏諸佛所
行衆寶莊嚴大功德殿與無央數大聲
聞衆大菩薩俱及諸天人阿素洛等無
量大衆前後圍遶
尒時會中有一菩薩示爲女相名德嚴華
承佛威神從座而起稽首作禮而白佛言
何等名爲菩薩惡友新學菩薩知已速
離尒時佛告德嚴華言我觀世間無有
天魔梵釋沙門婆羅門等與新學菩薩
於無上菩提爲惡知識如樂聲聞獨覺乘
者所以者何夫爲菩薩必爲利樂諸有情
故勤求無上正等菩提樂二乘人志意下劣
唯求自證般涅槃樂以是因緣新學菩薩
不應與彼同住一寺同止一房同處經行同
路遊適若諸菩薩已於大乘具足多聞得
不壞信我別開許與彼同居爲引發心趣
菩提故若彼種類善根未熟不應爲說大

《遼藏》山西應縣木塔發現
譯者為唐三藏法師玄奘
The Liao Tripitaka, found in a wooden pagoda in the Ying County, Shanxi.
The translator was the Buddhist monk Xuan Zang of the Tang Dynasty.

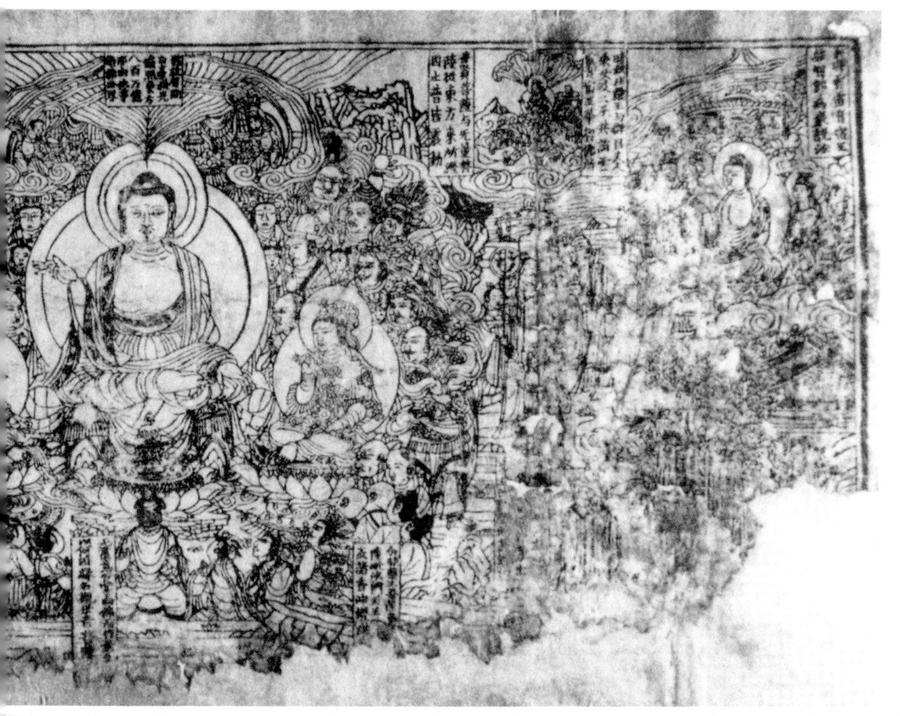

遼代刻印的《蒙求》
Answers to the Demands of the Ignorant, printed in the Liao Dynasty.

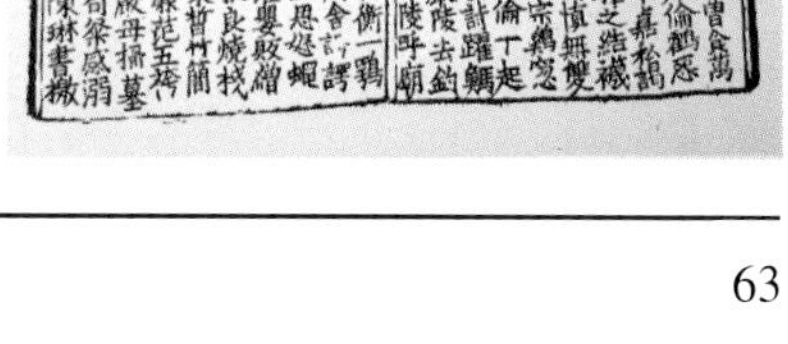

印刷敷彩工藝

遼代印刷品中，有一種先印刷圖畫的底紋及黑色部分，最後用手工塗彩。這是單色印刷向彩色的過渡。

金代印刷 (1115–1234 年)

金代最大的刻印工程是平陽廣勝寺通過民間集資刻印的《金藏》(1138–1173 年)，共 7,000 餘卷。

The Art of Hand-colouring in Printing

One type of print from the Liao had the outlines printed firstly in black and then they were coloured by hand. This shows the transition from single-colour to multi-colour printing.

Printing in the Jin Dynasty

The largest printing project of the Jin Dynasty was *The Jin Tripitaka* (1138–1173) published by the Guangsheng Monastery in Pingyang. The project, comprising more than seven thousand chapters, was supported by private funds.

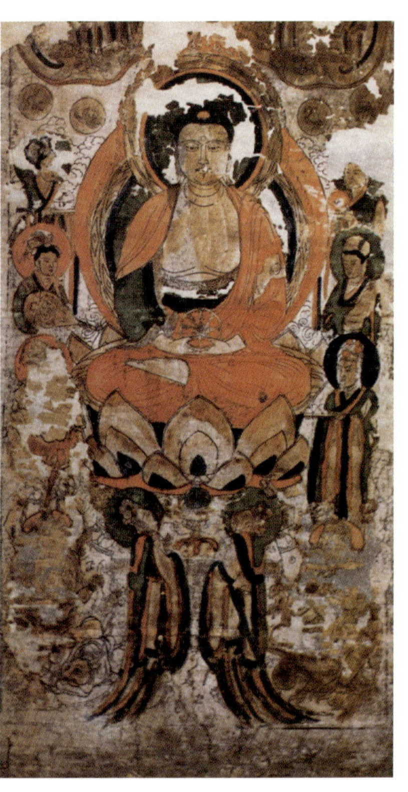

《熾盛光九曜圖》
遼代刻版印刷後手工塗彩佛像
The Nine Luminaries of the Buddha of Brilliant Light, a Liao Buddha portrait which was block-printed in black and coloured by hand.

趙城《金藏》
The Jin Tripitaka of Zhao Cheng.

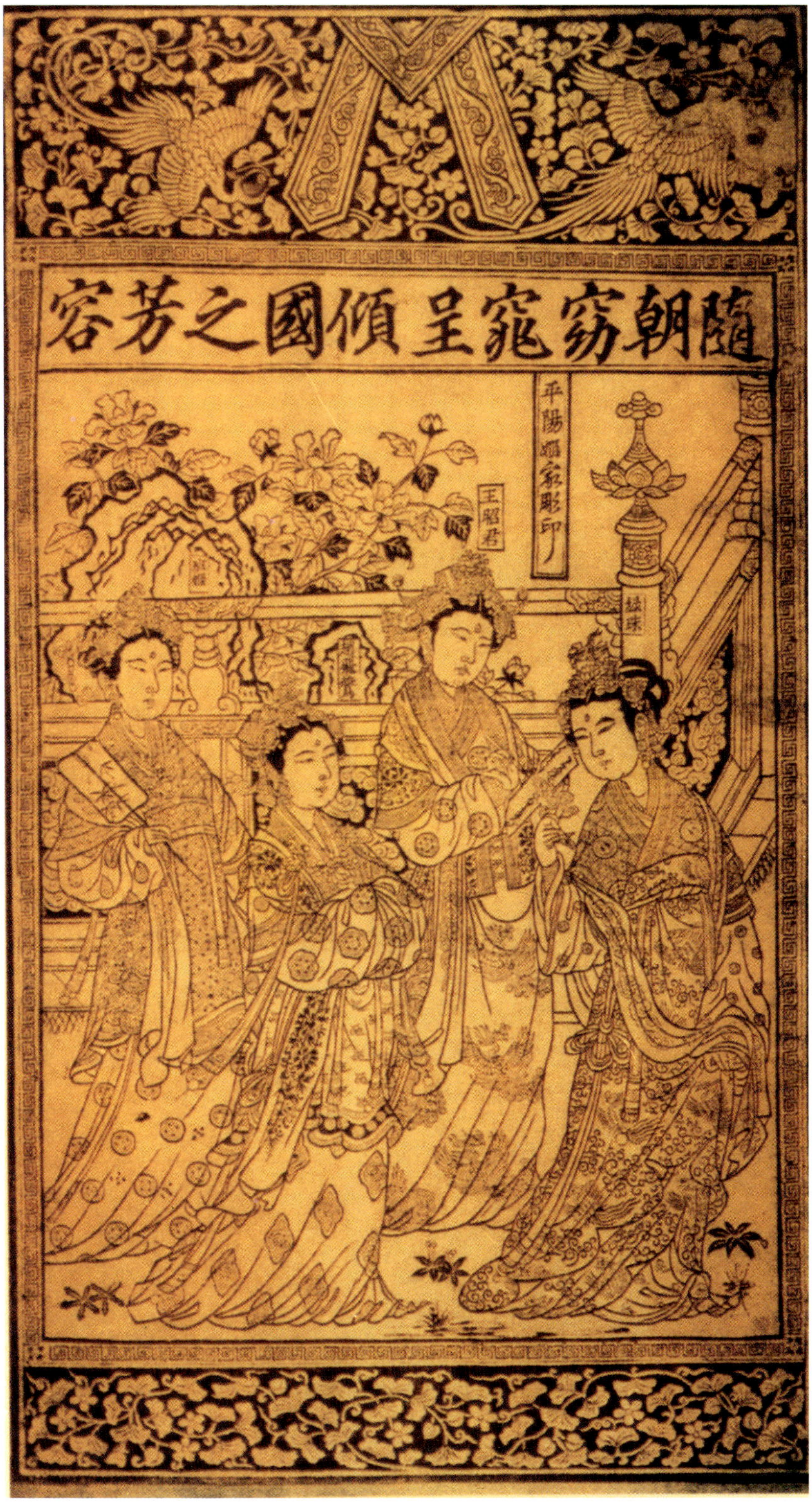

《黄帝內經素問》
金平陽刻印本
The Yellow Emperor's Classic of Internal Medicine, printed in Pingyang in the Jin Dynasty.

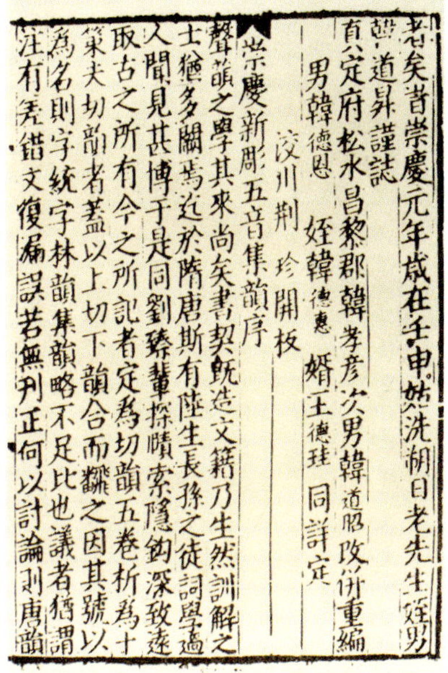
矣旹崇慶元年歲在壬申姑洗朔日老先生姪男
道昇謹誌
真定府松水昌黎郡韓孝彥次男韓道昭改併重編
男韓德恩 姪韓德惠 婿王德珪 同詳定
洨川荊珍開板
崇慶新彫五音集韻序
聲韻之學其來尚矣書契既造文籍乃生然訓解之
士猶多闕焉迨於隋唐斯有陸生長孫之徒詞學過
人聞見甚博于是同劉臻輩探賾索隱鉤深致遠
取古之所有今之所記者定為切韻五卷析為十
策夫切韻者蓋以上切下韻合而翻之因其號以
為名則字統字林韻集韻略不足比也議者猶謂
注有差錯文復漏誤若無刊正何以討論刊唐韻

《改併五音集韻》
金崇慶元年（1212 年），洨川荊珍刻印
Amending and Incorporating the Fives Scales in the Collection of Ryhmes, printed by Jing Zhen of Jiaozhou in the first year of the Chongqing period in the Jin Dynasty (1212).

金平陽姬家刻印的《四美人圖》刻工精細，為現存最早的年畫
The Four Beauties, engraved and printed by the Ji Family in Pingyang in the Jin Dynasty. The printing was of superior quality and the picture is the earliest extant New Year picture.

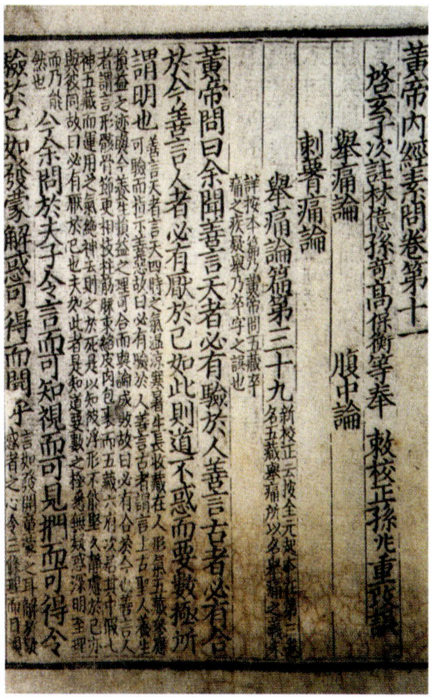

西夏印刷（1032–1227年）

黨項族建立的西夏國，京城為興慶府（今銀川市），據有今寧夏、甘肅、內蒙西部、陝西北部等大片地區。西夏政權重視文化，推崇佛教，興辦學校，除使用漢字外，也創造了本民族文字——西夏文。為滿足對書籍的需求，西夏曾向宋、金購買書籍，同時發展本地區的印刷業，印書品種包括佛經、曆書、軍事、詩集及儒家著作。

Printing in the Western Xia Dynasty

The Western Xia regime established by the Dangxiang tribe made Xingqing its capital and built up a kingdom covering a huge expanse of land that included the present-day Ningxia, Gansu, the western part of Inner Mongolia and the northern part of Shaanxi. The Western Xia regime attached great importance to culture, revered Buddhism and set up a large number of schools. Apart from using the Han characters, they also created their own tribal scripts, the scripts of Western Xia. To satisfy their needs for books, they purchased books from bookshops in the Southern Song and the Jin areas. At the same time, they developed their own printing industy and the books they produced included Buddhist scriptures, almanacs, books on military science, anthologies of poetry and Confucian works.

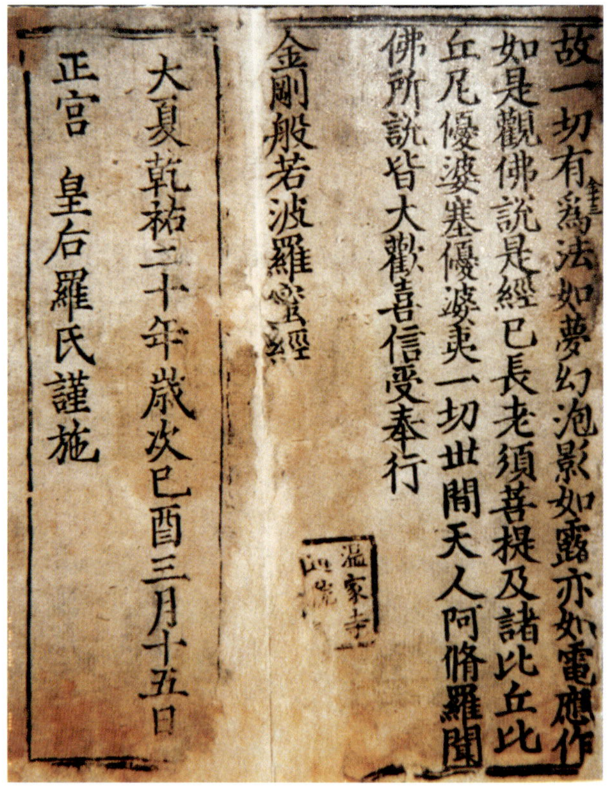
故一切有為法如夢幻泡影如露亦如電應作
如是觀佛說是經已長老須菩提及諸比丘比
丘尼優婆塞優婆夷一切世間天人阿脩羅聞
佛所說皆大歡喜信受奉行
金剛般若波羅蜜經
大夏乾祐二十年歲次己酉三月十五日
正宮皇后羅氏謹施

《金剛經》西夏乾祐二十年（1189年）
漢文刻本
The Diamond Sutra in the scripts of the Han, printed in the twentieth year of the Qianyou period of the Western Xia Dynasty (1189).

西夏文佛經《彌勒菩薩經》
西夏乾祐二十年（1189年）刻印
經折裝
Sutra of the Maitreya Buddha in pleated-leaf binding, printed in the twentieth year of the Qianyou period of the Western Xia Dynasty (1189).

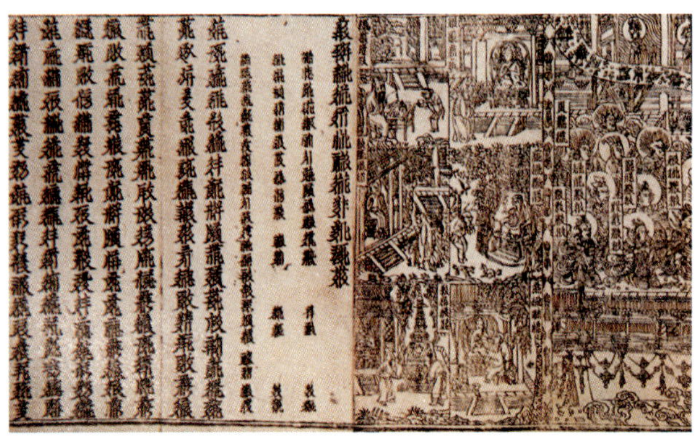

西夏韻書刻本《文海寶韻》
蝴蝶裝
A rhyming dictionary written in Western Xia characters and bound in butterfly format.

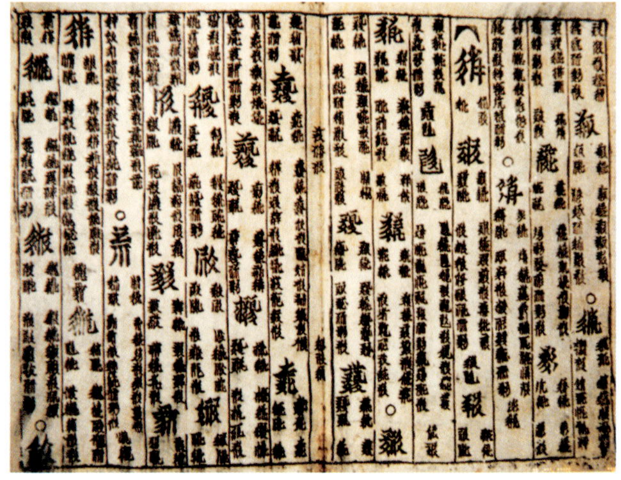

Printing in the Yuan Dynasty

1271–1368

元代印刷

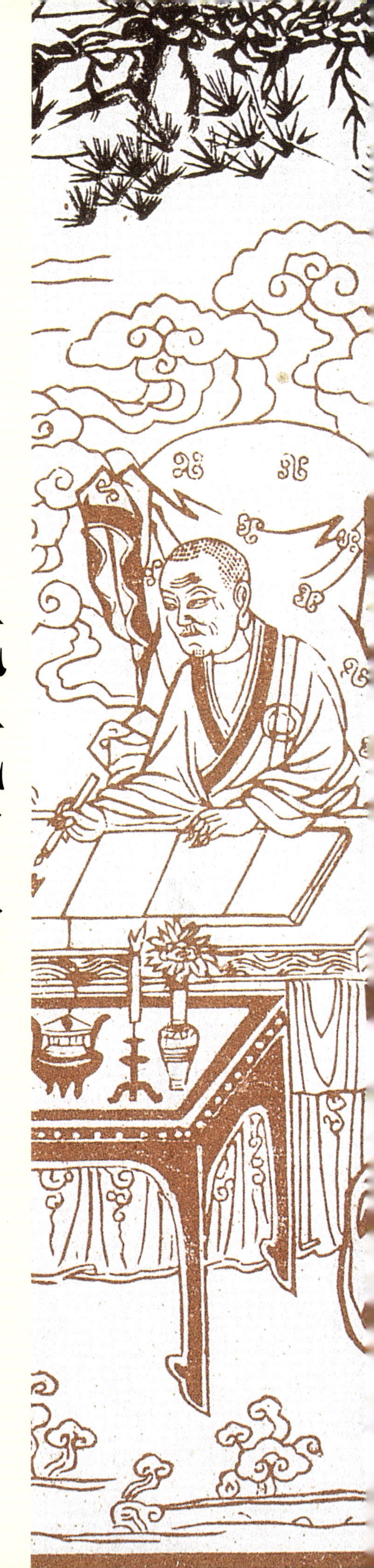

元代印刷（1271–1368）

元代的政府和民間印刷都很活躍，印書的中心有兩個：南方在杭州，北方在平陽。

元政府印刷

元政府的重要書籍，由中書省負責，委托地方政府組織刻印。如《宋史》、《金史》、《遼史》就是浙江行中書省在杭州刻印的。

Printing in the Yuan Dynasty (1271–1368)

Both government and private printing in the Yuan Dynasty were very active, with Hangzhou in the south and Pingyang in the north as major centres.

Government Printing in the Yuan Dynasty

The Secretariat Office was responsible for all the important government books while the organization of their printing was entrusted to the local governments. Histories such as *The History of Song*, *The History of Jin*, and *The History of Liao* were printed in Hangzhou by the Branch Secretariat located in Zhejiang.

《金史》杭州刻印
The History of Jin,
printed in Hangzhou.

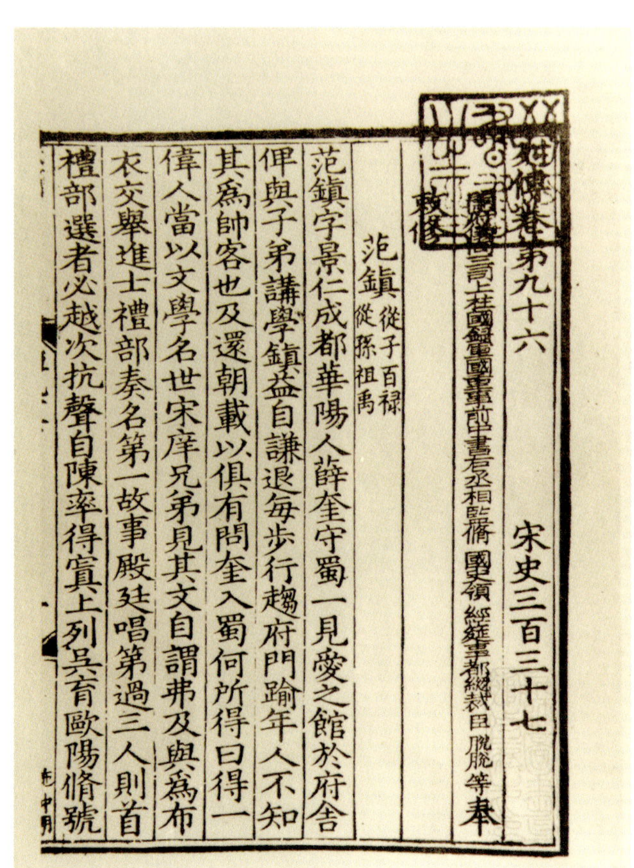

列傳卷第九十六　宋史三百三十七
開府儀同三司上柱國錄軍國重事中書右丞相監修國史領經筵事都總裁臣脫脫等奉
勅修
范鎮 從子百祿 從孫祖禹
范鎮字景仁成都華陽人薛奎守蜀一見愛之館於府舍
俾與子弟講學鎮益自謙退每步行趨府門踰年人不知
其爲帥客也及還朝載以俱有問奎入蜀何所得曰得一
偉人當以文學名世宋庠兄弟見其文自謂弗及與爲布
衣交舉進士禮部奏名第一故事殿廷唱第過三人則首
禮部選者必越次抗聲自陳率得寘上列吳育歐陽脩號

《宋史》杭州刻印
The History of Song,
printed in Hangzhou.

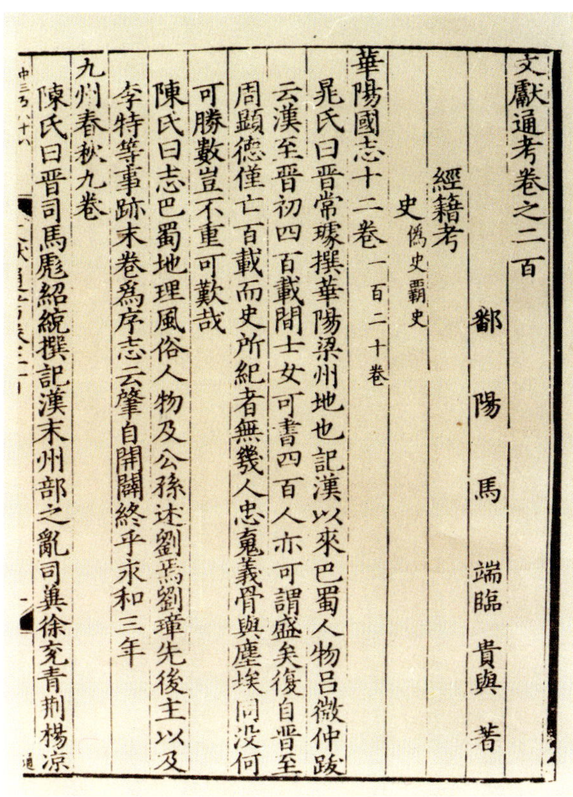

文獻通考卷之二百
鄱陽 馬端臨 貴與 著
經籍考
史 僞史霸史
華陽國志十二卷 一百二十卷
晁氏曰晉常璩撰華陽梁州地也記漢以來巴蜀人物呂微仲跋
云漢至晉初四百載間士女可書四百人亦可謂盛矣復自晉至
周顯德僅亡百載而史所紀者無幾人忠孝義骨與塵埃同沒何
可勝數豈不重可歎哉
陳氏曰志巴蜀地理風俗人物及公孫述劉焉劉璋先後主以及
李特等事跡末卷爲序志云肇自開闢終乎永和三年
九州春秋九卷
陳氏曰晉司馬彪紹統撰記漢末州部之亂司冀徐兗青荊楊涼

《文獻通考》
元泰定元年（1324 年）
西湖書院刻印
Comprehensive Study of the History of Civilization was printed by the West Lake Academy in the first year of the Taiding period of the Yuan Dynasty (1324).

學校印刷

西湖書院是在南宋國子監基礎上建立的，在元代刻印書籍較多。

由幾所學校聯合分工刻印大部頭書，是元代學校印刷的一大特點。

Academy Printing

The West Lake Academy was built on the foundation of the Southern Song National Academy which engraved and printed many publications during the Yuan Dynasty.

A major characteristic of academic printing in the Yuan period was the collective effort that several acedemies made in the engraving and printing of multi-volume books.

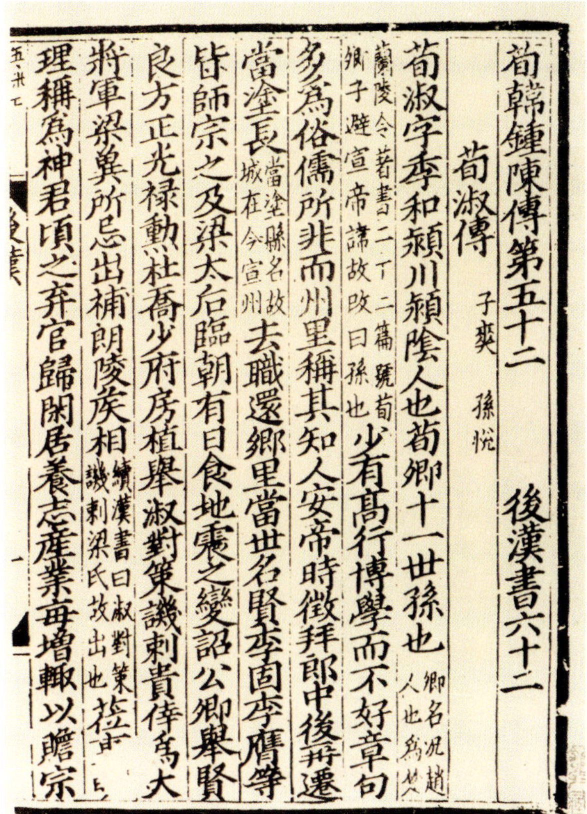

荀韓鍾陳傳第五十二 後漢書六十二
荀淑傳 子爽 孫悅
荀淑字季和潁川潁陰人也荀卿十一世孫也 卿名況趙人也爲楚
蘭陵令著書二十二篇號荀卿子避宣帝諱故改曰孫也 少有高行博學而不好章句
多爲俗儒所非而州里稱其知人安帝時徵拜郎中後再遷
當塗長 當塗縣名故城在今宣州 去職還鄉里當世名賢李固李膺等
皆師宗之及梁太后臨朝有日食地震之變詔公卿舉賢
良方正光祿勳杜喬少府房植舉淑對策譏刺貴倖爲大
將軍梁冀所忌出補朗陵侯相 續漢書曰淑對策譏刺梁氏故出也 莅事
理稱爲神君頃之弃官歸閑居養志產業每增輒以贍宗

寧國路儒學刻印的《後漢書注》
Commentaries on the History of the Later Han Dynasty,
printed by the Confucian Academy in the Ningguo Route.

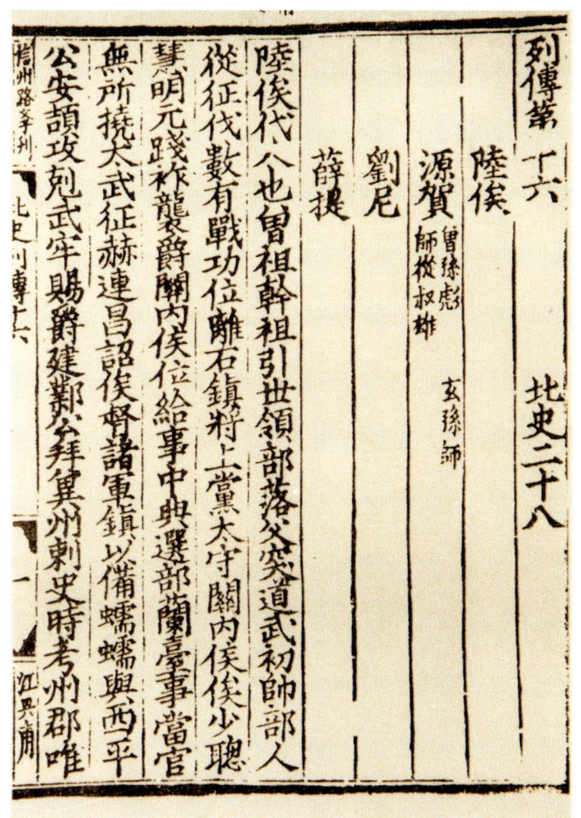

列傳第十六 北史二十八
陸俟
源賀 曾孫彪 師從叔雄 玄孫師
劉尼
薛提
陸俟代人也曾祖幹祖引世領部落父突道武初帥部人
從征伐數有戰功位離石鎮將上黨太守關內侯俟少聰
慧明元踐祚襲爵關內侯位給事中典選部蘭臺事當官
無所撓太武征赫連昌詔俟督諸軍鎮以備蠕蠕與西平
公安頡攻剋武牢賜爵建鄴公拜冀州刺史時考州郡唯

信州路儒學刻印的《北史》
The History of the Northern Dynasty,
printed by the Confucian Academy in the Xinzhou Route.

元代印刷技術

元代的雙色套印技術已很精湛。在字體方面，出現行書體。

Printing Techniques in the Yuan Dynasty

Two-colour printing techniques were fairly sophisticated in the Yuan Dynasty. With regards to typeface, the *running* script made its first appearance.

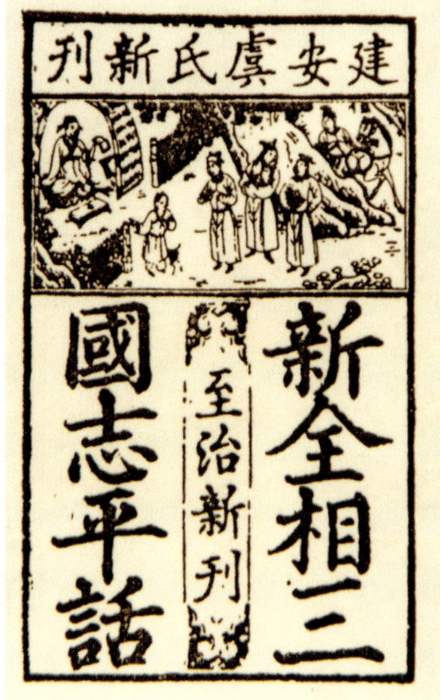
建安虞氏新刊

新全相三國志平話

至治新刊

《三國志平話》
元至治間（1321–1327 年）建安虞氏刻印
最早有插圖的書名頁
A Story-telling Version of the Romance of the Three Kingdoms, printed by the Lu Family in Jian'an during the Zhizhi period of the Yuan (1321–1327).

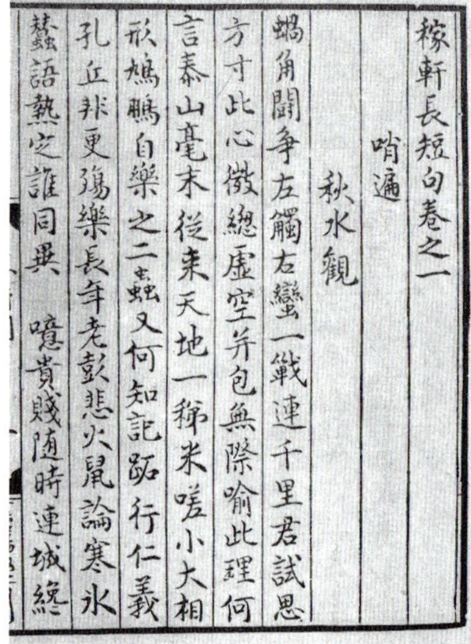
稼軒長短句卷之一

哨遍

秋水觀

蝸角鬭爭左觸右蠻一戰連千里君試思
方寸此心微總虛空并包無際喻此理何
言泰山毫末從來天地一稊米嗟小大相
形鳩鵬自樂之二蟲又何知記跖行仁義
孔丘非更殤樂長年老彭悲火鼠論寒氷
蠶語熱定誰同異 噫貴賤隨時連城纔

《稼軒長短句》用趙孟頫行書體刻印
Poems of Xin Qiji, engraved in the calligraphic style of Zhao Mengfu.

朱墨雙色套印《金剛經注》
至正元年（1341 年）中興路刻印
Commentaries on the Diamond Sutra,
in red and black,
was printed in the Chongxing Route in the first year of the Zhiyuan period of the Yuan Dynasty (1341).

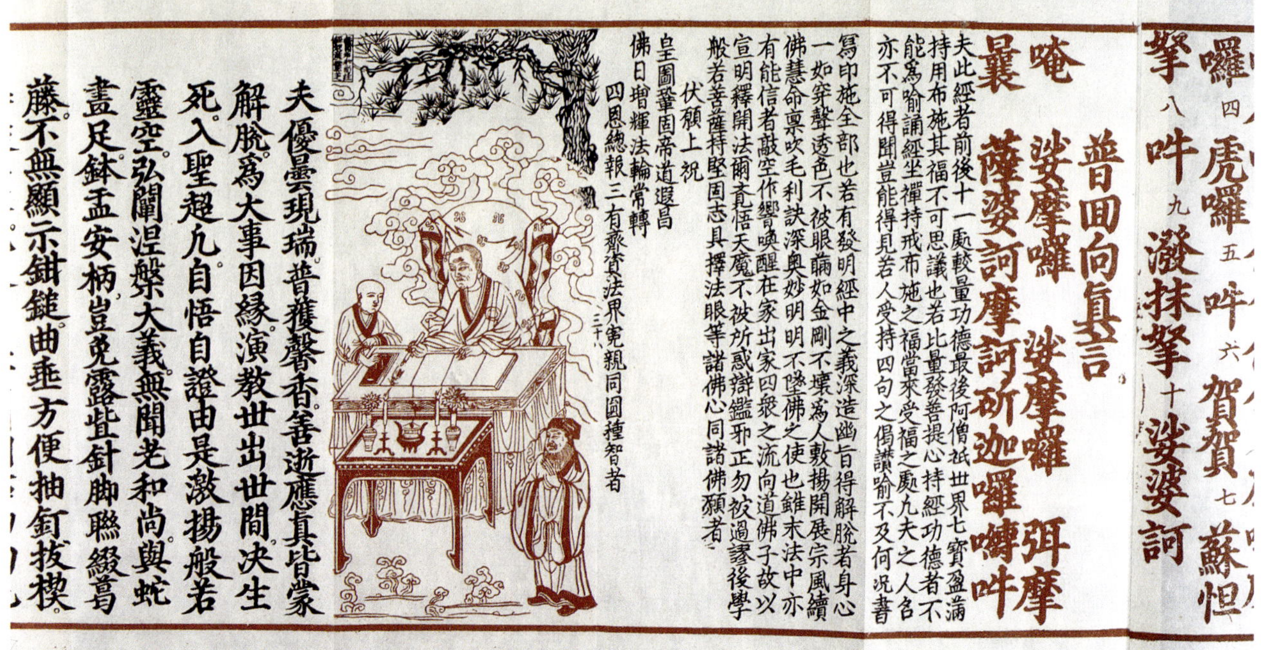
囉四虎囉五吽六賀賀七蘇怛
拏八吽九潑抹拏十娑婆訶

普回向眞言

唵 娑摩囉 娑摩囉 弭摩
曩 薩婆訶 摩訶 斫迦囉 嚩吽

夫此經者前後十一處較量功德最後阿僧祇世界七寶盈滿
持用布施其福不可思議也若比量發菩提心持經功德者不
能爲喻誦經坐禪持戒布施之福當來受福之處凡夫之人名
亦不可得聞豈能得見若人受持四句之偈讚喻不及何況書
寫印施全部也若有發明經中之義深造幽旨得解脫者身心
一如穿聲透色不被眼瞞如金剛不壞爲人敷揚開展宗風續
佛慧命稟吹毛利訣深奥妙明明不墜佛之使也雖末法中亦
有能信者敲空作響喚醒在家出家四衆之流向道佛子故以
宣明釋開法爾竟悟天魔不被所惑辯鑑邪正勿被過謬後學
般若菩薩持堅固志具擇法眼等諸佛心同諸佛願者
伏願上祝
皇圖鞏固帝道遐昌
佛日增輝法輪常轉
四恩總報三有齊資法界冤親同圓種智者

三十八

夫優曇現瑞普獲馨香善逝應眞皆蒙
解脫爲大事因緣演教世出世間決生
死入聖超凡自悟自證由是激揚般若
靈空弘闡涅槃大義無聞老和尚與蛇
畫足鉢盂安柄豈免露出針脚聯綴葛
藤不無顯示鉗鎚曲垂方便抽釘拔楔

元代民間印刷

元代民間印刷以平陽，建陽，杭州為最興盛，其他各地也都分布有印刷業。

Private Printing in the Yuan Dynasty

Private printing in the Yuan Dynasty flourished in Pingyang, Jianyang, and Hangzhou. Printing was also found elsewhere in the country.

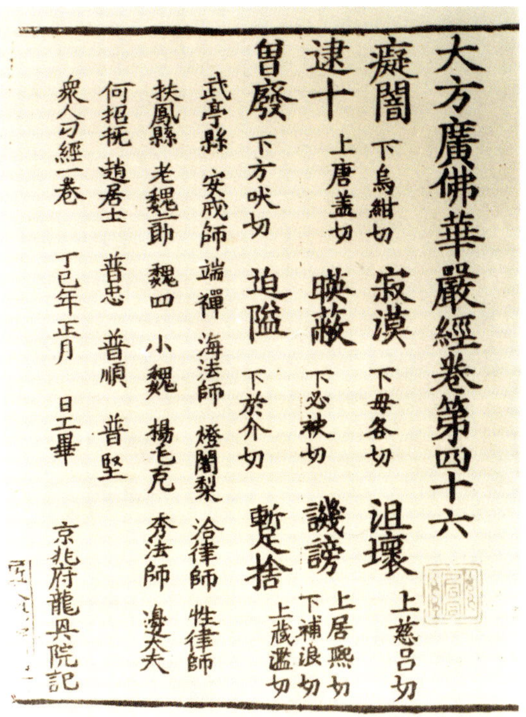

大方廣佛華嚴經卷第四十六

癡闇 下烏紺切 寂漠 下毋各切 沮壞 上慈呂切

逮十 上唐蓋切 暎蔽 下必袂切 譏謗 上居熙切 下補浪切

曾廢 下方吠切 迫隘 下於介切 暫捨 上藏濫切

武亭縣 安戒師 端禪 海法師 燈闍梨 洽律師 性律師

扶鳳縣 老魏郎 魏四 小魏 楊毛充 秀法師 淩大夫

何招撫 趙居士 普忠 普順 普堅

衆人句經一卷 丁巳年正月 日工畢 京兆府龍興院記

《大方廣佛華嚴經》蒙古憲宗八年（1257 年）京兆府刻印
The Garland Sutra, engraved and printed by the Metropolitan Prefecture in the eighth year of the reign of Emperor Xianzong of Mongolia (1257).

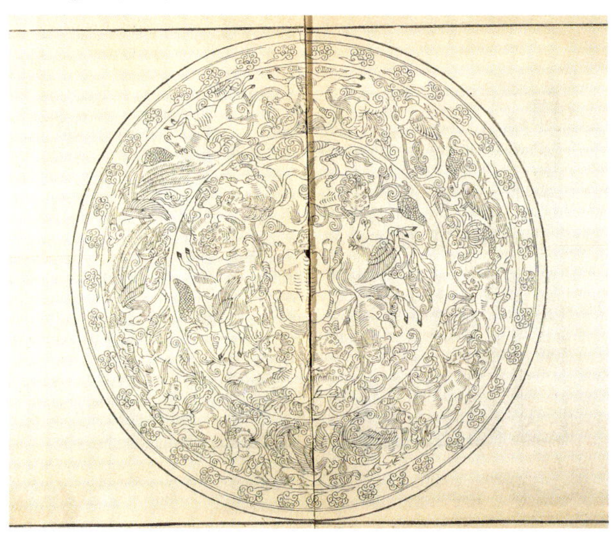

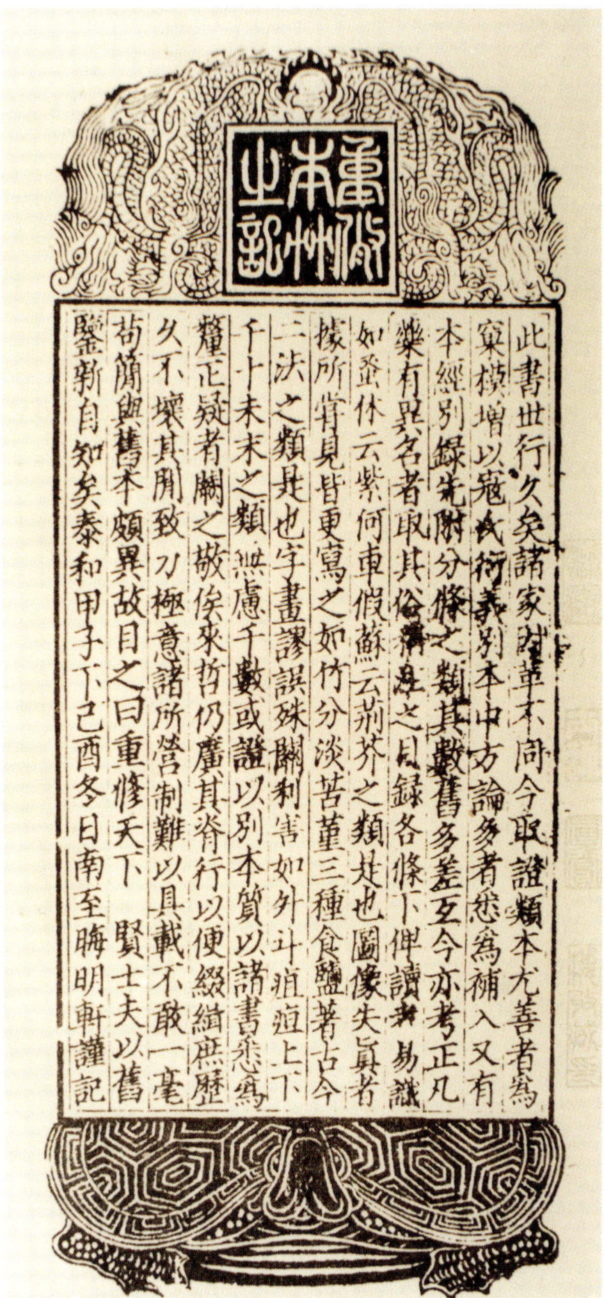

此書世行久矣諸家隨革不同今取證類本尤善者為窠模增以寇氏衍義別本中方論多者悉為補入又有本經別錄先附分條之類其數舊多差互今亦考正凡藥有異名者取其俗稱注之目錄各條下俾讀者易識如蚤休云紫河車假蘇云荊芥之類是也圖像失真者據所嘗見皆更寫之如竹分淡苦董三種食鹽著古今二法之類是也字畫謬誤殊關利害如升斗疽疸上下千十未末之類無慮千數或證以別本質以諸書悉為釐正疑者闕之敬俟來哲仍廣其脊行以便綴緝庶歷久不壞其用致刀極意諸所營制難以具載不敢一毫苟簡與舊本頗異故目之曰重修天下 賢士夫以舊鑒新自知矣泰和甲子下己酉冬日南至晦明軒謹記

《備用本草》一書刊記
蒙古憲宗四年平陽張存惠刻印（1254 年）
The "Publisher's Notes" of *Main Points for Materia Medica Usage*. The book was printed by Zhang Cunhui of Pingyang in the fourth year of Emperor Xianzong of Mongolia (1254).

《博古圖錄》
元至大年間（1308–1311 年）
杭州刻印
An Illustrated Catalogue of Antiques, engraved and printed in Hangzhou during the Zhida period of the Yuan Dynasty (1308–1311).

Printing in the Ming Dynasty

1368–1644

明代印刷

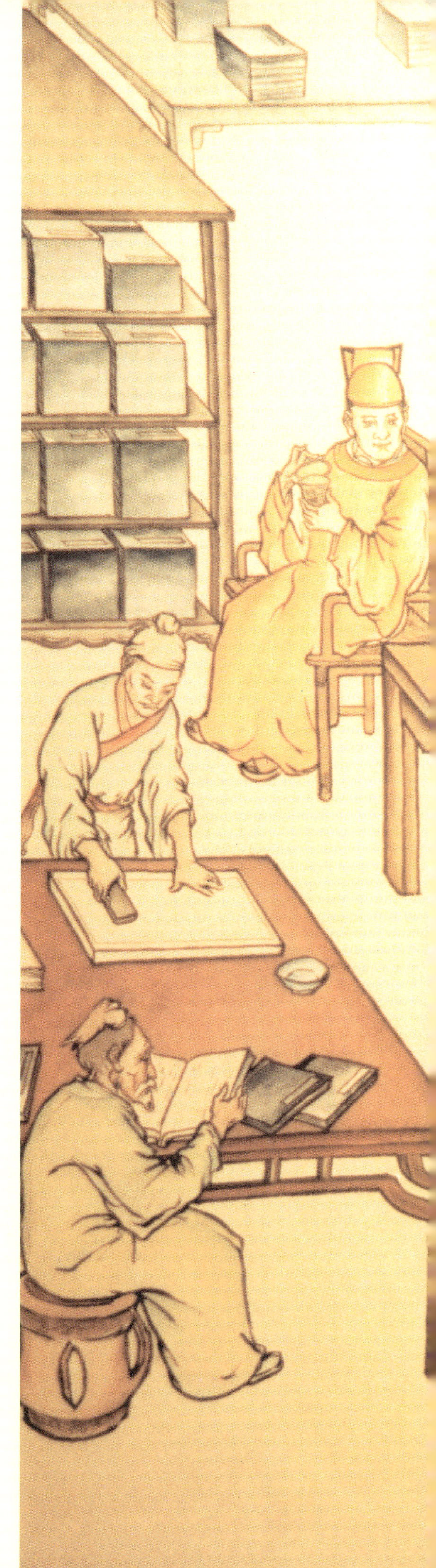

明代印刷
(1368–1644 年)

明代是中國古代印刷的全盛時期，其特點是印刷規模大、分布廣、品種多、質量精。在技術方面，圖版刻印更為精良，並且首創彩色套印。金屬活字廣泛使用。印刷字體——宋體——更為成熟。

Printing in the Ming Dynasty (1368–1644)

The Ming Dynasty was the golden period of printing in ancient China. The scale of printing was large, the distribution wide, the types varied and the quality superior. Technologically, the engraving of printing plates was sophisticated, and colour-printing was invented during the Ming. Metal movable-type printing was also widely used. The printing typeface — the Song typeface — became more refined.

司禮監經廠圖
明政府最大的印刷廠，有刻版工 350 名，刷印工 134 名，擺配工 189 名，裝訂工 293 名，製筆、墨工數十名，總數超過 1,000 人。
An illustration of the classics being printed by the factory run by the Directorate of Ceremonies. The Directorate was the largest government printing house, employing 350 engravers, 134 printers, 189 printing assistants, 293 binders, and scores of brush-makers and ink-makers, totalling more than one thousand workers.

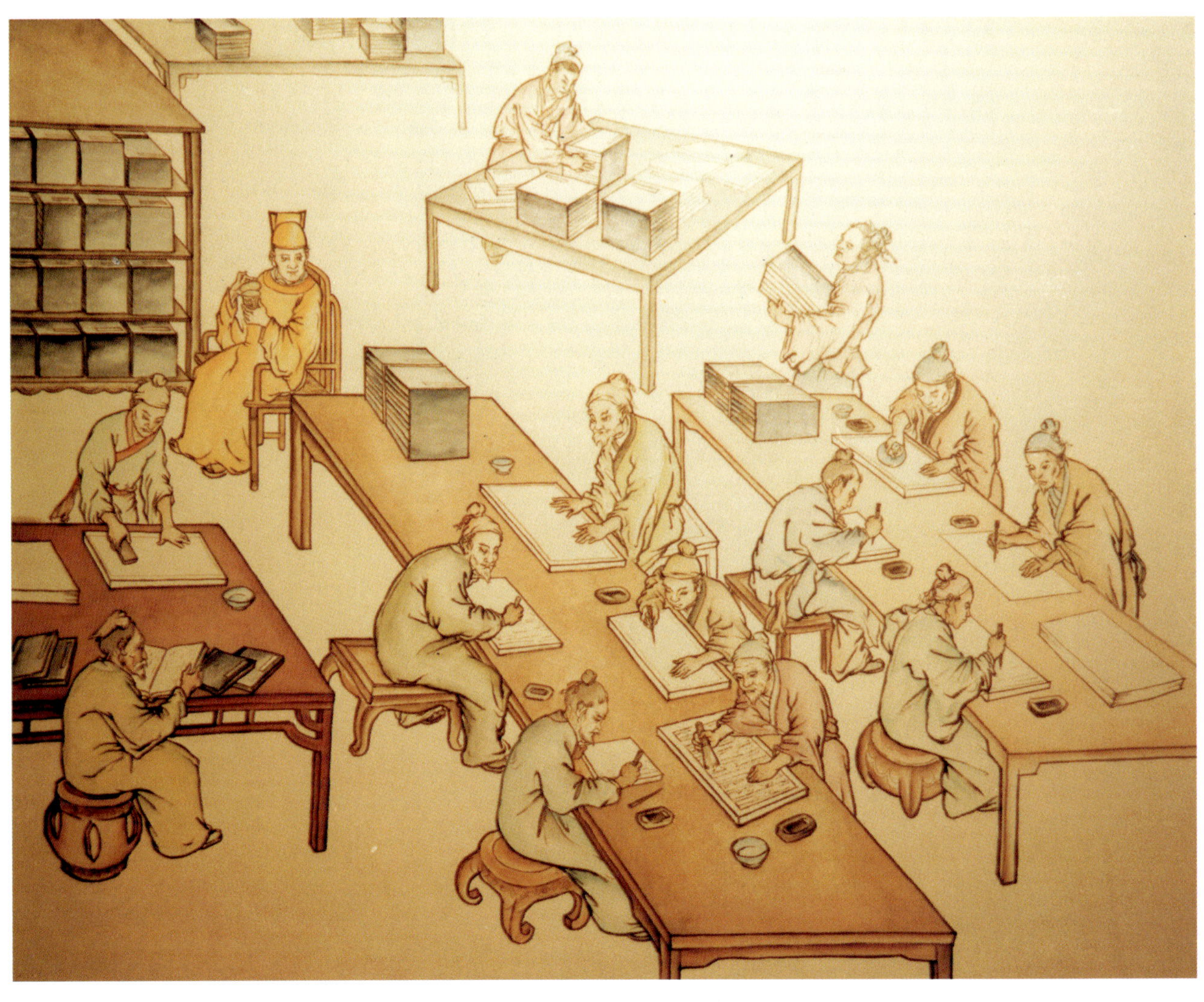

明代政府的印刷

明代國子監分南北二處，俗稱南監、北監。南京國子監規模大，刻書種類比北監多。

Government Printing in the Ming Dynasty

The National Academy of the Ming Dynasty was located in the south and also in the north. The National Academy at Nanjing was larger in scale and the types of books printed were more varied than those of the Northern Academy.

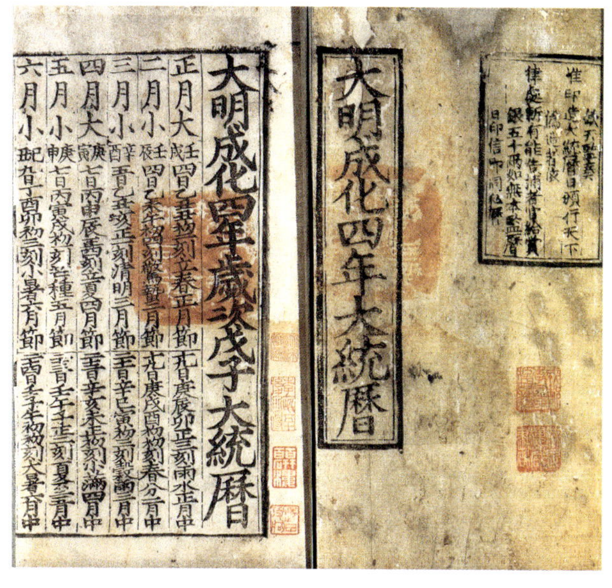

《大明成化四年大統曆》明成化四年（1468 年）刊
The Annual Almanac for the Fouth Year of the Chenghua Period of the Ming Dynasty, printed in 1468.

《周易傳義》明正統十二年（1447 年）司禮監經廠刻印本
Exegesis of the Book of Changes, printed by the workshop run by the Directorate of Ceremonies in the twelfth year of the Zhengtong period of the Ming Dynasty (1447).

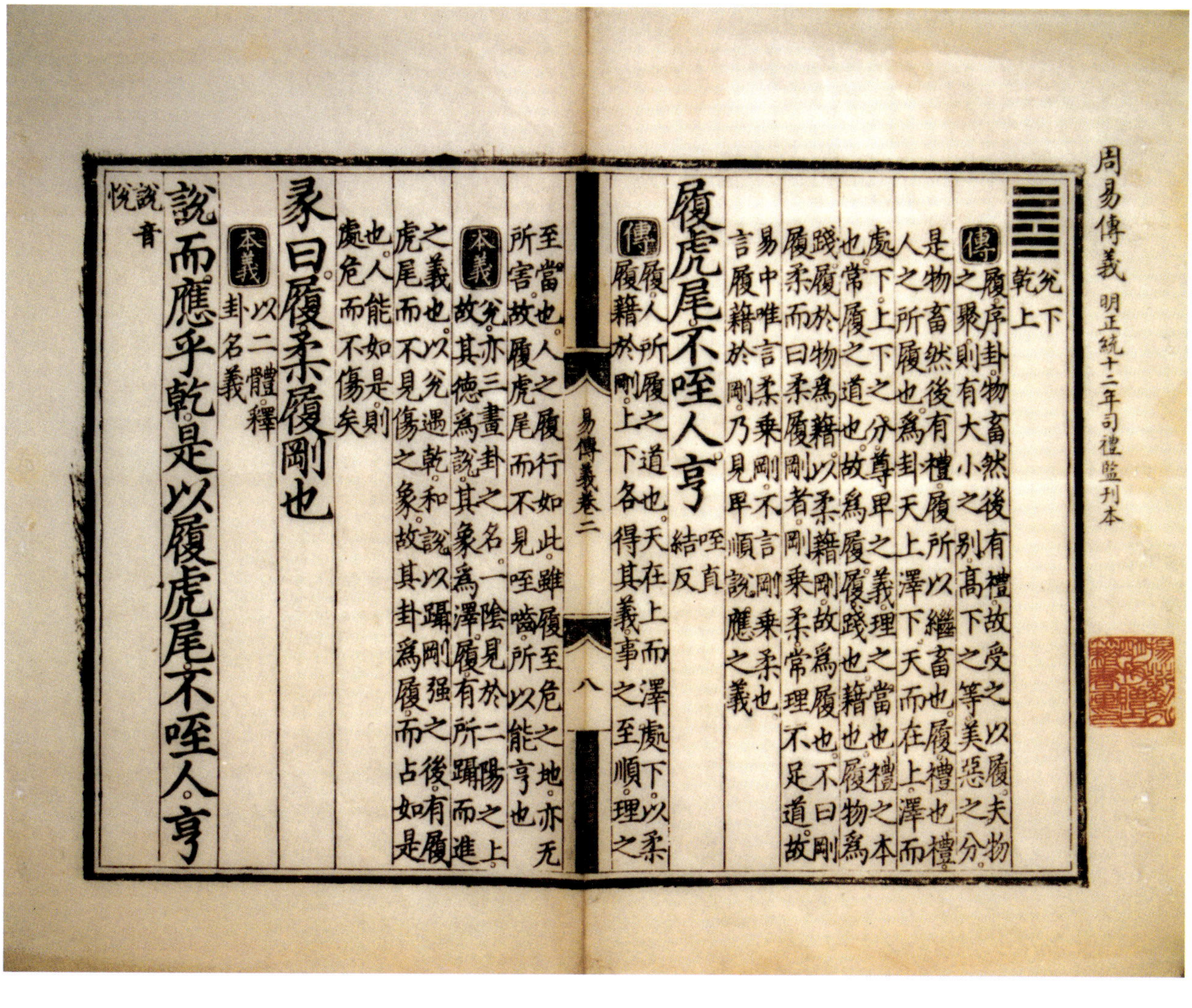

《大明集禮》明嘉靖九年 (1530 年) 內府刻本
The Ming Dynasty Encyclopedia of Rituals, printed by the Imperial Printer in the nineth year of the Jiajing period (1530).

《三國志注》明萬曆二十四年（1596 年）南京國子監刻印
Commentaries on the History of the Three Kingdoms, printed by the National Academy at Nanjing in the twenty-fourth year of the Wanli period (1596).

《道藏・墨子》明正統十年（1445 年）北京刻印
The book of *Mozi* as collected in *The Taoist Tripitaka,* printed in Beijing in the tenth year of the Zhengtong period of the Ming Dynasty (1445).

明藩王府印刷

藩王府印書是明代的特有現象。駐在各地的藩王，由於沒有實際政務，有的研究學問，有的則熱衷於雇工印刷書籍。他們印的書，質量都十分考究，史稱這種書為“藩本”。據史料統計，藩本有 500 多種。藩本中有一些特有的書，如醫學書、棋書、音樂書、茶譜、花卉、法帖、地理等書。

Printing at the Ming Provincial Commanders' Offices

The printing of books at the Provincial Commanders' Offices was a special phenomenon of the Ming Dynasty. As the commanders stationed at the various places did not have any real administrative duties to perform, some dabbled in academic pursuits, others developed an interest in printing and hired workers to print books. The books they printed were exquisite and were known as "commander editions." Historical statistics show that there were over 500 commander editions. Some of these publications were books of a very special nature, such as books on medicine, chess, music, tea, flowers, model calligraphy and geography.

《普濟方》明永樂周藩刻本 (1403–1424)
Prescriptions for Curing All People, printed by Zhou Commander's Office in the Yongle period of the Ming (1403–1424).

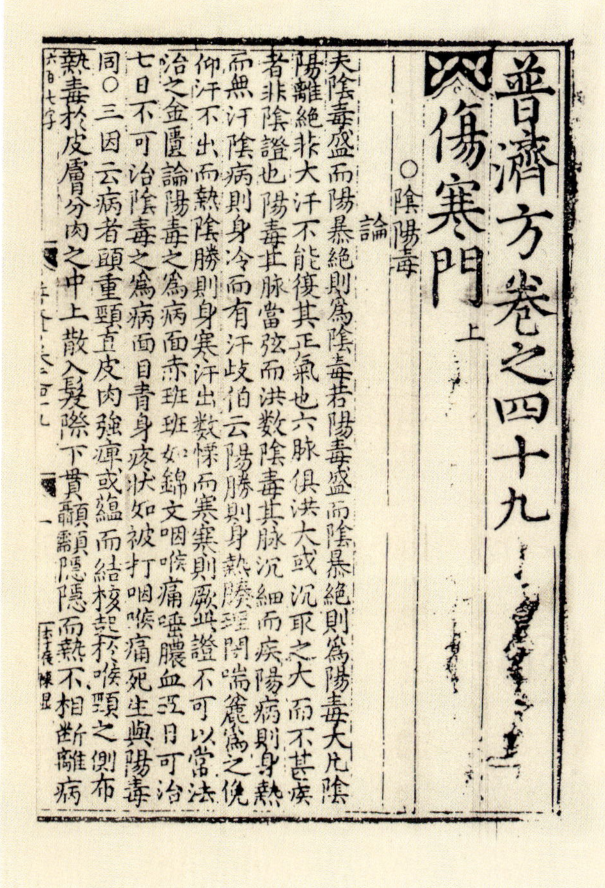

普濟方卷之四十九
傷寒門 上
○陰陽毒
論
夫陰毒盛而陽暴絕則為陰毒若陽毒盛而陰暴絕則為陽毒大凡陰
陽離絕非大汗不能復其正氣也六脈俱洪大或沉取之大而不甚疾
者非陰證也陽毒其脉當弦而洪數陰毒其脉沉細而疾陽病則身熱
而無汗陰病則身冷而有汗岐伯云陽勝則身熱腠理閉喘麤為之俛
仰汗不出而熱陰勝則身寒汗出數慄而寒寒則厥與證不可以常法
治之金匱論陽毒之為病面赤斑斑如錦文咽喉痛唾膿血五日可治
七日不可治陰毒之為病面目青身疼狀如被打咽喉痛死生與陽毒
同○三因云病者頭重頸直皮肉強痺或蘊而結核起於喉頸之側布
熱毒於皮膚分肉之中上散入髮際下貫顳顬隱隱而熱不相斷離病

《欒城集》明萬曆二十年 (1592 年) 蜀藩刻印
The Luan Cheng Anthology, a collection of poetry printed by the Sichuan Commander's Office in the twentieth year of the Wanli period of the Ming Dynasty (1592).

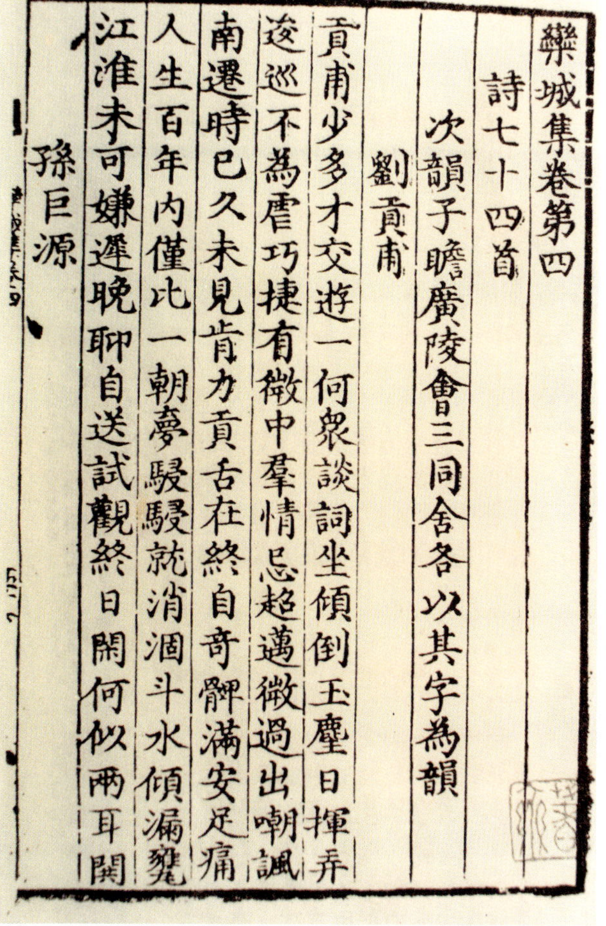

欒城集卷第四
詩七十四首
次韻子瞻廣陵會三同舍各以其字為韻
劉貢甫
貢甫少多才交遊一何衆談詞坐傾倒玉麈日揮弄
逡巡不為嚚巧捷有微中羣情忌超邁微過出嘲諷
南遷時已久未見肯力貢舌在終自奇斛滿安足痛
人生百年內僅比一朝夢騷騷就消涸斗水傾漏甕
江淮未可嫌遲晚聊自送試觀終日閑何似兩耳閧
孫巨源

明代各地民間印刷

明代民間印刷業遍及全國各地，印刷品種多，刻印精良。尤以江浙、安徽最為興盛。

Private Printing in Other Parts of the Ming Empire

Many fine publications were produced by the private-printing industry that thrived in different parts of the Ming Empire, especially in the Jiangsu, Zhejiang and Anhui region.

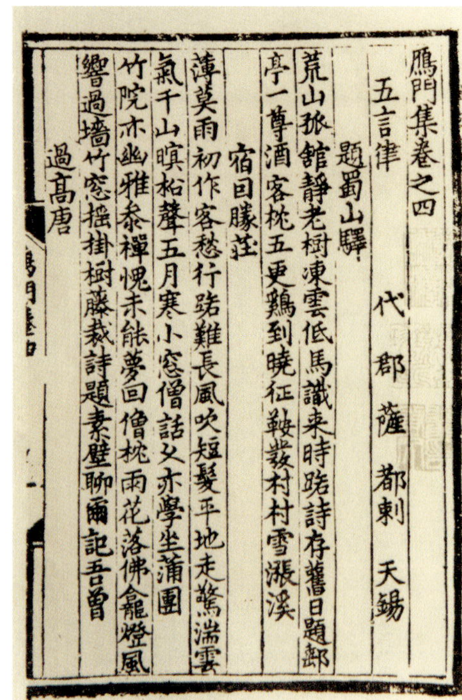

鴈門集卷之四
五言律　代郡薩都剌天錫
題蜀山驛
荒山孤館靜老樹凍雲低馬識来時路詩存舊日題郵
亭一尊酒客枕五更鷄到曉征鞍發村村雪漲溪
宿回滕莊
薄莫雨初作客愁行路難長風吹短髮平地走驚湍雲
氣千山暝松聲五月寒小窗僧話久亦學坐蒲團
竹院亦幽雅參禪愧未能夢回僧枕雨花落佛龕燈風
響過墻竹窗搖掛樹藤裁詩題素壁聊爾記吾曾
過高唐

《雁門集》
明成化四年（1468）
蘇州張習刻印
The Yanmen Anthology, engraved and printed by Zhang Xi in Suzhou in the fourth year of the Chenghua period (1468).

《人鏡陽秋》
明萬曆休寧汪氏環翠堂刻印，徽州名刻工黃應祖刻版
Mirrors of Human Behaviour and Morals of History, engraved and printed by the Huanchui Hall of the Wang Family in Xiuning during the Wanli period of the Ming. The book was engraved by the famous engraver Huang Yingzu, a native of Huizhou.

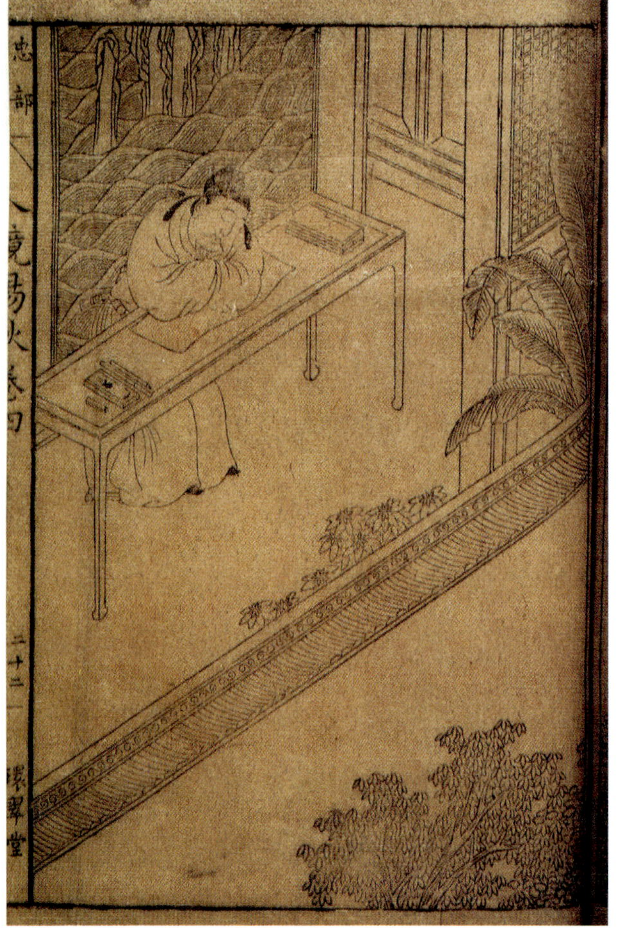

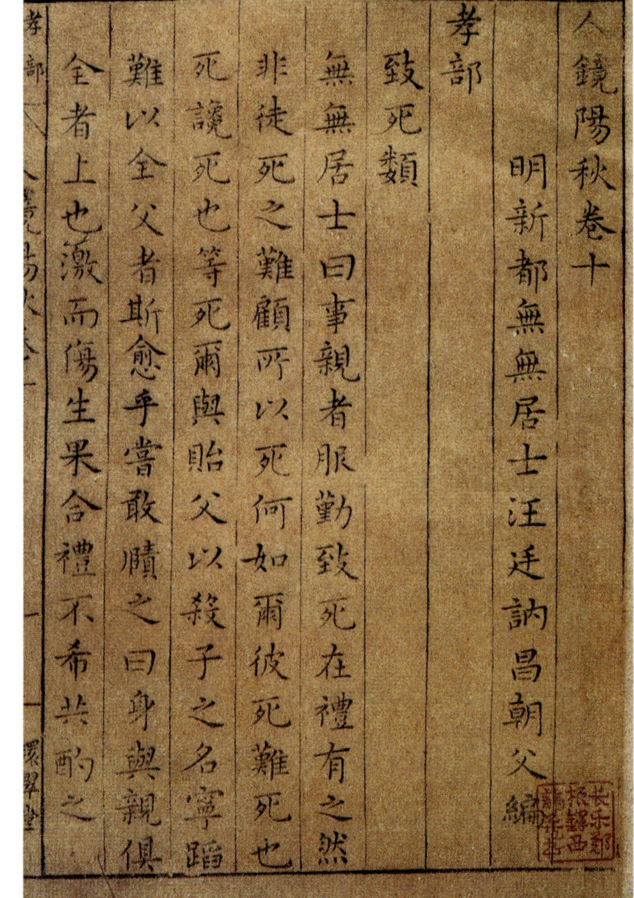

人鏡陽秋卷十
明新都無無居士汪廷訥昌朝父編
孝部
致死類
無無居士曰事親者服勤致死在禮有之然
非徒死之難顧所以死何如爾彼死難死也
死讒死也等死爾與貽父以殺子之名寧蹈
難以全父者斯愈乎嘗敢贖之曰身與親俱
全者上也激而傷生果合禮不希共酌之

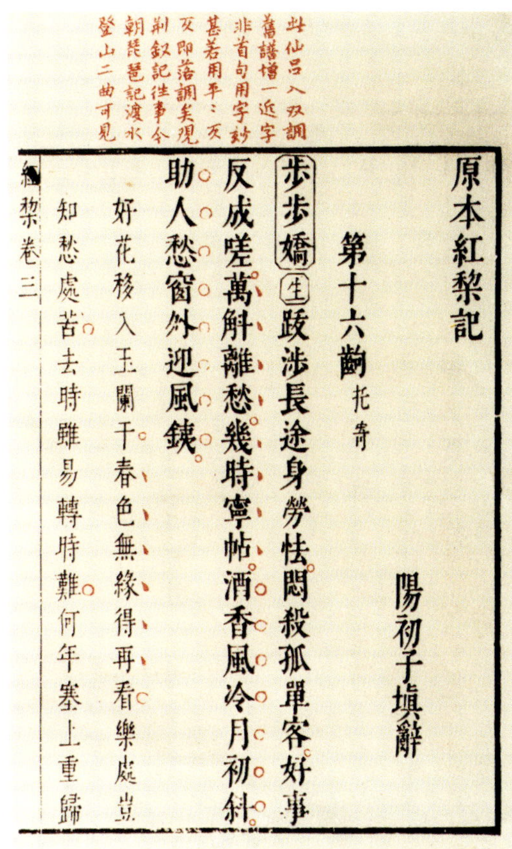

此仙呂入双調舊譜增一近字非首句用字妙甚若用平平亦可即落調矣觀荊釵記往事今朝琵琶記渡水登山二曲可見

原本紅梨記

陽初子塡辭

第十六齣 托寄

步步嬌（生）跋涉長途身勞怯悶殺孤單客好事反成嗟萬斛離愁幾時寧帖酒香風冷月初斜助人愁窗外迎風鐵

好花移入玉闌干春色無緣得再看樂處豈知愁處苦去時雖易轉時難何年塞上重歸

紅梨卷三

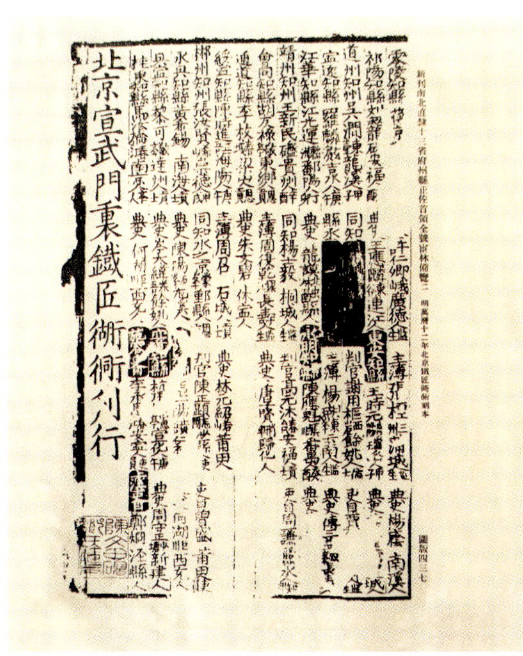

北京宣武門裏鐵匠衚衕刊行

（上） 《紅梨記》吳興刻套印本

(Top) *Red Pears,* colour printing by Wu Xing.

（下） 《宦林備覽》萬歷十二年（1584 年）北京書坊刻印本

(Bottom) *Directory of Officials,* printed by workshops in Beijing in the twelfth year of the Wanli period of the Ming Dynasty (1584).

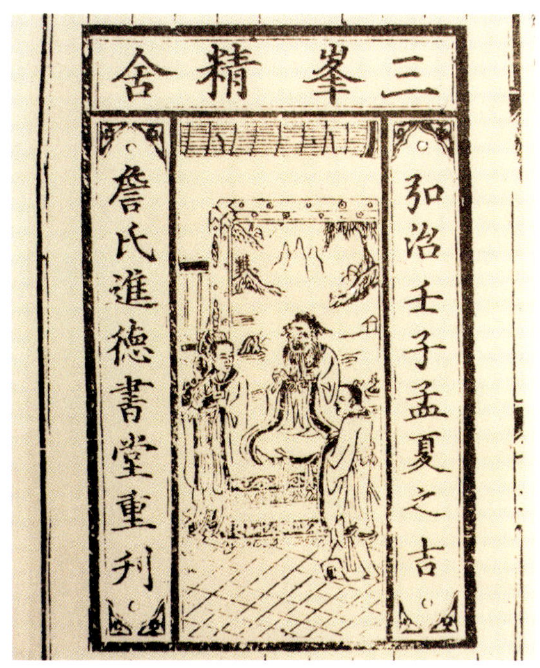

三峯精舍

弘治壬子孟夏之吉

詹氏進德書堂重刊

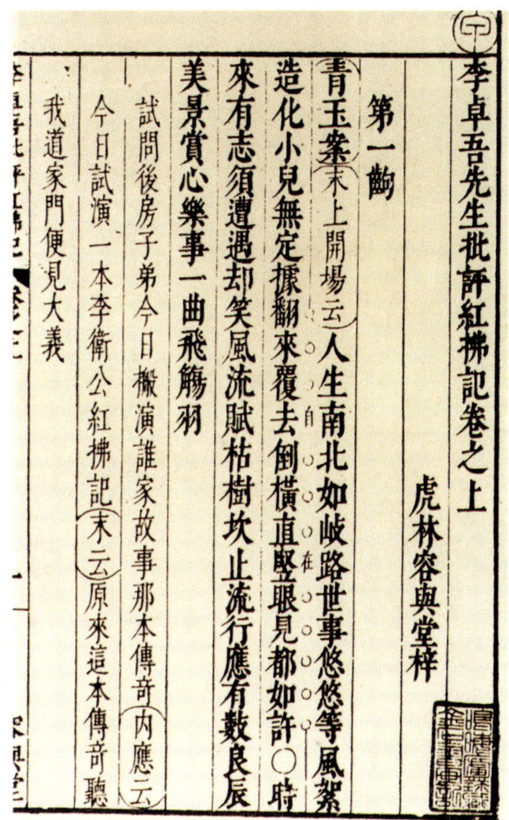

李卓吾先生批評紅拂記卷之上

虎林容與堂梓

第一齣

青玉案（末上開場云）人生南北如岐路世事悠悠等風絮造化小兒無定據翻來覆去倒橫直豎眼見都如許○時來有志須遭遇却笑風流賦枯樹坎止流行應有數良辰美景賞心樂事一曲飛觴羽

試問後房子弟今日搬演誰家故事那本傳奇（內應云）今日試演一本李衛公紅拂記（末云）原來這本傳奇聽我道家門便見大義

（上） 《玉篇》明弘治五年（1492 年）建陽進德書堂刻印

(Top) *Yübian* (China's earliest dictionary in regular script dated to A.D. 1013), printed by the Jinde Printing House in Jianyang in the fifth year of the Hongzhi period in the Ming Dynasty (1492).

（下） 《紅拂記》杭州容與堂刻印，所刻宋體字有粗細兩種，十分精美

(Bottom) *A Story of Courtesan Red Whisk,* printed by the Rongyu Hall in Hangzhou. The Song typeface engraving nicely delineated the bold and light fonts.

明圖版雕刻及徽派刻工

明代圖版雕刻技藝十分精湛，尤以徽州為最著名，徽州又以虬村黃氏最有代表性。

Plate Engraving in Ming and Engravers of the Huizhou School

Plate engraving techniques in Ming were sophisticated, and the Huizhou engravers, represented by the Huang family of Qiu Village, were best known for their craftsmanship.

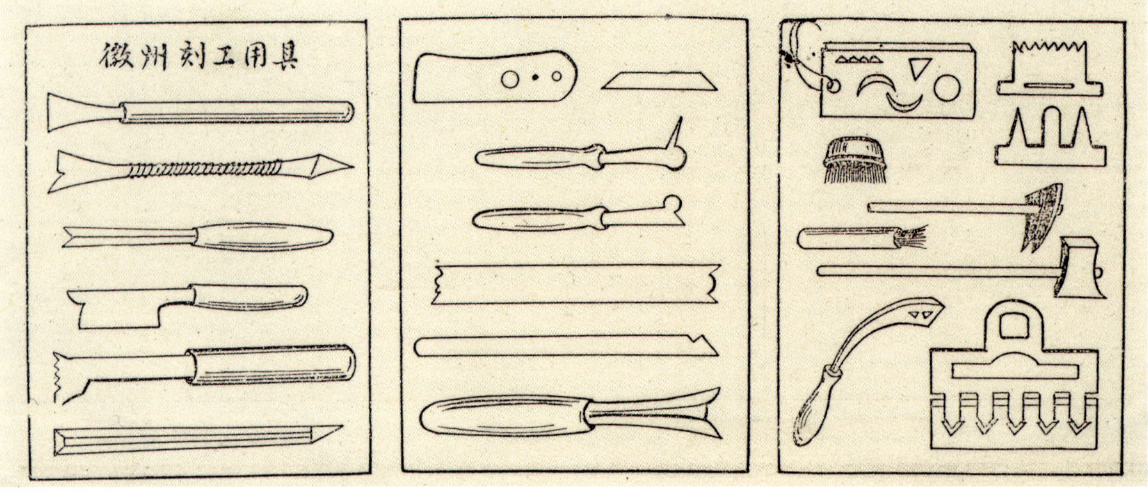

徽州刻工使用的工具
Tools used by the Huizhou engravers.

《仙媛紀事》明代版畫
Chronicles of Female Immortals,
engraved illustrations of the Ming Dynasty.

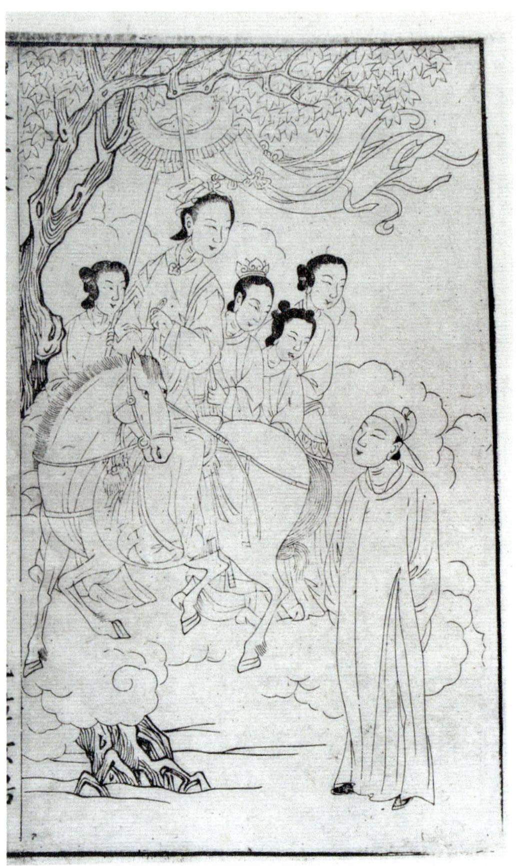

《玉杵記》明萬曆刊
Story of the Jade Rod,
engraved and printed in the Wanli period of the Ming Dynasty.

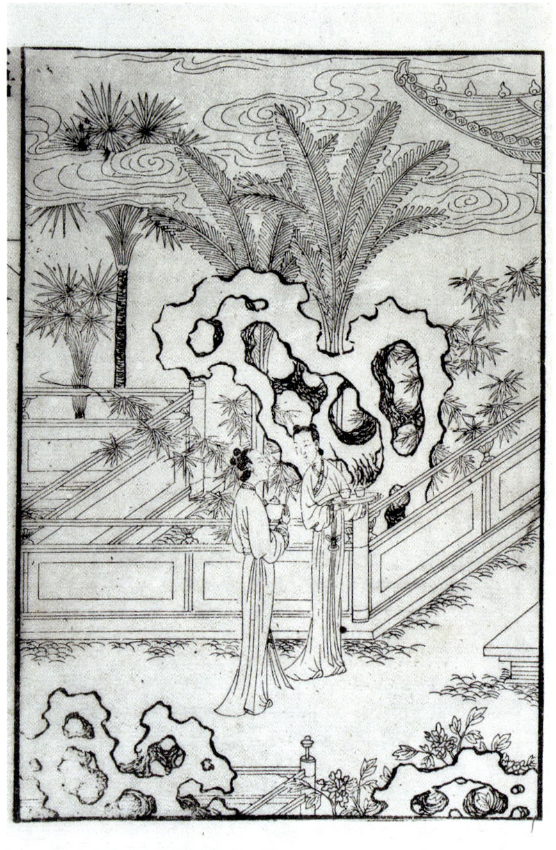

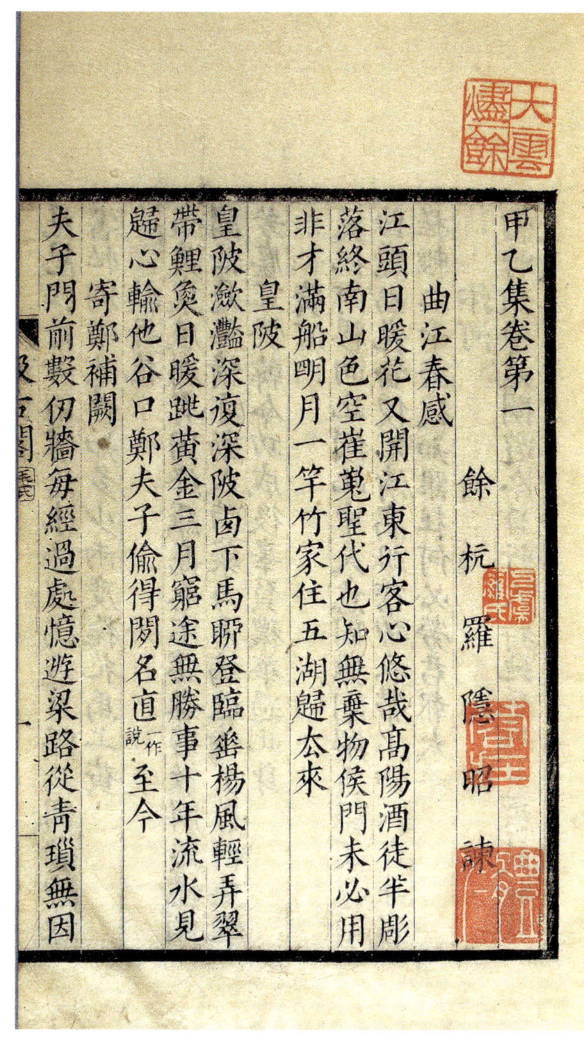

甲乙集卷第一　　餘杭羅隱昭諫

曲江春感

江頭日暖花又開江東行客心悠哉高陽酒徒半彫落終南山色空崔嵬聖代也知無棄物侯門未必用非才滿船明月一竿竹家住五湖歸去來

皇陂

皇陂瀲灧深復深陂西下馬聊登臨鸂鶒風輕弄翠帶鯉魚日暖跳黃金三月窮途無勝事十年流水見歸心輸他谷口鄭夫子偷得閑名直一作說至今

寄鄭補闕

夫子門前數仞牆每經過處憶遊梁路從青瑣無因

《甲乙集》（詩集）
常熟毛氏汲古閣刻本
Jiayi Anthology
(collection of poems),
engraved and printed by
the Xigu Hall of the Mao
Family in Changshu.

明常熟毛晉印刷

毛晉（1599–1659）字子晉，號潛在，常熟人，明代大藏書家、出版家。家雇工幾十人，從事刻書事業，所印著名書有《十三經》、《十七史》、《津逮秘書》等，在中國古代印刷史上具有重要影響。

The Printing of Mao Jin of Changshu in the Ming Dynasty

Mao Jin (1599–1659), styled Zijin, also known as Qianzai, was a native of Changshu. He was a great collector of calligraphy and hired several dozen workers to engrave and print books. Among the books he printed were the famous *The Thirteen Classics, The Seventeen Histories,* and *Rare Scholarly Books*. He was an important figure in the history of printing in China.

《剪綃集》常熟毛氏汲古閣刻本
Cutting Raw Silk: An Anthology of Poems,
engraved and printed by the Xigu Hall of the Mao Family in Changshu.

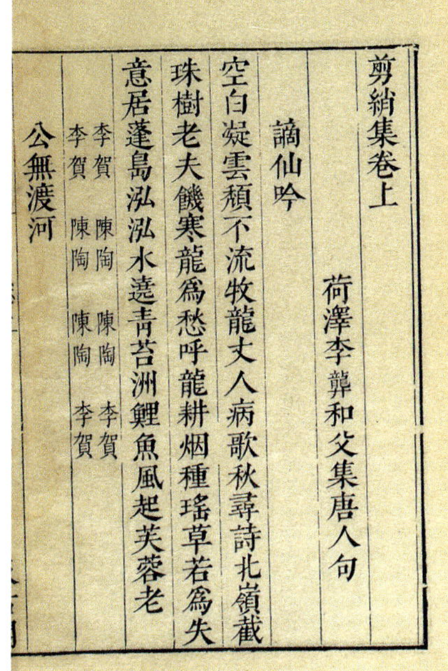

剪綃集卷上　　荷澤李龏和父集唐人句

謫仙吟

空白凝雲頹不流　牧龍丈人病歌秋　尋詩北嶺截珠樹　老夫饑寒龍為愁　呼龍耕烟種瑤草　若為失意居蓬島　泓泓水遶青苔洲　鯉魚風起芙蓉老

李賀　陳陶　陳陶　李賀
李賀　陳陶　陳陶　李賀

公無渡河

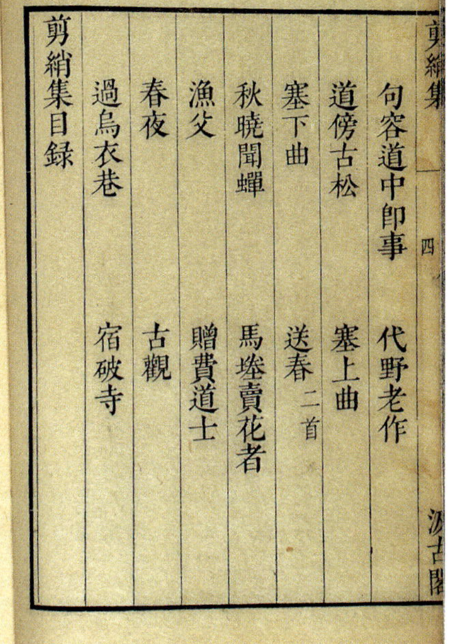

剪綃集　四　汲古閣

句容道中即事　代野老作
道傍古松　塞上曲
塞下曲　送春二首
秋曉聞蟬　馬塍賣花者
漁父　贈費道士
春夜　古觀
過烏衣巷　宿破寺

剪綃集目録

《青樓韻語》明代版畫
Rhymed Stories of the Houses of Pleasure,
engraved illustrations of the Ming Dynasty.

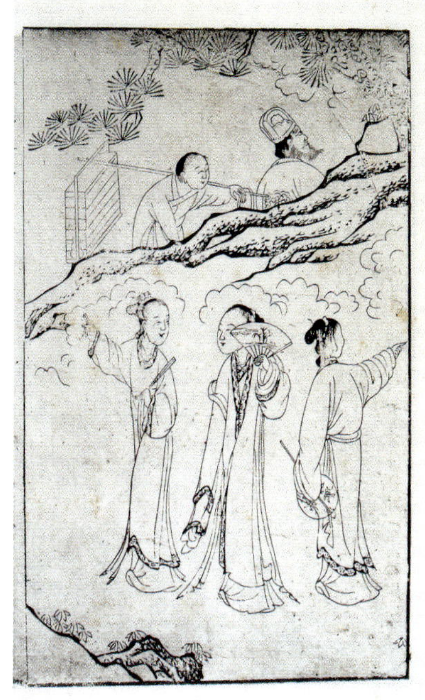

明代多色及彩色印刷

中國是世界上使用彩色套印最早的國家，明中期，從雙色套印，多色套印，發展到彩色套印。

Multi-colour Printing and Colour Printing in the Ming Dynasty

China was the first country in the world to use colour processing printing. In the middle part of the Ming Dynasty, the method of painting several colours on one plate was developed into the process of multi-colour printing, and eventually into full colour-printing.

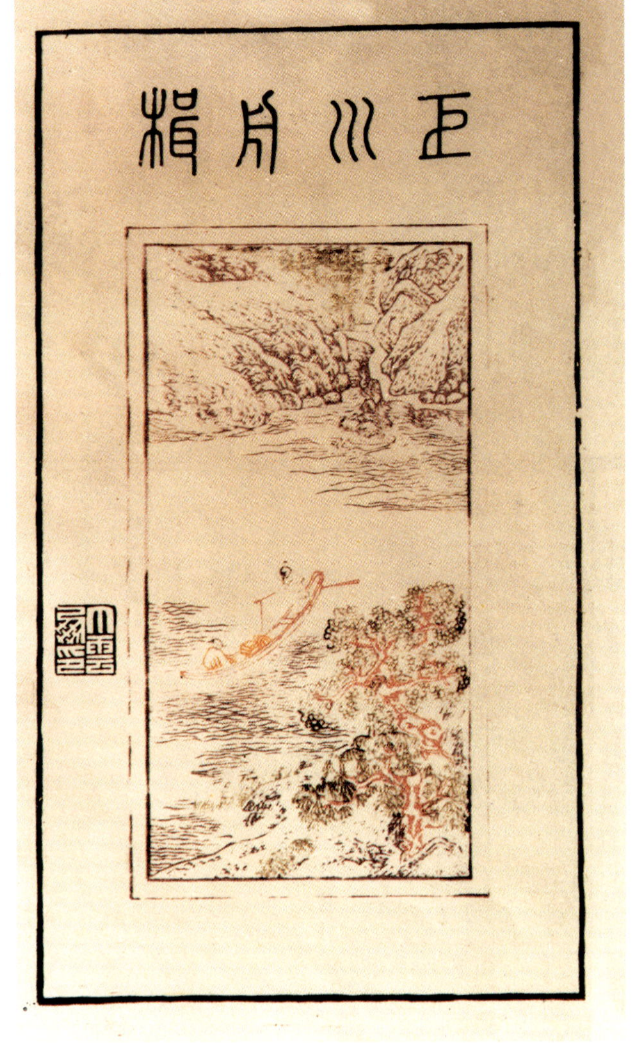

《巨川舟楫圖》
明萬歷年間休寧程氏滋蘭堂
刻彩色套印
A Boat on a Big River,
engraved and printed in colour,
by the Zilan Hall of the Cheng Family
at Xiuning during the Wanli period of
the Ming Dynasty.

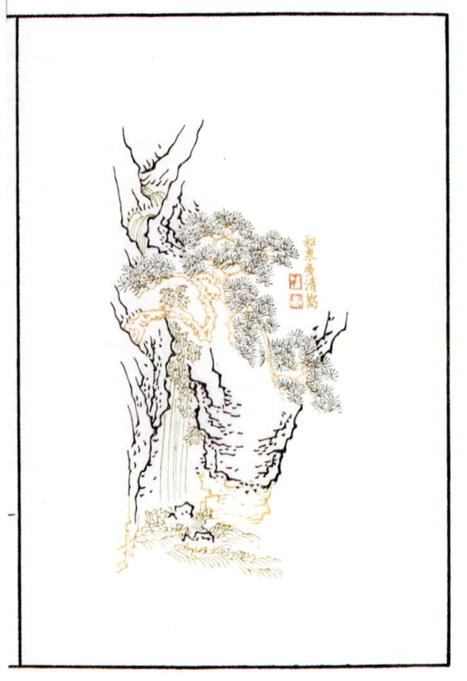

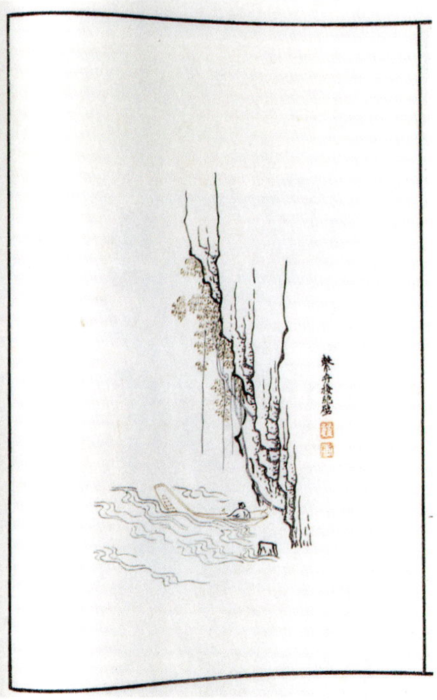

《蘿軒變古箋譜》
明天啟六年（1626 年）
吳發祥分色版套印於南京，使用了餖版、拱花工藝。
Letter-designs of the Sunglo Studio, printed by Wu Faxiang in Nanjing by colour-separation printing. The techniques of watercolour block printing and blind stamping were used.

餖版印刷工藝
Technology of Water Colour Blocks

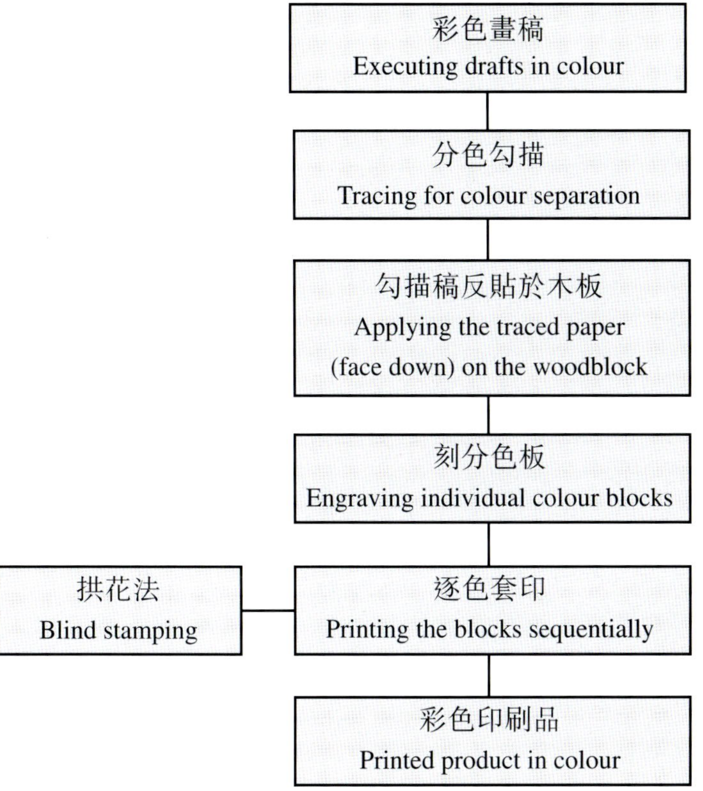

胡正言（1581-1672 年），字曰從，徽州休寧人，後居南京，官至中書舍人。萬歷四十七年（1619 年）起，與徽派刻工合作，採用餖版（即分色版）方法，刻印《十竹齋箋譜》和《十竹齋畫譜》。是歷史上最早可印出層次彩色的技術。為印刷術的發展作出貢獻。

Hu Zhengyan (1581–1672), styled Ruocong, was a native of Xiuning of Huizhou. He later moved to Nanjing and held the position of Great Secretary of the Great Imperial Secretariat. Since the forty-seventh year of Wanli (1619), he collaborated with engravers of the Huizhou School and used the watercolour block printing method (colour-separation printing) in the engraving and printing of *Letter-paper Designs of the Ten-bamboo Studio* and *Painting Manual the Ten-bamboo Studio*. That was the first time in history printing techniques were used to produce colour gradations. He thus made a great contribution to the development of printing.

《十竹齋畫譜》明胡正言餖版套印（南京）
Painting Manual of the Ten-bamboo Studio, printed with watercolour blocks by Hu Zhengyan (in Nanjing) of the Ming Dynasty.

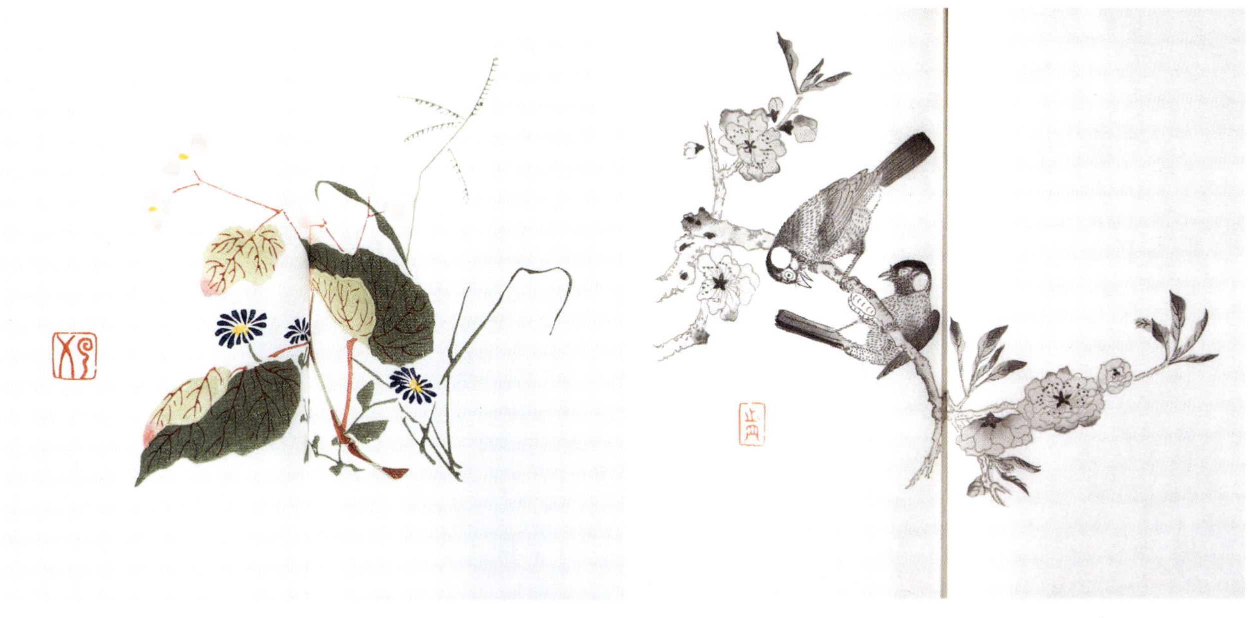

Printing in the Qing Dynasty

1644–1911

清代印刷

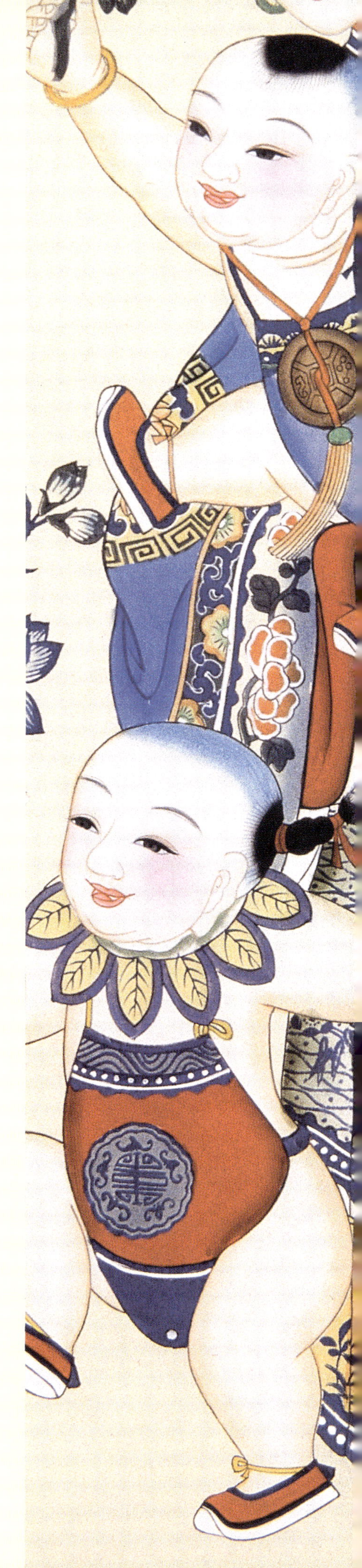

清代印刷
(1644–1911 年)

清代是中國古代印刷事業發展的又一高峯。古代開創的雕版、泥活字版、木活字版、金屬活字版以及木版彩色套印技術，都有應用，而且有所發展。

清代政府的印刷

清政府十分重視書籍的編纂和印刷。除內府設有專門的編印機構外，各地還設立官書局。

Printing in the Qing Dynasty (1644–1911)

In the Qing Dynasty, all the printing techniques invented in the ancient period — woodblock printing, clay movable-type printing, wooden movable-type printing, metal movable-type printing and watercolour block printing — were used and further developed.

Government Printing in the Qing Dynasty

The Qing court laid great store on the compilation and publication of books. Apart from setting up publication units in the Imperial Household Department, official bookstores were established throughout the country.

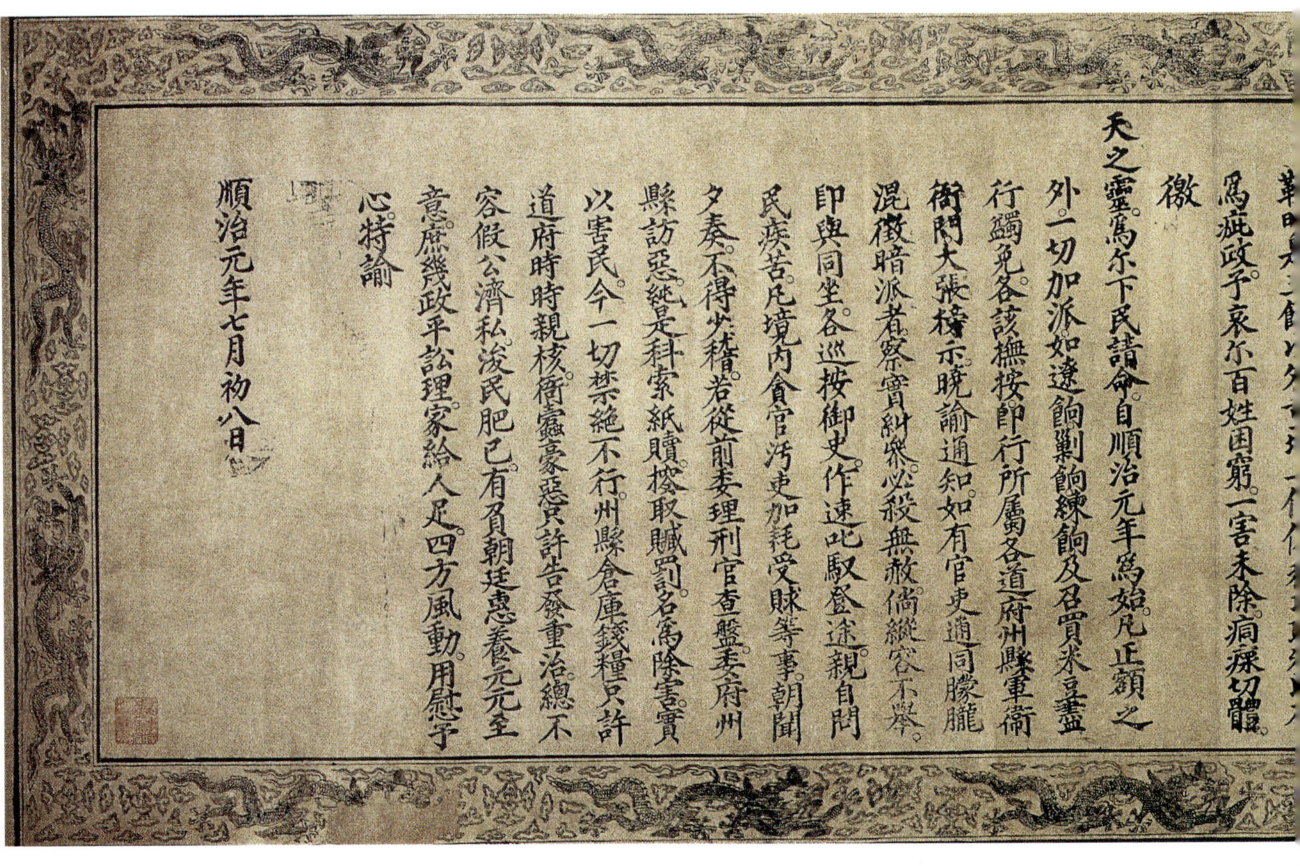

爲疵政。予哀爾百姓困窮。一害未除。痌瘝切體。
徵
天之靈。爲爾下民請命。自順治元年爲始。凡正額之
外一切加派如遼餉剿餉練餉及召買米豆盡
行蠲免。各該撫按即行所屬各道府州縣軍衛
衙門大張榜示曉諭通知。如有官吏通同朦朧
混徵暗派者。察實糾參。必殺無赦。倘縱容不舉。
即與同坐。各巡按御史作速叱馭登途。親自問
民疾苦。凡境內貪官污吏加耗受賕等事。朝聞
夕奏。不得少稽。若從前委理刑官查盤委府州
縣訪惡。總是科索紙贖。搜取贓罰。名爲除害。實
以害民。今一切禁絕不行。州縣倉庫錢糧只許
道府時時親核。衙蠹豪惡。只許告發重治。總不
容假公濟私。浚民肥己。有負朝廷惠養元元至
意。庶幾政平訟理。家給人足。四方風動。用慰予
心。特諭
順治元年七月初八日

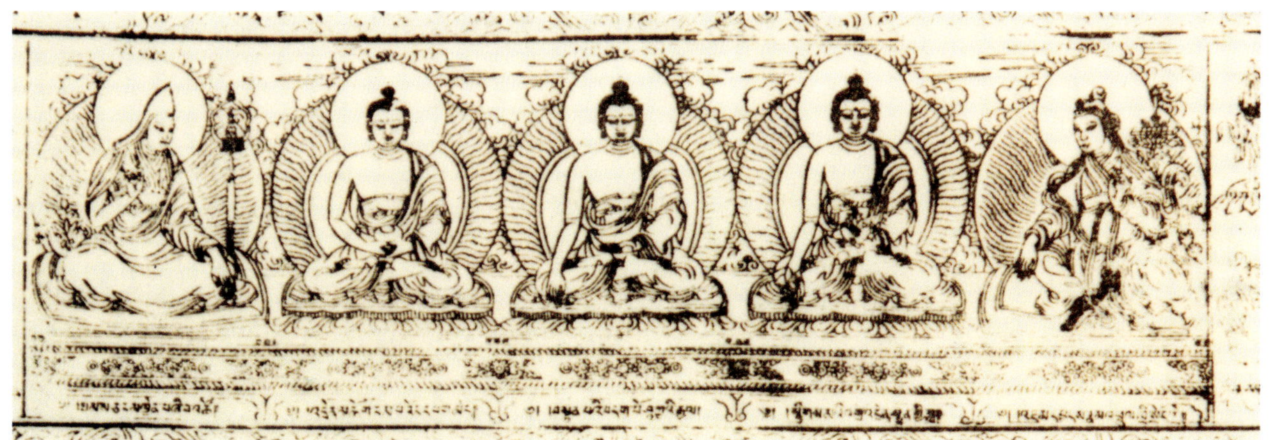

蒙文《七佛如來供養儀軌經》，清康熙二十一年 (1682 年) 刻於北京
Rites to Worship Seven Buddhas Sutra in Mongolian script, engraved and printed in Beijing in the twenty-first year of the Kangxi period of the Qing Dynasty (1682).

下圖是 1644 年清軍進入北京後第四天印刷發布的《安民告示》，是清軍入關後第一件印刷品 。用整塊木板雕刻，是現今發現古代幅面最大的雕版 。雕刻精細，印刷墨色厚重 。

The photograph below was the *Notice to Reassure the Public* printed and issued by the Qing army four days after entering Beijing in 1644 and was the first item printed after the army marched through the gate at Shanhaiguan. The notice was engraved on a single woodblock that was the largest block carved in ancient China. The engraving was exquisite and the printing ink was thick and solid.

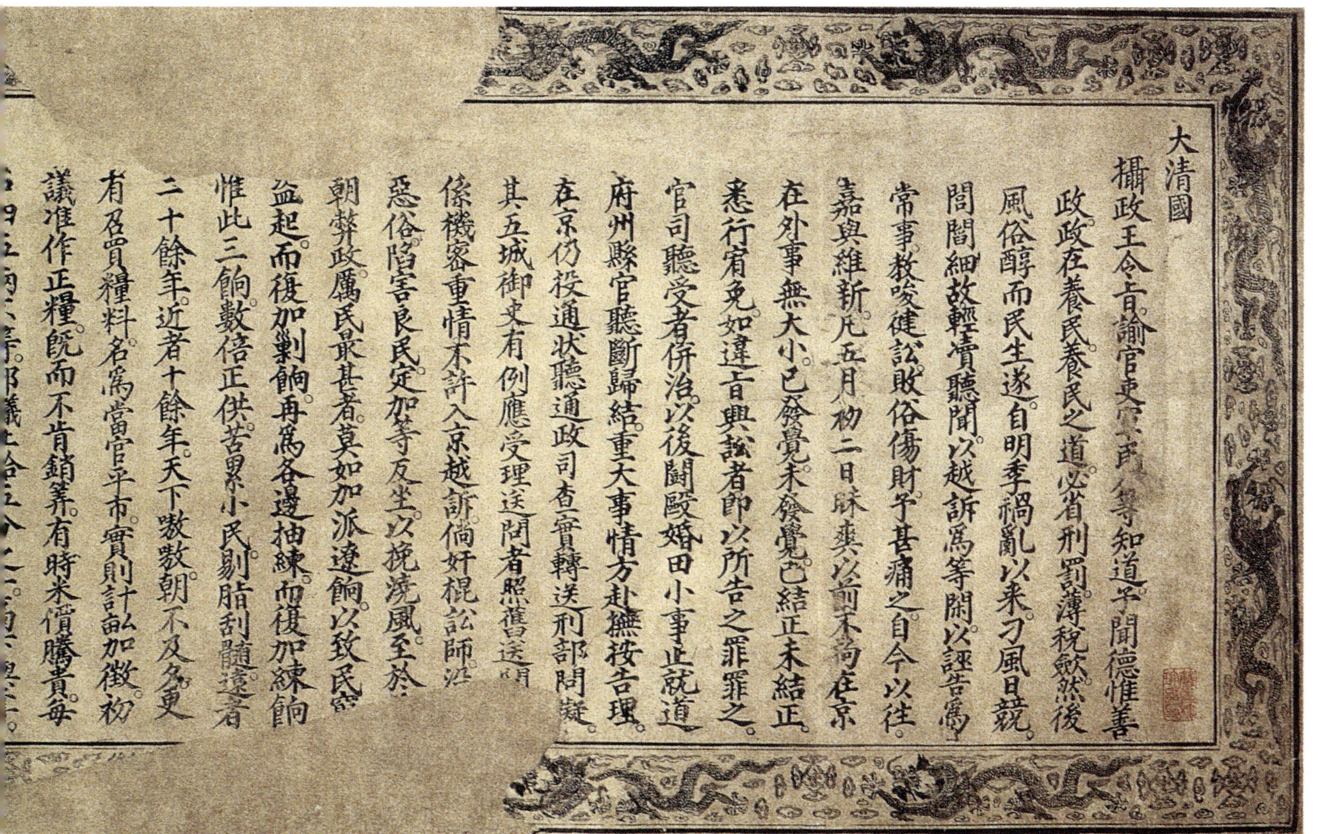

大清國
攝政王令旨諭官吏軍民人等知道予聞德惟善
政政在養民養民之道必省刑罰薄稅斂然後
風俗醇而民生遂自明季禍亂以來刁風日競
閭閻細故輕瀆聽聞以越訴爲等閑以誣告爲
常事教唆健訟敗俗傷財予甚痛之自今以往
嘉與維新凡五月初二日昧爽以前未向在京
在外事無大小已發覺未發覺已結正未結正
悉行宥免如違旨興訟者卽以所告之罪罪之
官司聽受者併治以後鬬毆婚田小事止就道
府州縣官聽斷歸結重大事情方赴撫按告理
在京仍投通狀聽通政司查實轉送刑部問擬
其五城御史有例應受理送問者照舊送問
係機密重情不許入京越訴倘奸棍訟師混
惡俗陷害良民定加等反坐以挽澆風至於
朝弊政厲民最甚者莫如加派遼餉以致民窮
盜起而復加剿餉再爲各邊抽練而復加練餉
惟此三餉數倍正供苦累小民剔脂刮髓遠者
二十餘年近者十餘年天下嗷嗷朝不及夕更
有召買糧料名爲當官平市實則計畝加徵初
議准作正糧旣而不肯銷算有時米價騰貴每

清政府刻書

順、康、雍、乾四朝，清政府刻書盛極一時。

《龍藏》是清政府據明《北藏》校刻的佛經總集。開刻於雍正十三年（1735 年），完成於乾隆三年（1738 年）共 718 函，7168 卷。近年由文物出版社以原版刷印，並贈中國印刷博物館一部。

揚州詩局

清康熙年間政府設於揚州的刻版印刷機構。所刻印的《全唐詩》、《楝亭十二種》等，寫刻極為工緻。

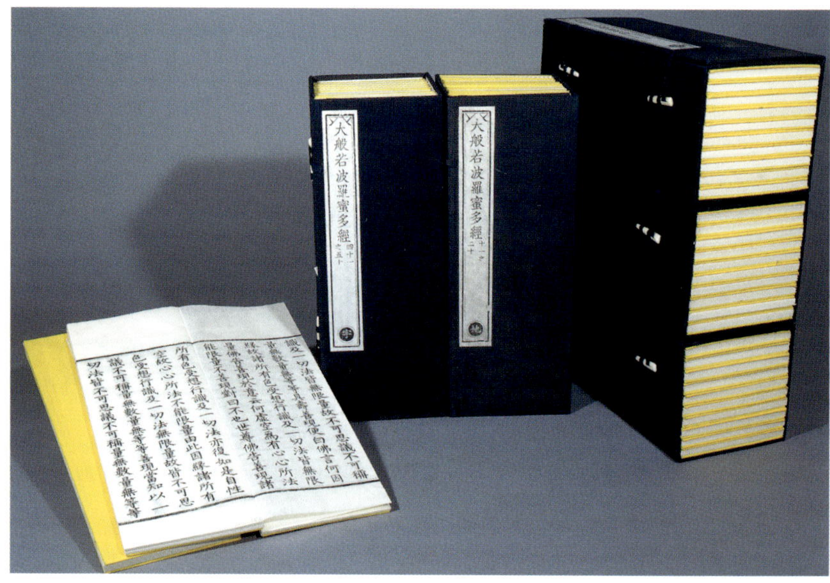

乾隆版《大藏經》（《龍藏》）
The *Dragon Tripitaka* printed during the Qianlong period (1736–1795).

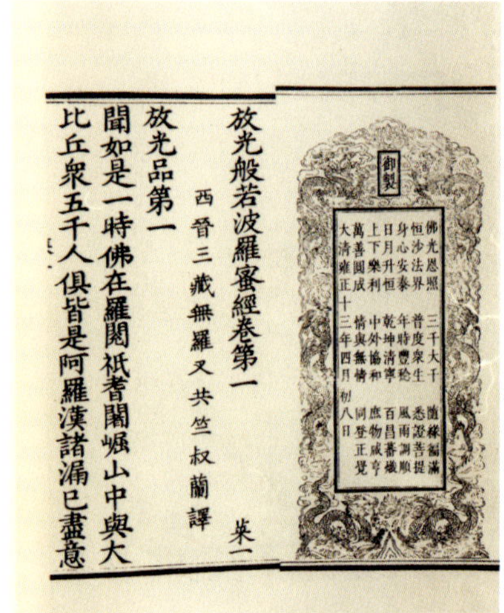

《龍藏》清雍正十三年（1735 年）
至乾隆三年（1738 年）
清內府刻印於北京
The *Dragon Tripitaka*, engraved and printed by the Qing Imperial Household Department from the thirteenth year (1735) of Yongzheng to the third year of the Qianlong period (1738) of the Qing Dynasty.

《藏文六字真言經》
清康熙五十六年（1717）
刻印於北京
True Words Sutra in Tibetan, engraved and printed in Beijing in the fifty-sixth year of the Kangxi period of the Qing Dynasty (1717).

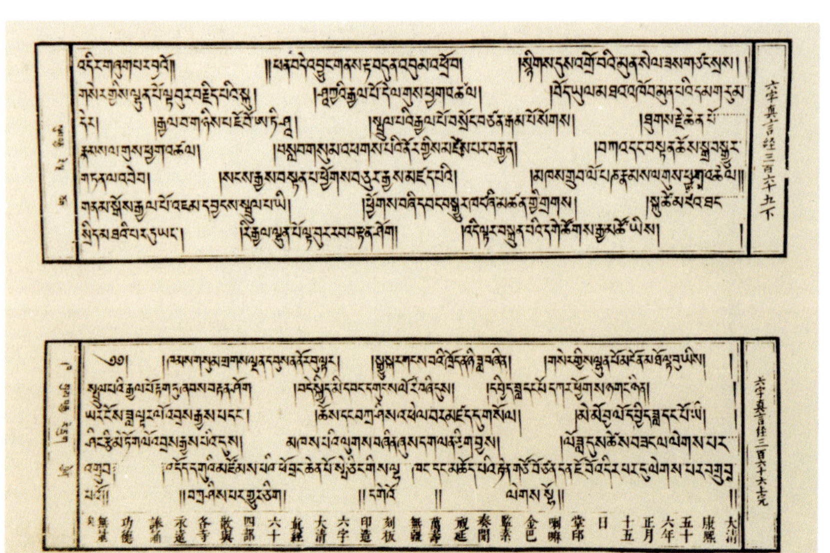

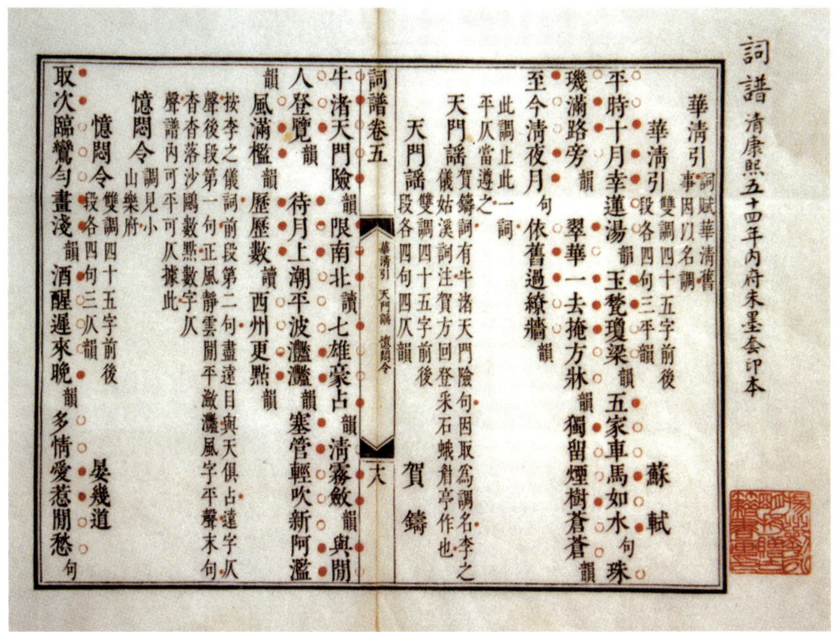

詞譜 清康熙五十四年內府朱墨套印本

華清引 蘇軾
華清引 詞賦華清舊事因以名調
雙調四十五字前後段各四句三平韻
平時十月幸蓮湯 韻 玉甃瓊梁 韻 五家車馬如水 句 珠
璣滿路旁 韻 翠華一去掩方牀 韻 獨留煙樹蒼蒼 韻
至今清夜月 句 依舊過繚牆 韻
此調止此一詞平仄當遵之
天門謠 賀鑄詞有牛渚天門險句因取為調名李之儀姑溪詞注賀方回登采石蛾眉亭作也
天門謠 雙調四十五字前後段各四句四仄韻 賀鑄

華清引 天門謠 憶悶令
大

詞譜卷五
牛渚天門險 韻 限南北 讀 七雄豪占 韻 清霧斂 韻 與閒
人登覽 韻 待月上潮平波灩灩 韻 塞管輕吹新阿濫
韻 風滿檻 韻 歷歷數 讀 西州更點 韻
按李之儀詞前段第二句畫達目與天俱占達字仄聲後段第一句正風靜雲閒平激灩風字平聲末句杳杳落沙鷗數點數字仄聲譜內可平可仄據此
憶悶令 調見小山樂府
憶悶令 雙調四十五字前後段各四句三仄韻 晏幾道
取次臨鸞勻畫淺 韻 酒醒遲來晚 韻 多情愛惹閒愁 句

《詞譜》 清康熙五十四年 (1715 年) 內府刻本
Classic Verses with Annotations, engraved and printed by the Imperial Household Department in the fifty-fourth year of the Kangxi period of the Qing Dynasty (1715).

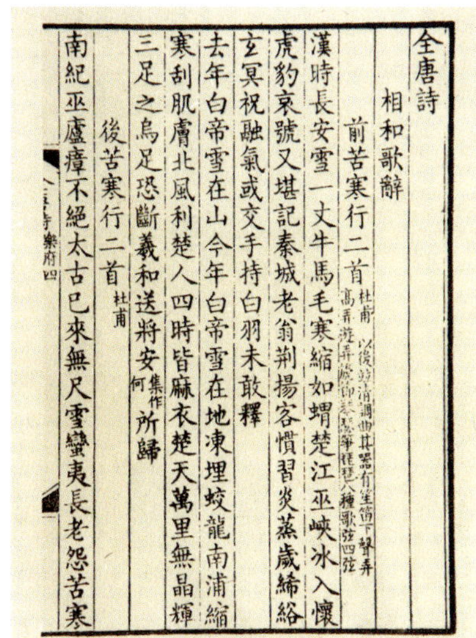

全唐詩
相和歌辭
前苦寒行二首 杜甫
漢時長安雪一丈牛馬毛寒縮如蝟楚江巫峽冰入懷
虎豹哀號又堪記秦城老翁荊揚客慣習炎蒸歲絺綌
玄冥祝融氣或交手持白羽未敢釋
去年白帝雪在山今年白帝雪在地凍埋蛟龍南浦縮
寒刮肌膚北風利楚人四時皆麻衣楚天萬里無晶輝
三足之烏足恐斷羲和送將安所歸
後苦寒行二首 杜甫
南紀巫盧瘴不絕太古已來無尺雪蠻夷長老怨苦寒

《全唐詩》清康熙四十六年（1707 年）揚州詩局刻印
The Complete Poems of the Tang Dynasty, engraved and printed by Yangzhou Poetry Bureau in the forty-sixth year of the Kangxi period of the Qing Dynasty (1707).

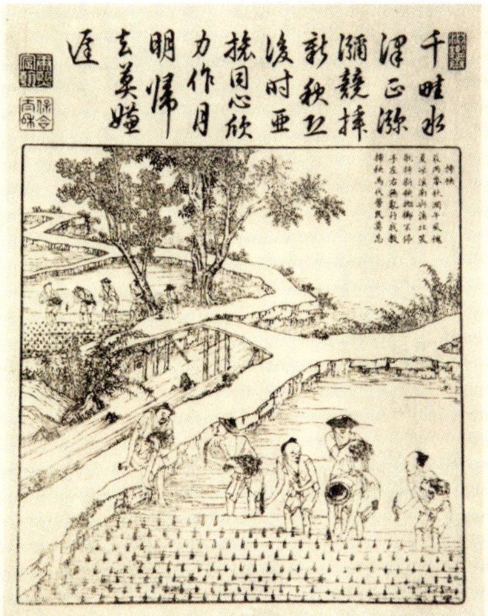

《耕織圖》清康熙三十五年（1696 年）清內府銅版刻印，名刻工朱圭刻版
Pictures of Tilling and Weaving, engraved and printed with bronze plates by the Imperial Household Department in the thirty-fifth year of the Kangxi period of the Qing Dynasty (1696). The famous engraver Zhu Gui did the engraving.

Government Printing

During the reign of emperors Shunzhi, Kangxi, Yongzheng and Qianlong, the Qing government printed books in unprecedented quantities.

The Dragon Tripitaka was a collection of Buddhist scriptures printed by the Qing court. It was based on the Ming edition of the *Northern Tripitaka*, but was engraved with revisions. The engraving of the *Tripitaka* started in the thirteenth year of the Yongzheng period (1735) and was completed in the third year of the Qianlong period (1738). It fills 718 cases in 7,168 volumes. In recent years, the Cultural Relics Publishing House reprinted the original edition and donated a copy to The Printing Museum of China.

Yangzhou Poetry Bureau

This was a bureau of engraving and printing set up in Yangzhou by the government in the Kangxi period of the Qing Dynasty. *The Complete Poems of the Tang Dynasty* printed by the Bureau was exquisite and detailed in its engraving.

清代民間印刷

清代民間印刷品比明代更精細，色彩更佳。最大特色為滿文、藏文、蒙文字書與佛經之大量印刷及深入民間之年畫彩印。各類小說、畫譜、韻書普遍採用雙色及多色套印，蔚為大觀。

Private Printing in the Qing Dynasty

Printing during the Qing was more sophisticated and refined than during the Ming and there was obvious progress in colour printing. Characteristics of the period were private printing of foreign language dictionaries in Manchurian, Tibetan and Mongolian, and especially colourful large-format New Year pictures. Novels, painting albums and rhyming dictionaries were liberally illustrated with bi- and multi-coloured block prints. Traditional Chinese printing reached a pinnacle during the Qing in terms of the abundance and brilliance of colour.

《水經注釋》
清乾隆五十一年（1786 年）
杭州趙氏小山堂刻印
Glosses on Shuijingzhu, engraved and printed by the Xiaoshan Hall of the Zhao family in Hangzhou in the fifty-first year of the Qianlong period of the Qing Dynasty (1786).

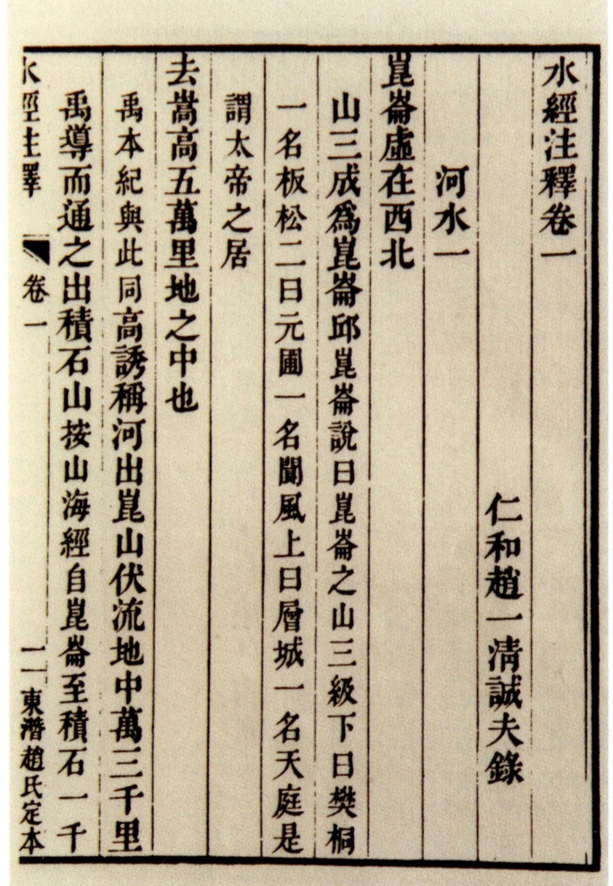

水經注釋卷一
仁和趙一清誠夫錄
河水一
崑崙虛在西北
山三成爲崑崙邱崑崙說曰崑崙之山三級下曰樊桐
一名板松二曰元圃一名閬風上曰層城一名天庭是
謂太帝之居
去嵩高五萬里地之中也
禹本紀與此同高誘稱河出崑山伏流地中萬三千里
禹導而通之出積石山按山海經自崑崙至積石一千
水經注釋 卷一 二 東潛趙氏定本

《滿漢字書經》
乾隆三年（1738 年）北京鴻遠堂刻印
The Book of History in Manchurian and Chinese, engraved and printed by the Hongyuan Hall in Beijing in the third year of the Qianlong period (1738).

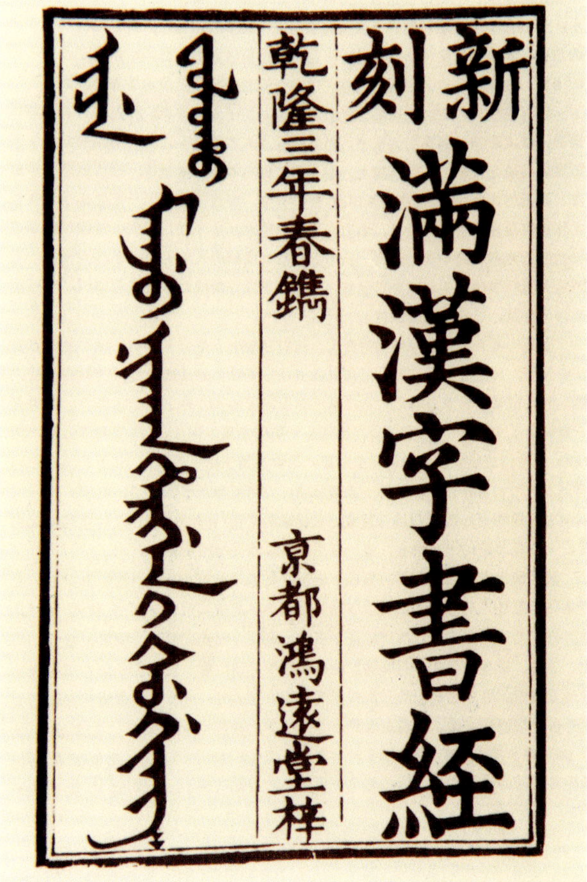

新刻滿漢字書經
乾隆三年春鐫
京都鴻遠堂梓

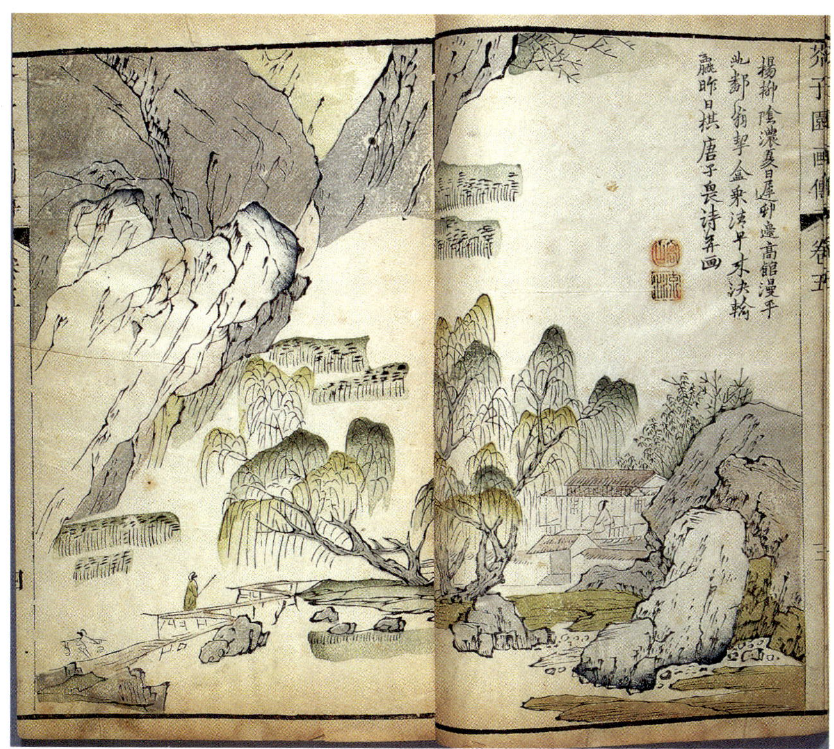

《芥子園畫傳第一集，山水》
The Mustard-seed Garden Painting Album, Volume One, Scenery.

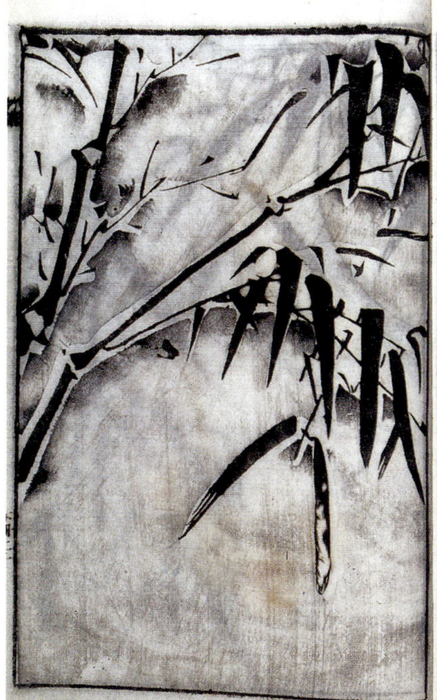

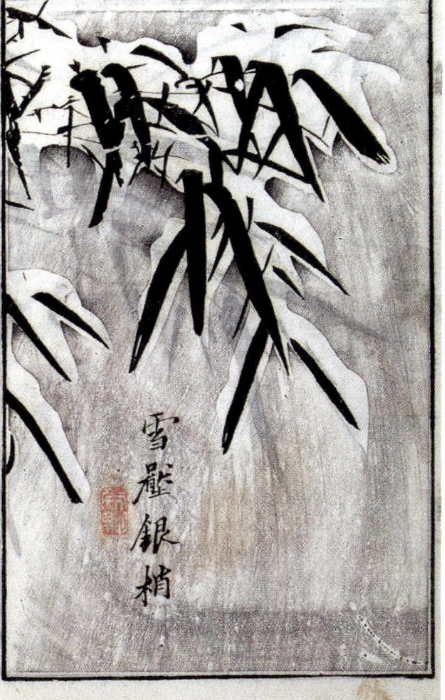

《芥子園畫傳第二集，竹》
The Mustard-seed Garden Painting Album, Volume Two, Bamboo

《芥子園畫傳》的刻印

《芥子園畫傳》繼承了明代餖版套印工藝，並有所發展。共四集，開刻於康熙十八年，完成於嘉慶二十三年。上圖為該《畫傳》初集，刻印於康熙十八年（1679年），下圖為《畫傳》二集，刻印於康熙四十年（1701年）。

The Engraving and Printing of *The Mustard-seed Garden Painting Album*

The Mustard-seed Garden Painting Album inherited and improved on the watercolour printing techniques of the Ming Dynasty. The album is in four volumes. The engraving of the work began in the eighteenth year of the Kangxi period and was completed in the twenty-third year of the Jiaqing period. The upper illustration on this page is from the first edition of the album which was engraved and printed in the eighteenth year of the Kangxi period (1679). The lower illustration on this page is from the second edition of the album which was engraved and printed in the fortieth year of the Kangxi period (1701).

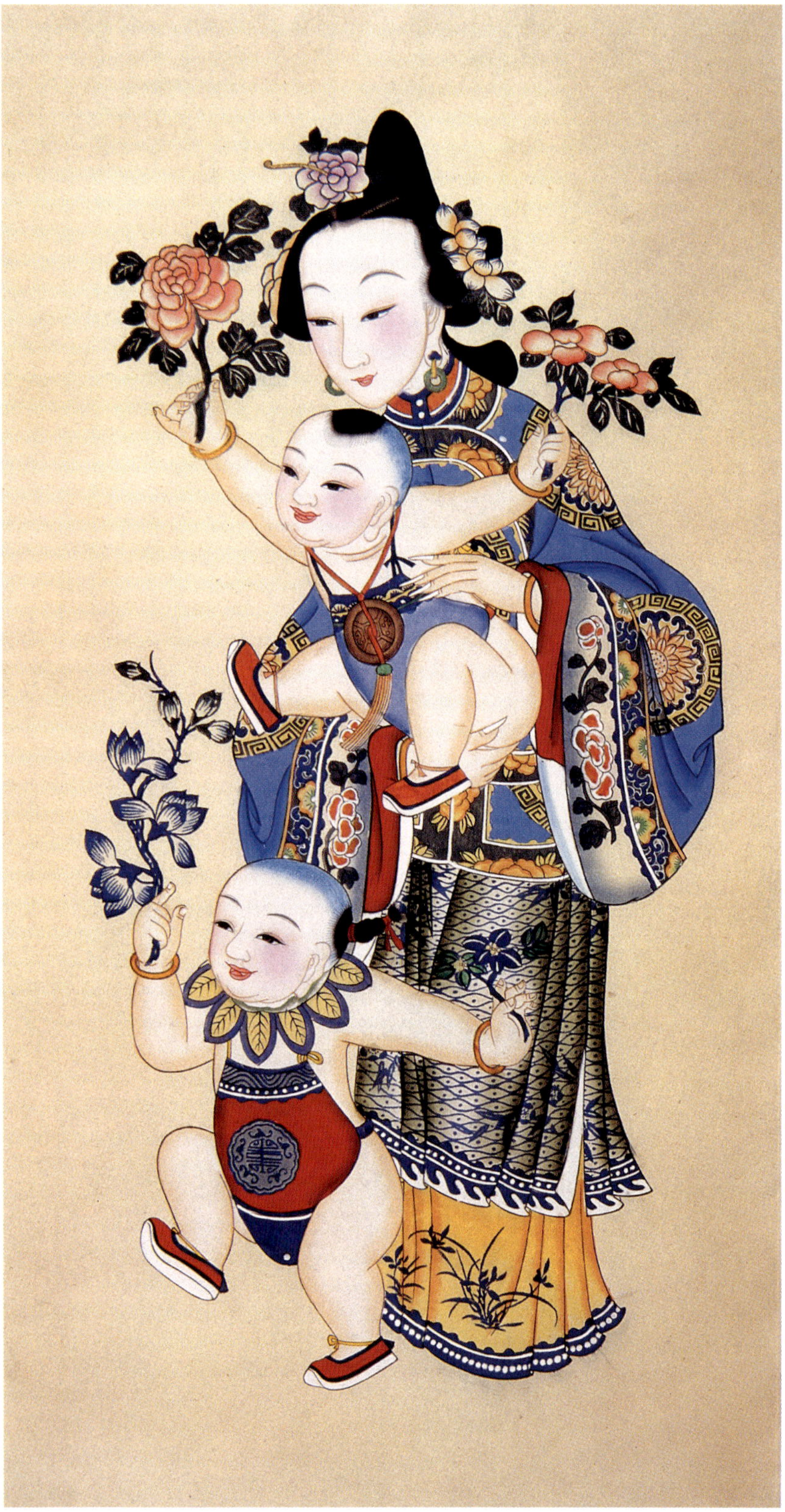

清代民間年畫印刷

用木板彩色套印年畫，起源於明代後期，清初開始，木版年畫印刷在各地發展很快，印刷作坊遍及全國各地，著名者有天津楊柳青，江蘇蘇州桃花塢，山東濰坊楊家埠，以及山西臨汾、陝西鳳翔、四川綿陽、河南朱仙鎮、廣東佛山、河北武強等地。

《仕女戲嬰圖》天津楊柳青
A Lady Playing with a Baby, printed by a workshop in Yangliuqing, Tianjin.

《福》蘇州桃花塢
Good Fortune, printed by a workshop in Taohuawu in Suzhou, Jiangsu.

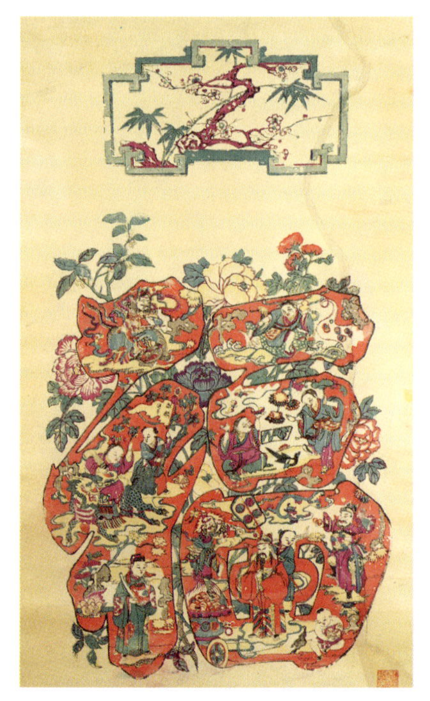

Private Printing of New Year Pictures in the Qing

The use of colour woodblocks in the printing of New Year pictures originated in the latter half of the Ming Dynasty. In the early Qing Dynasty, woodblock printing of New Year pictures grew rapidly and printshops were found in all parts of the country. Places such as Yangliuqing in Tianjin, Taohuawu in Suzhou (Jiangsu), Yangjiabu in Weifang (Shandong), Linfen in Shanxi, Fengxiang in Shaanxi, Mianyang in Sichuan, Zhuxianzhen in Henan, Foshan in Guangdong and Wuqiang in Hebei were all known for their production of New Year pictures.

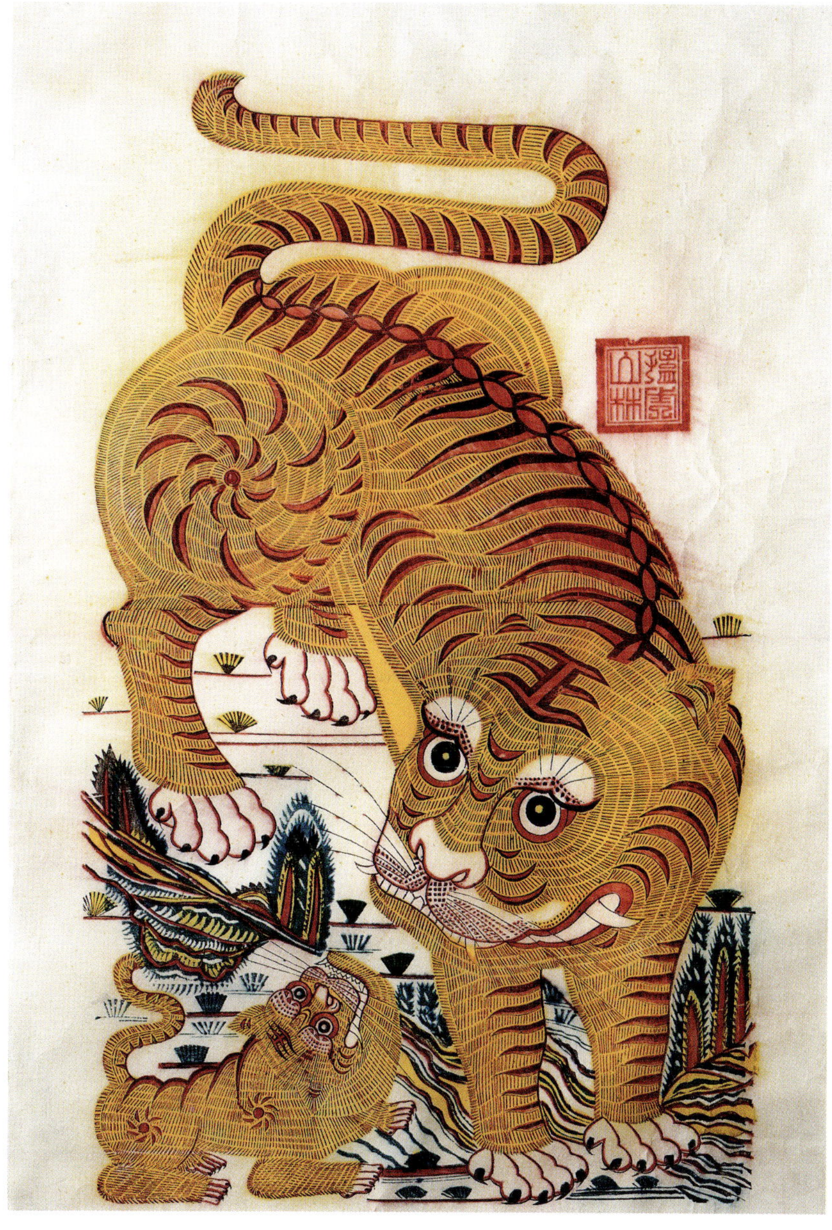

《山林猛虎》山東濰坊楊家埠
A Fierce Tiger in a Forest, printed at Yangjiabu, Weifang, Shandong.

《壽》蘇州桃花塢
Longevity, by a workshop in Taohuawu in Suzhou, Jiangsu.

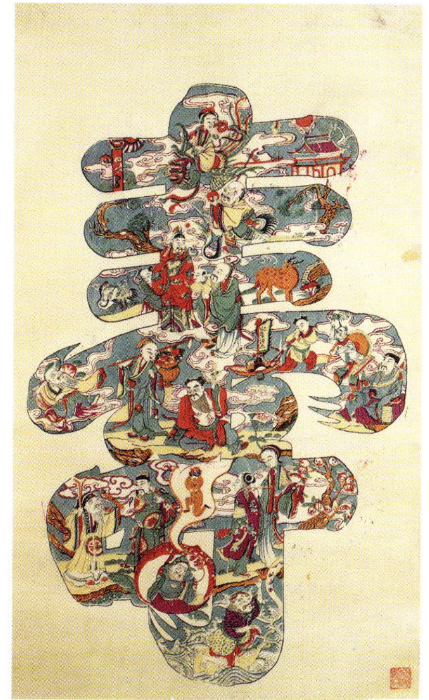

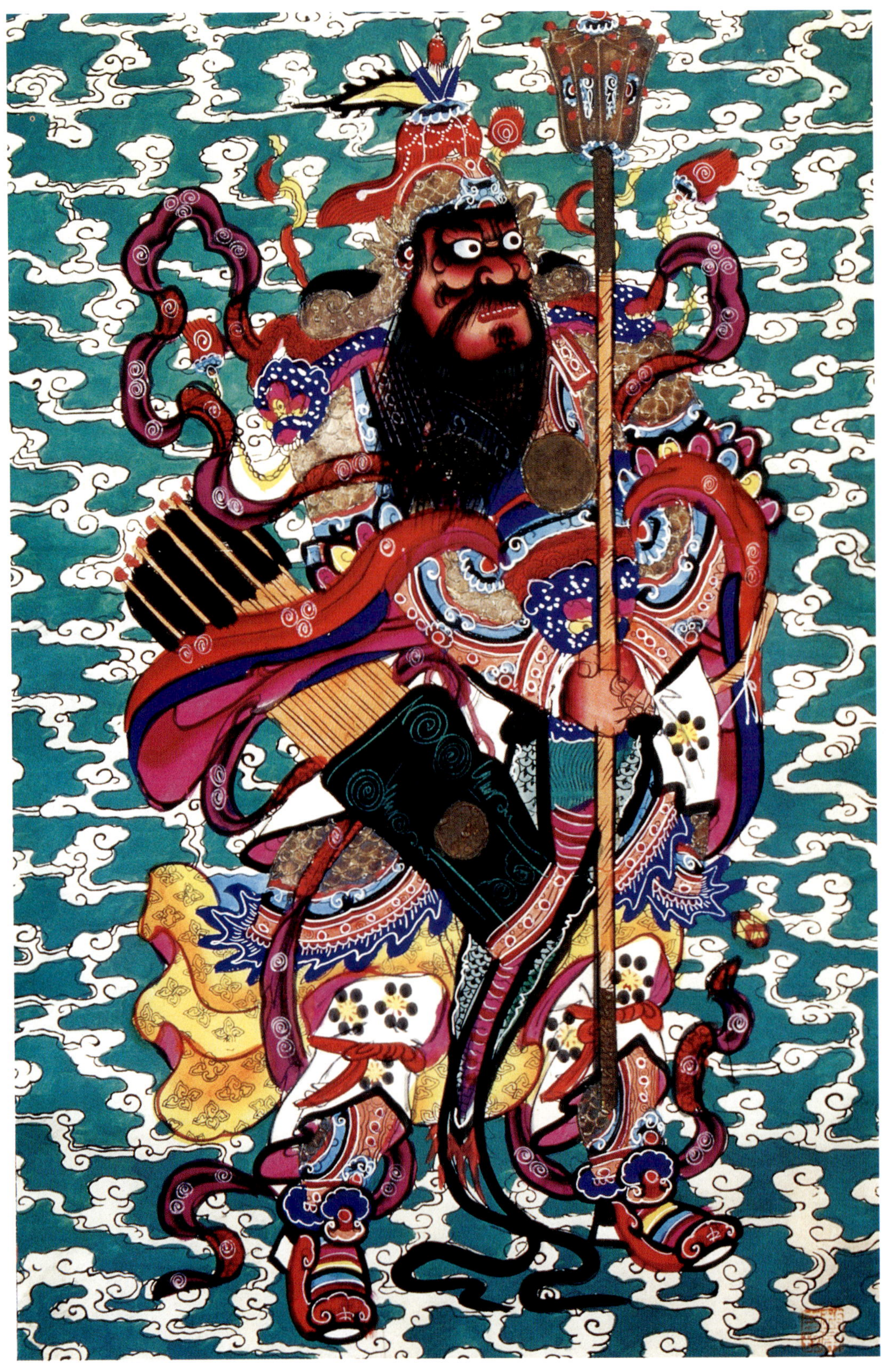

《宮庭武門神》（左）北京
Armed Palace Door Gods (Left), printed in Beijing.

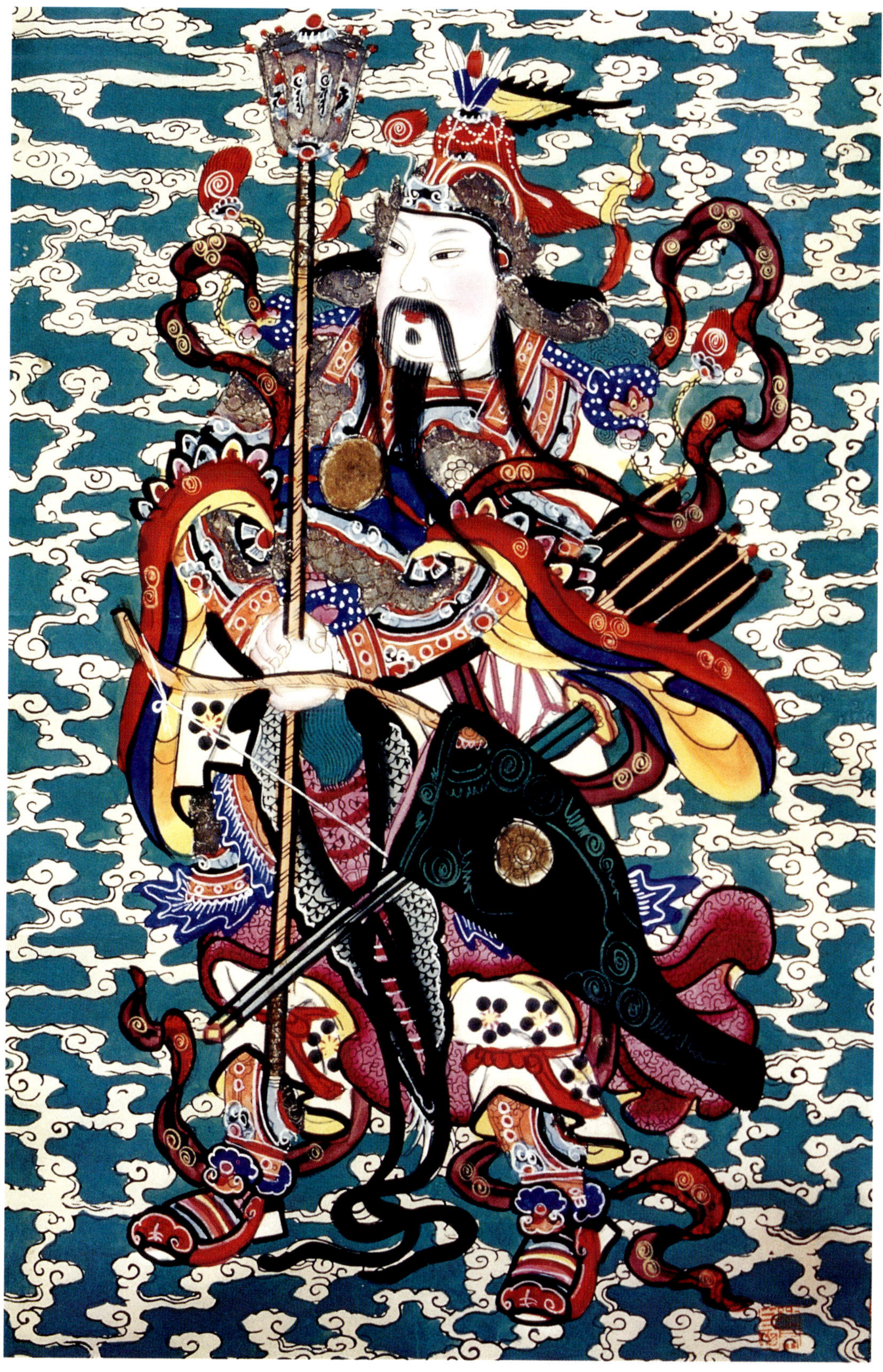

《宮庭武門神》（右）北京
Armed Palace Door Gods (Right), printed in Beijing.

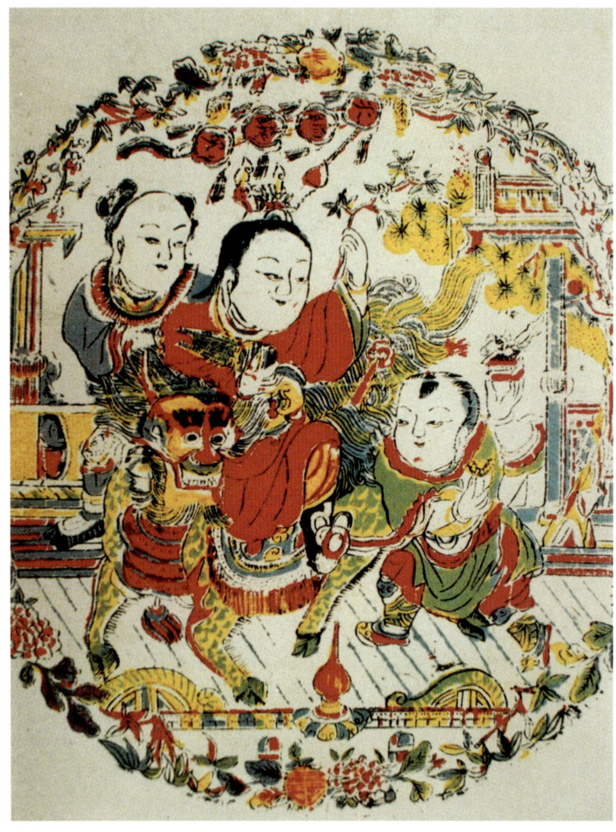

《麒麟送子》清代南京年畫
The Unicorn Escorting a Child, a New Year Picture printed in Nanjing during the Qing period.

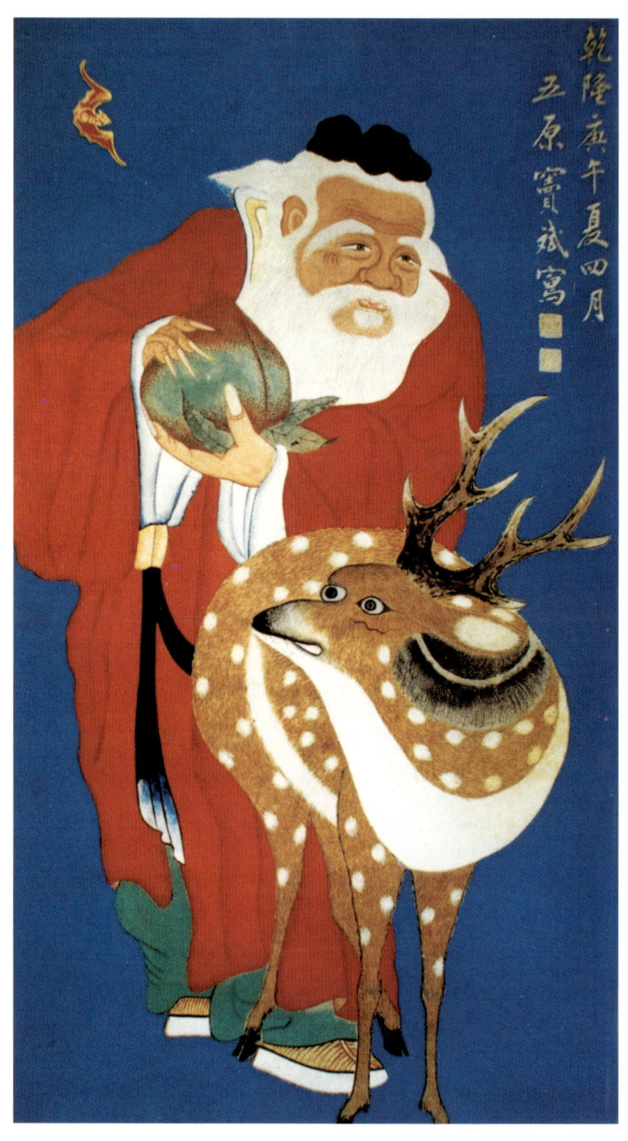

《壽星》清代廣西年畫
The God of Longevity, a New Year Picture printed in Guangxi during the Qing period.

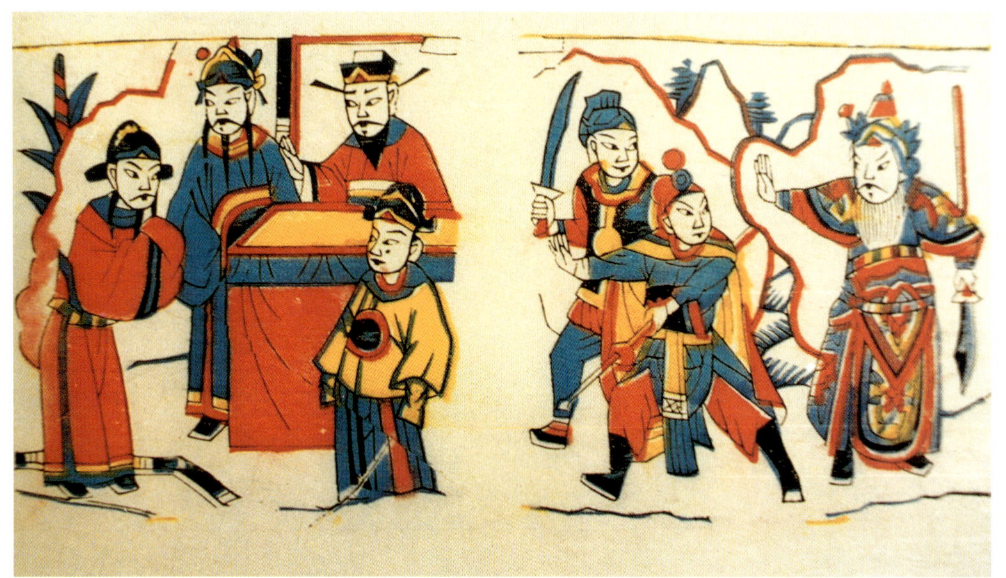

《戲曲故事》
（山西臨汾年畫）
An Opera Story, a New Year picture printed at Linfen, Shanxi.

紙幣及商標印刷

The Printing of Paper Money and Trademarks

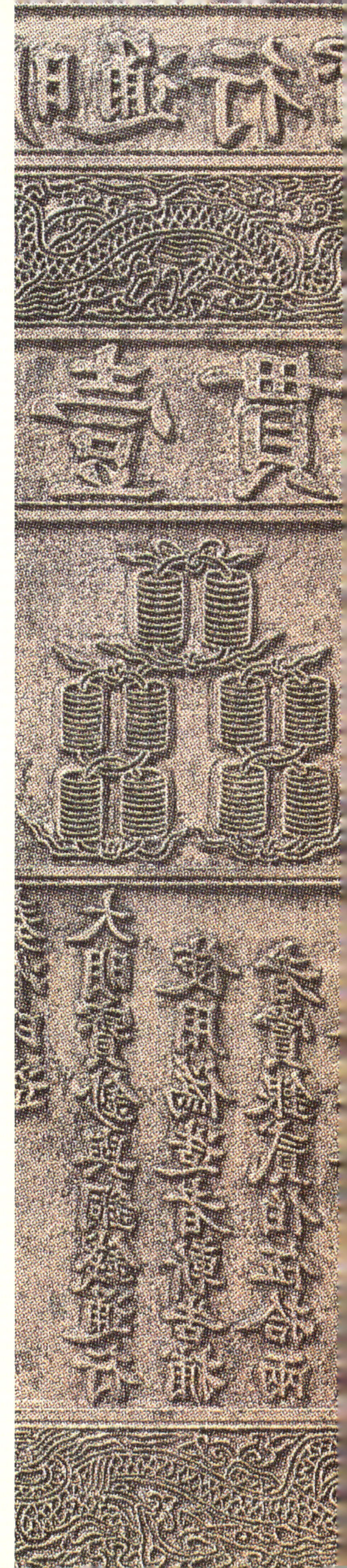

紙幣及商標印刷

中國在世界上最早印製紙幣。唐代後期，四川就出現一種代金證券，稱“飛錢”。宋初，四川民間興起印製發行紙幣，後由地方政府管理，稱“交子”。南宋時，紙幣的印製發行由中央管理，名稱有“錢引”、“關子”、“會子”、“便錢”等。紙幣除木版外，還有銅版，這是金屬印版的開始。

The Printing of Paper Money and Trademarks

China was the first country in the world to print paper money. In the latter part of the Tang Dyansty, Sichuan had a kind of currency known as “flying money”. In the early years of Song, people in Sichuan were actively involved in the printing and issuing of paper notes, but this was later taken over by the local government, and the notes were called “exchange media”. In the Southern Song, the printing and issue of paper money was managed by the central government, and the notes were known variously as “money vouchers”, “gate vouchers”, “check media”, and “convenient coins”. In addition to woodblocks, bronze plates were also used to print paper money. This was the beginning of metal-plate printing.

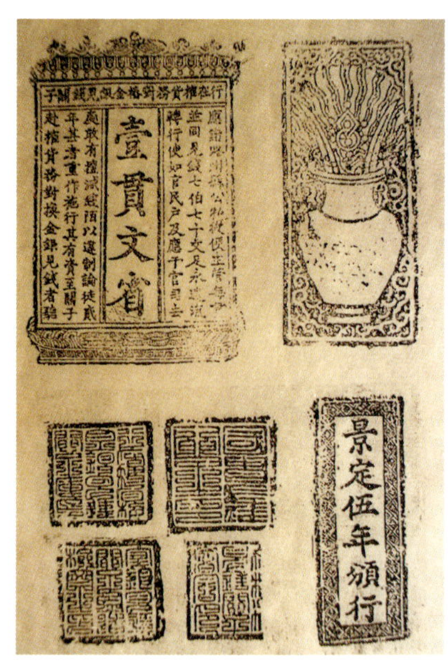

南宋紙幣“關子”印版一套，包括：印版、花飾、頒行印及四枚有關印章版。1983 年發現於安徽東至縣。
A set of plates for the printing of “gate vouchers”, a form of paper currency in the Southern Song. The set includes the printing plates, decorative designs, issue-enforcement stamp, and four seal plates. They were found in Dongzi County, Anhui in 1983.

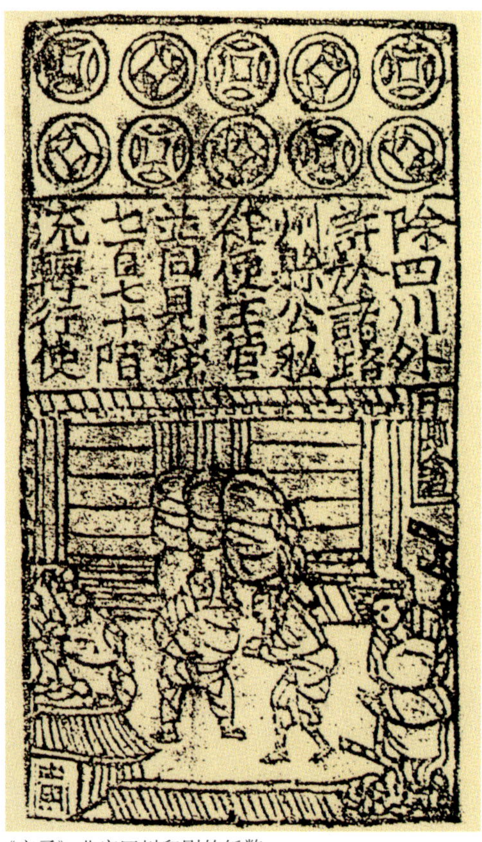

《交子》北宋四川印刷的紙幣
“Exchange media”, a form of paper currency printed in Sichuan in the Northern Song.

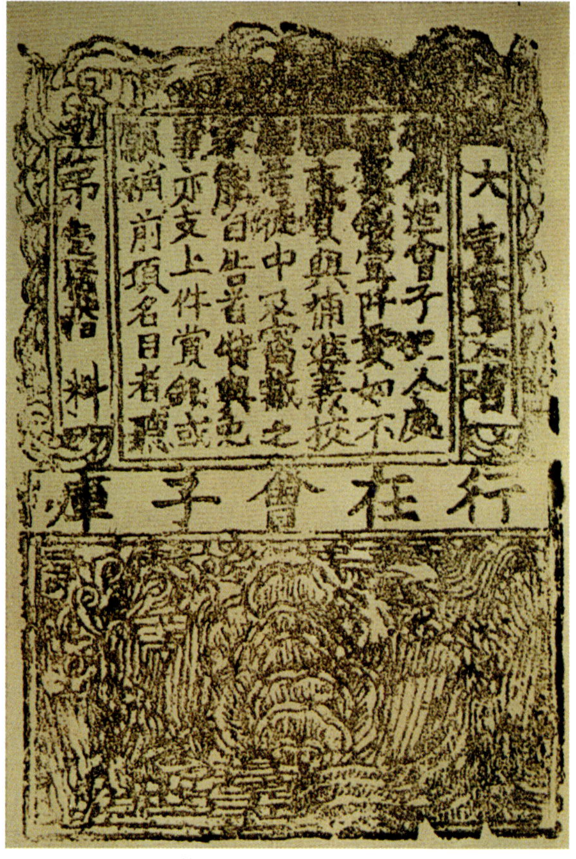

《會子》南宋印刷的紙幣
“Check media”, a form of paper currency printed in the Southern Song.

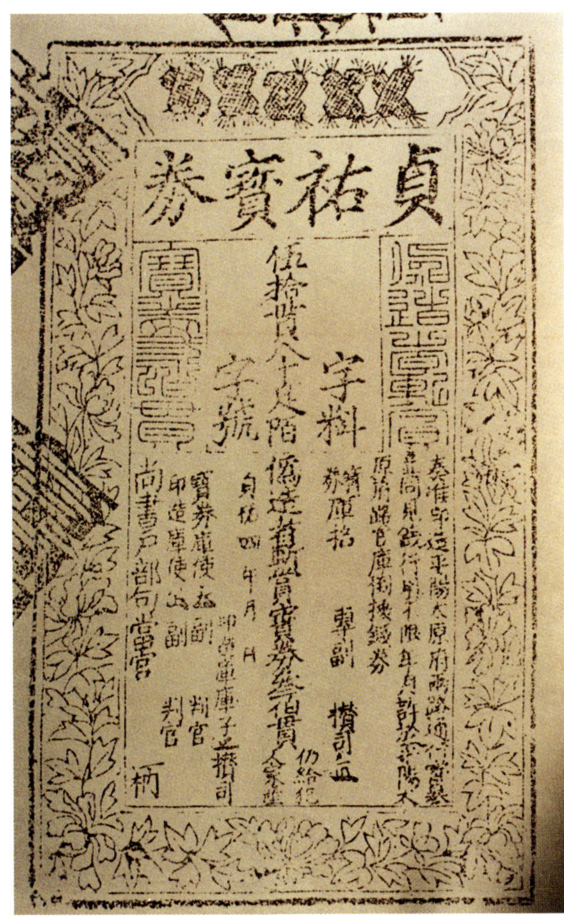

金代刻印的紙幣《貞祐寶券》
"Precious Notes of Zhenyou", a form of paper currency block-printed in the Jin.

金代紙幣印刷量也很大，共有十種面值的紙幣，京城設有專門的機構管理。

Paper notes were printed in large quantities in the Jin Dynasty. There were ten currencies of different denominations and a special organization was set up in the capital to administer matters relating to currency.

世界最早商標

下圖為世界最早的商標印刷品，宋代，文字為："收買上等鋼條，造功夫細針，不誤宅院使用，客轉與販，別有加饒，請記白。"

Earliest Trademark

The world's earliest trademark, shown below, dates to the Song Dynasty. The title on top says, "Fine needles made by the Liu Family in Ji'nan." The copy here shows a rabbit kissing a needle and customers are reminded by the vertical caption to remember the white rabbit trademark. At the bottom, there is a promise of "additional discount for resale" and a claim that high quality steel is used in making the needle.

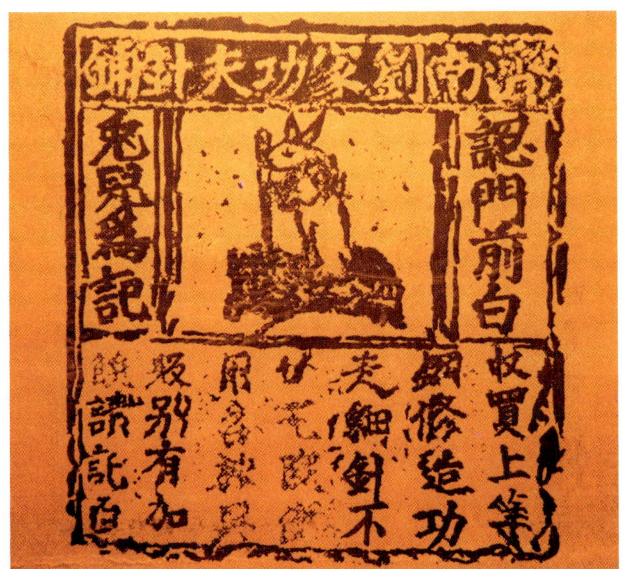

商標印版拓印件　宋代
A rubbing of a trademark printing block of the Song Dynasty.

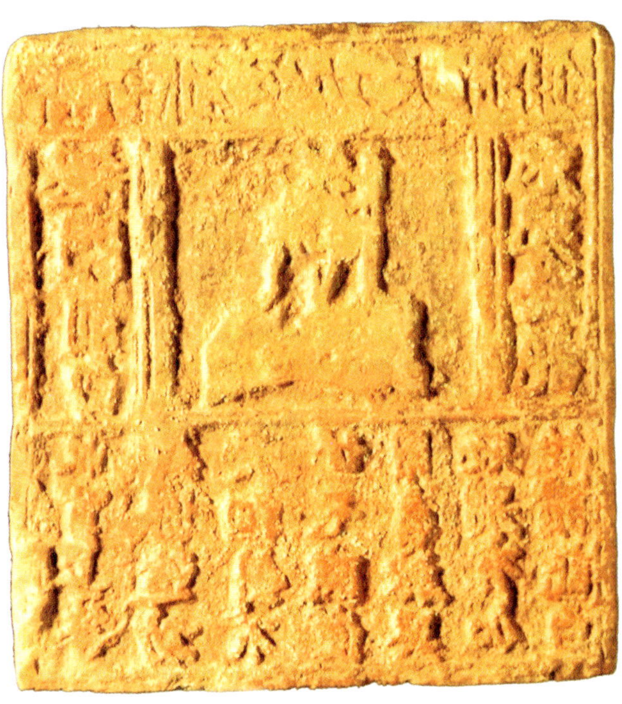

宋代濟南劉家針鋪商標銅印版
A copperplate trademark of the Liu Family needle shop in Ji'nan, Song Dynasty.

元代紙幣印刷

元代印行過中統鈔和至元鈔兩套，票有多種面值，其發行量大大超過宋代。

Printing of Paper Currency in the Yuan Dynasty

The two Yuan currencies printed were notes of the Zhongtong era and those of the Zhiyuan era, which had differect denominations. The volume of these notes issued was much greater than during the Song Dynasty.

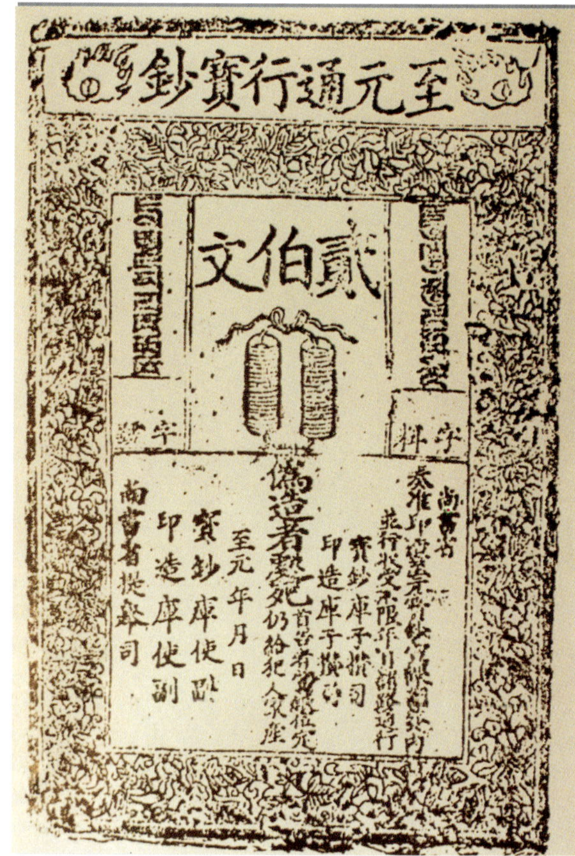

至元鈔
Notes of the Zhiyuan era.

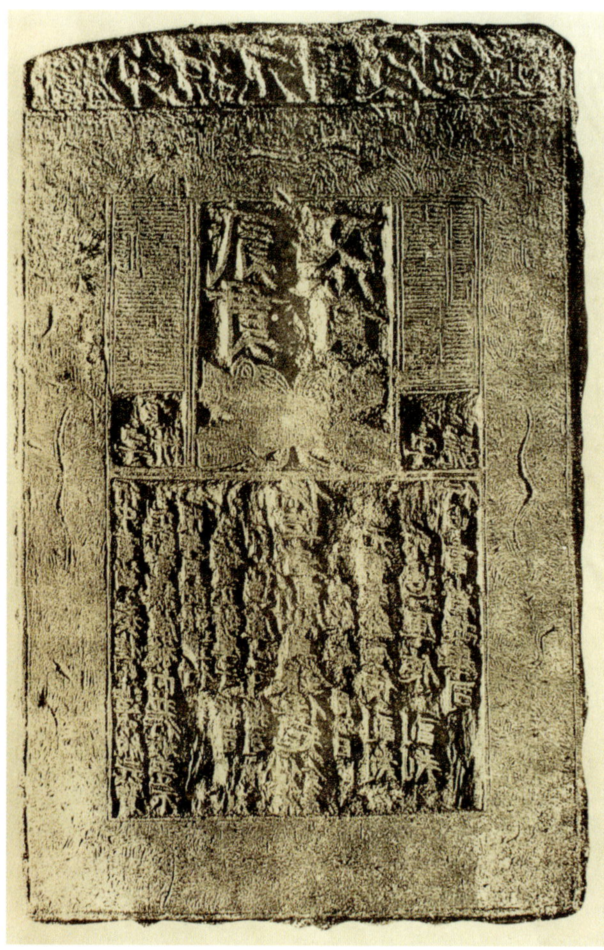

中統鈔版
Printing plate of the notes of the Zhongtong era.

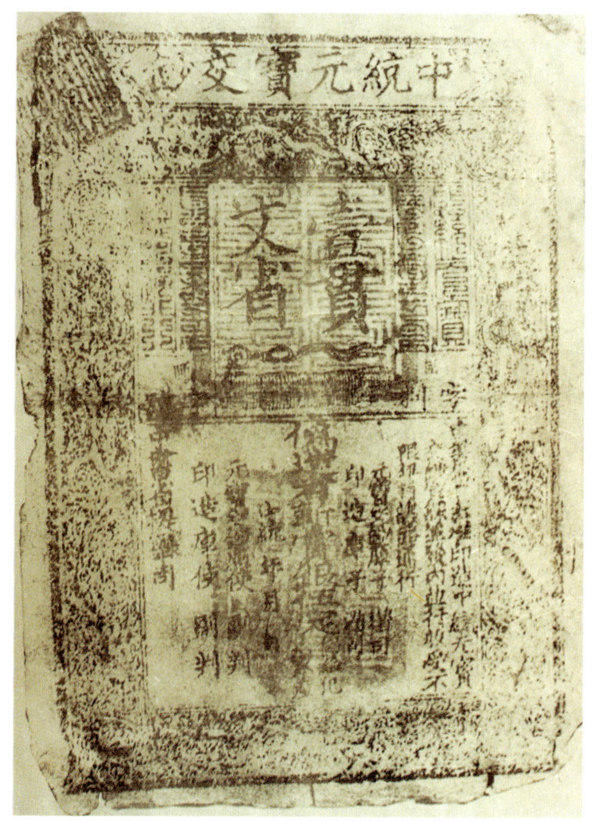

中統鈔
Notes of the Zhongtong era.

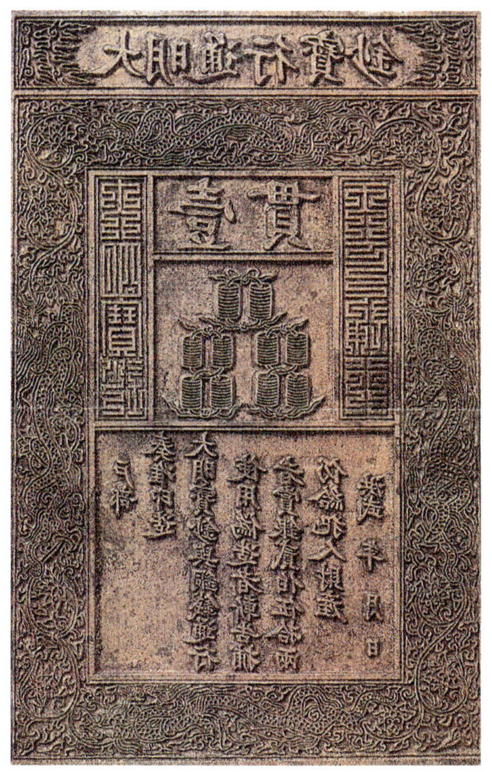

銅鈔版
Bronze plates for paper money.

明代紙幣印刷

明代初年，就開始印刷發行紙幣，洪武年間，在南京設寶鈔局。其印鈔工場內有各種工匠五百八十名。所印紙幣稱"大明通行寶鈔"。洪武十八年（1385年），所印紙幣合銀6,946,599錠。永樂年間，紙幣發行量更大，造成紙幣貶值，信譽降低。

The Printing of Paper Currency in the Ming Dynasty

In the early Ming, paper notes began to be printed. During the Hongwu period, the Bureau of Precious Notes was set up in Nanjing. Here, 580 craftsmen were employed to print the paper notes called "Precious Notes of the Great Ming". In the eighteenth year of the Hongwu period (1385), the printed paper notes issued had a face value of 6,946,599 ounces of silver. In the Yongle period, the issue of paper currency increased in volume, which devalued the currency and lowered its credibility.

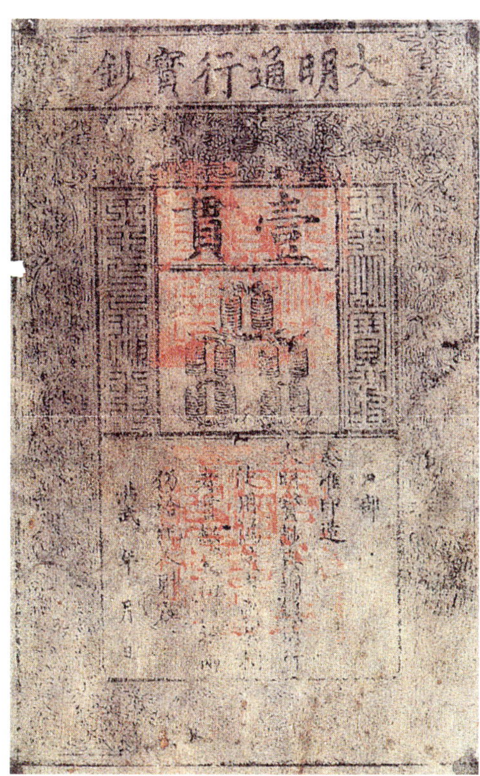

壹貫面額寶鈔，上刻有警告字句及發行機構名字
A one *guan* paper note with a warning against counterfeiting and the name of the issuing ministry.

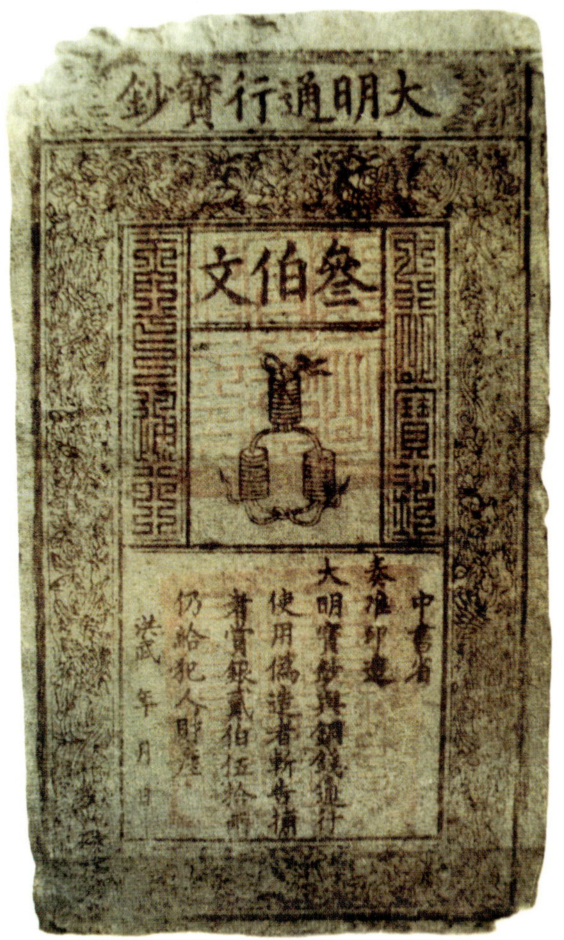

叁佰文面額寶鈔
A 300 *wen* paper note.

清代證券

清代後期，政府大量印刷各種執照和有價證券。

Negotiable Securities in the Qing Dynasty

In the latter part of the Qing Dynasty, the government printed in large volumes a great variety of certificates and negotiable securities.

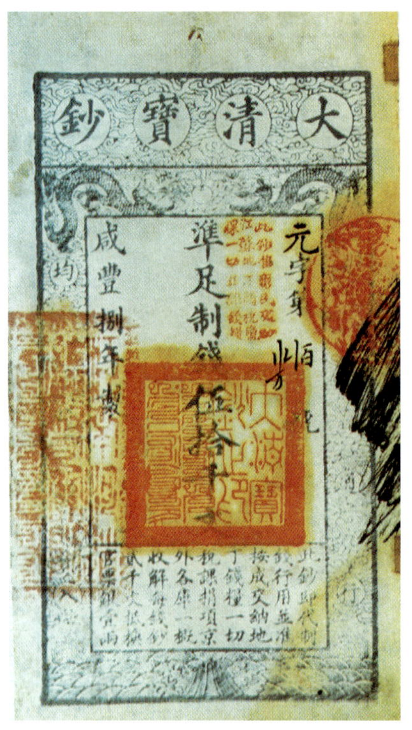

《大清寶鈔》清咸豐八年 (1858 年) 印
Paper Money of the Great Qing Dynasty, printed in the eighth year of the Xianfeng period of the Qing Dynasty (1858).

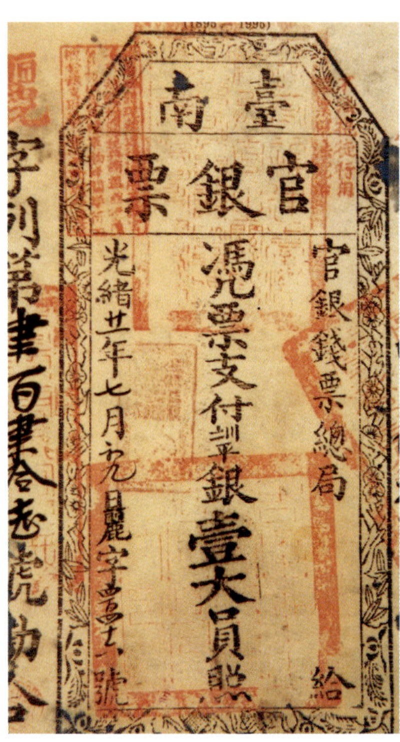

《官銀票》清光緒年印
Official Bank-notes, printed in the Guangxu period of the Qing Dynasty.

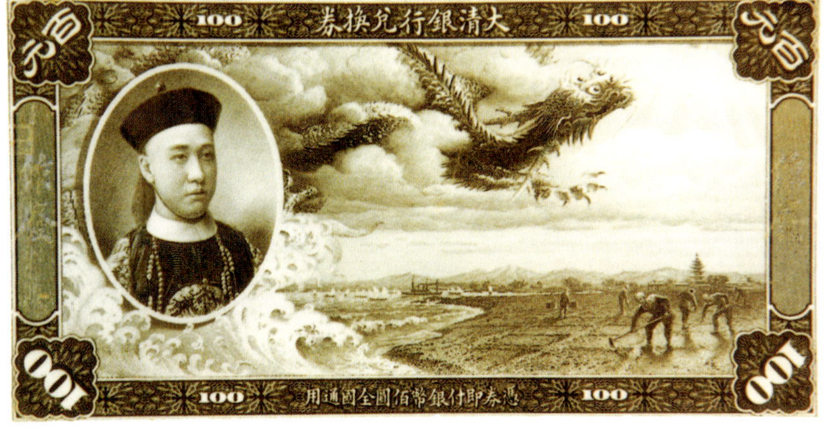

宣統紙幣（正面）
Notes of the Xuantong period. (the front)

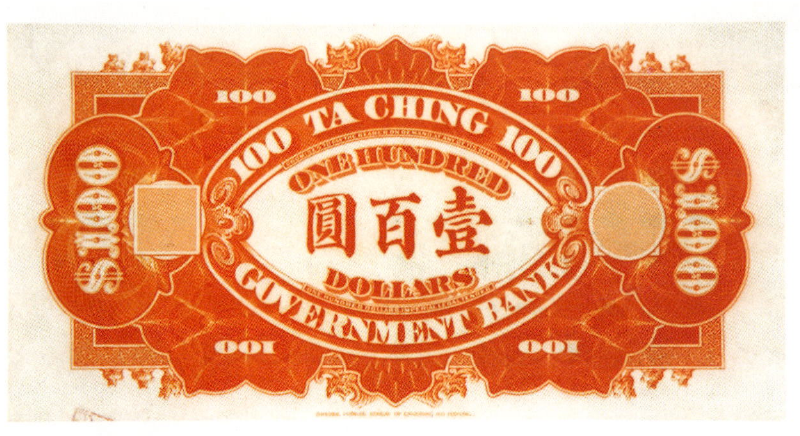

宣統紙幣（背面）
Notes of the Xuantong period. (the back)

活字版的發明和發展

The Invention and Development of Movable-type Printing

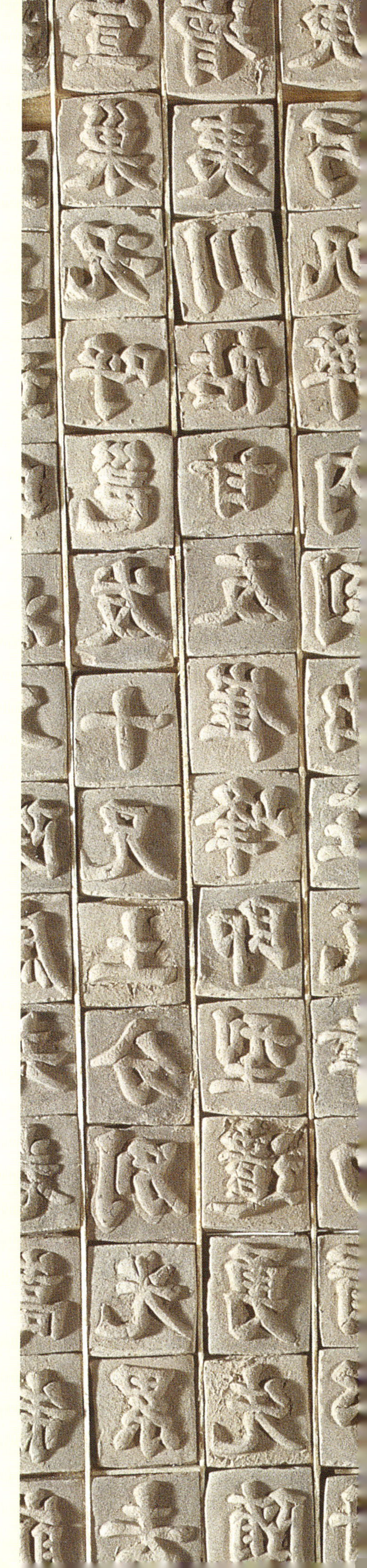

活字版的發明與發展

活字版的發明是印刷史上又一偉大創舉，它向人類提供了一種更為快速排印書籍的技術。自北宋畢昇發明泥活字版後，南宋又出現木活字，元代有錫活字，明代銅活字廣泛應用。

活字版發明者——畢昇

據北宋文人沈括的《夢溪筆談》一書記載，北宋慶歷年間（1041-1048），布衣畢昇發明活字版。

畢昇（？-1052 年），淮南人，布衣（刻版工匠），曾在南京、杭州一帶刻版，並發明活字版。

The Invention and Development of Movable-type Printing

The invention of movable-type printing was another great pioneering endeavour in the history of printing. It provided mankind with technique to speed up the typesetting of books. The invention of clay movable-type was by Bi Sheng of the Northern Song; wooden movable-type appeared in the Southern Song; tin movable-type in the Yuan, and bronze movable-type was widely used in the Ming Dynasty.

The Inventor: Bi Sheng

According to the *Dream Pool Jottings* by Shen Kuo, a man of letters in the Northern Song, a commoner by the name of Bi Sheng invented movable-type printing in the Qingli period of the Northern Song (1041–1048).

Bi Sheng (?–1052), a native of Huainan (present-day Yingshan County, Hubei), worked as an engraver in places such as Nanjing and Hangzhou and he was the inventor of movable-type printing.

泥活字仿製品
Reproduction of clay movable-type.

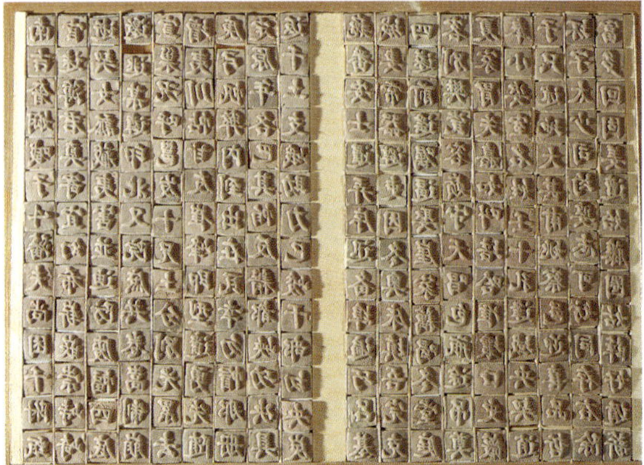

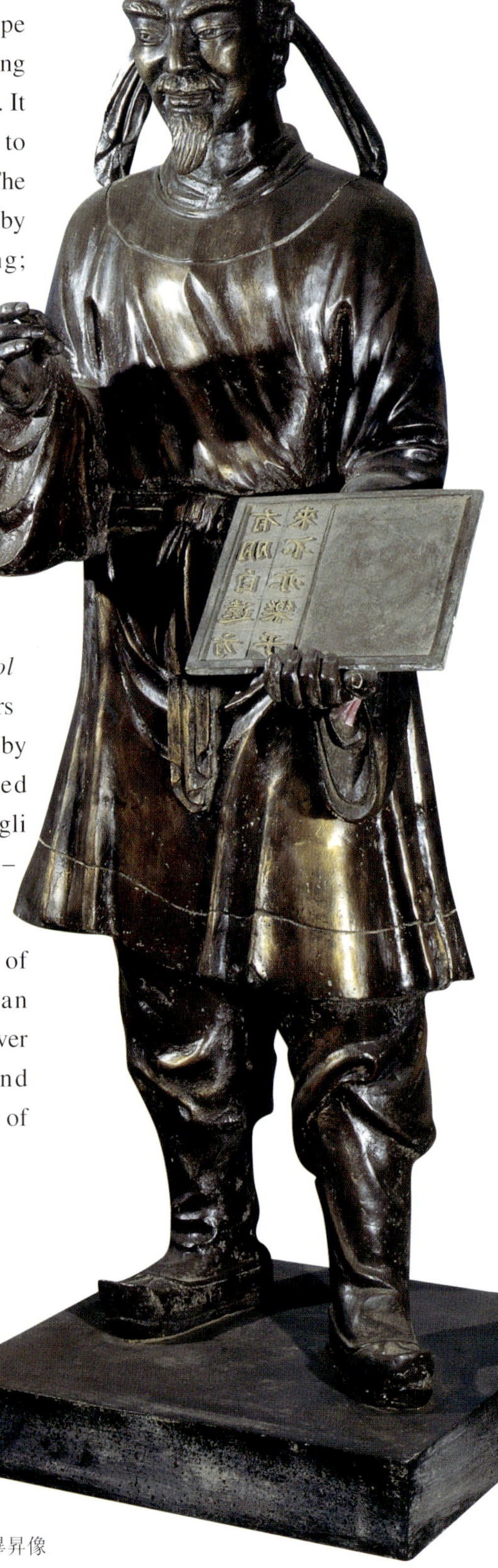

中國印刷博物館內的畢昇像
A statue of Bi Sheng in The Printing Museum of China.

畢昇的活字版印刷工藝　Bi Sheng's Printing Method

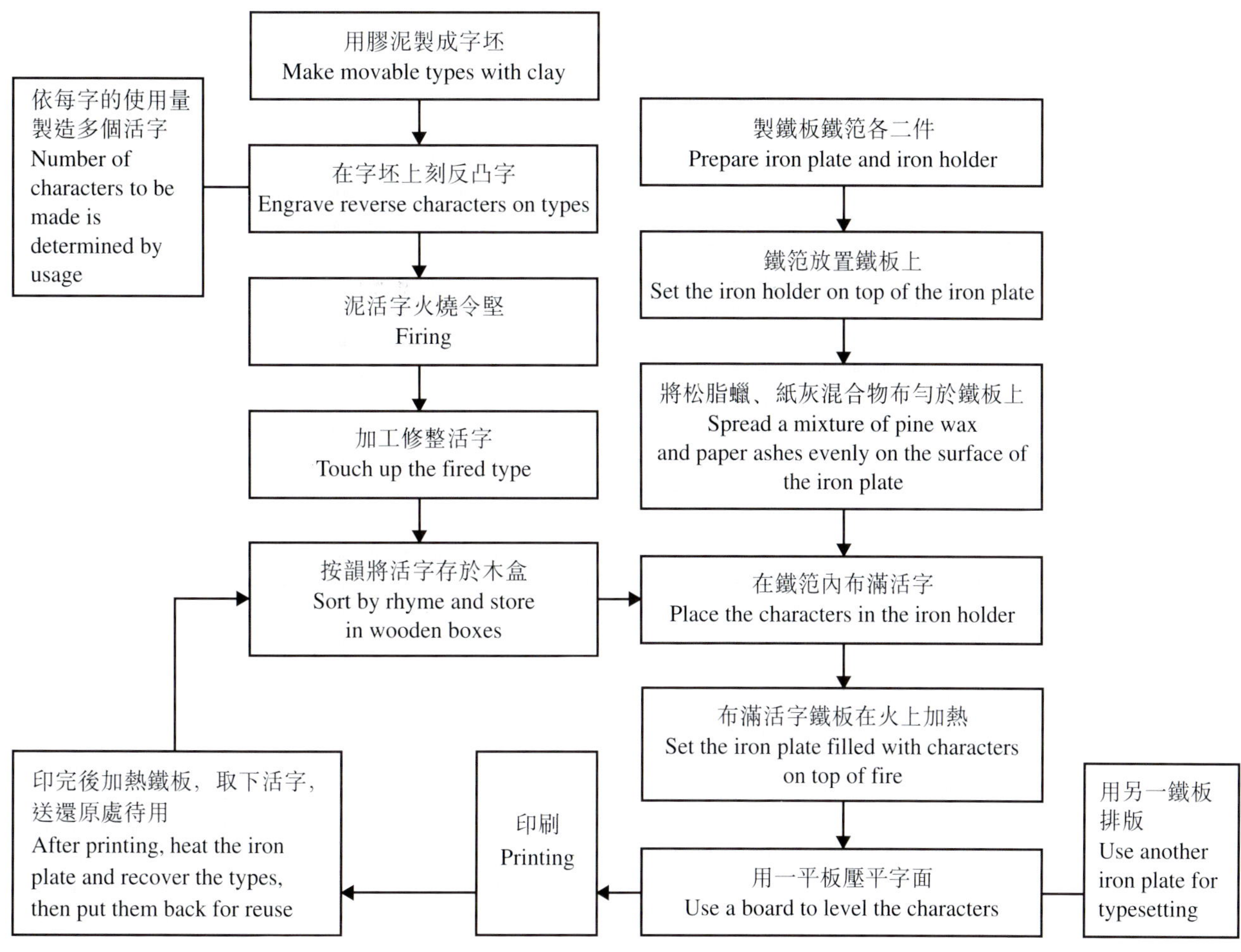

版印書籍唐人尚未盛為之自馮瀛王始印五經已後典籍皆為版本慶曆中有布衣畢昇又為活版其法用膠泥刻字薄如錢脣每字為一印火燒令堅先設一鐵版其上以松脂臘和紙灰之類冒之欲印則以一鐵範置鐵板上乃密布字印滿鐵範為一板持就火煬之藥稍鎔則以一平板按其面則字平如砥若止印三二本未為簡易若印數十百千本則極為神速常作二鐵板一板印刷一板已自布字此印者纔畢則第二板已具更互用之瞬息可就每一字皆有數印如之也等字每字有二十餘印以備一板內有重複者不用則以紙貼之每韻為一貼木格貯之有奇字素無備者旋刻之以草火燒瞬息可成不以木為之者木理有疎密沾水則高下不平兼與藥相粘不可取不若燔土用訖再火令藥鎔以手拂之其印自落殊不沾汙昇死其印為余羣從所得至今保藏

淮南人衛朴精於曆術一行之流也春秋日

《夢溪筆談》一書中關於畢昇用泥活字印書的記載

In the *Dream Pool Jottings*, there is a passage saying that Bi Sheng used movable-type to print books.

沈括（1031–1095），字存中，錢塘（今杭州）人，北宋嘉祐進士，所著《夢溪筆談》一書，記載了畢昇的活字版技術。

Shen Kuo (1031–1095), styled Cunzhong, was a native of Qiantang (present-day Hangzhou). He received the *jinshi* degree in the Jiayou period of the Northern Song. In his book *Dream Pool Jottings*, he recorded Bi Sheng's movable-type printing technique.

活字版的革新：木活字

畢昇在創製泥活字前，就試製過木活字，但由於技術問題而未能成功，南宋時木活字開始應用，而且傳到西北地區。現存最早的木活字版印刷品為 1993 年發現於寧夏賀蘭縣拜寺溝方塔內的西夏文佛經印本，約為 12 世紀下半葉之物。

Wooden Movable-type: An improvement in Movable-type

Before Bi Sheng invented clay movable-type, he had tried to make wooden movable-type. He did not succeed due to technological problems. In the Southern Song period, wooden movable-type began to be used and the technique spread to the northwest. The earliest extant items printed by wood movable-type are the Buddhist scriptues in the Western Xia language found in the Goufang Pagoda of the Bai Temple in Helan County, Ningxia in 1993. It was determined that they were printed in the latter half of the twelfth century.

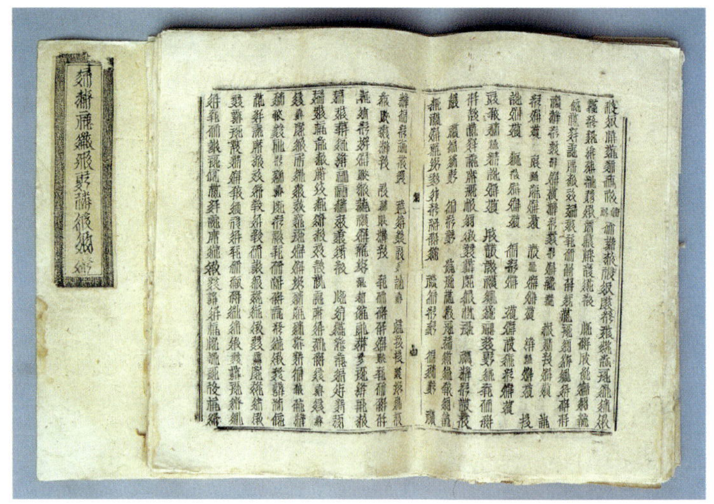

西夏文木活字印本《吉祥遍至口合本續》封面
The title-page of the *Propitiousness Has Spread to Everywhere* in the Western Xia characters by wooden movable-type.

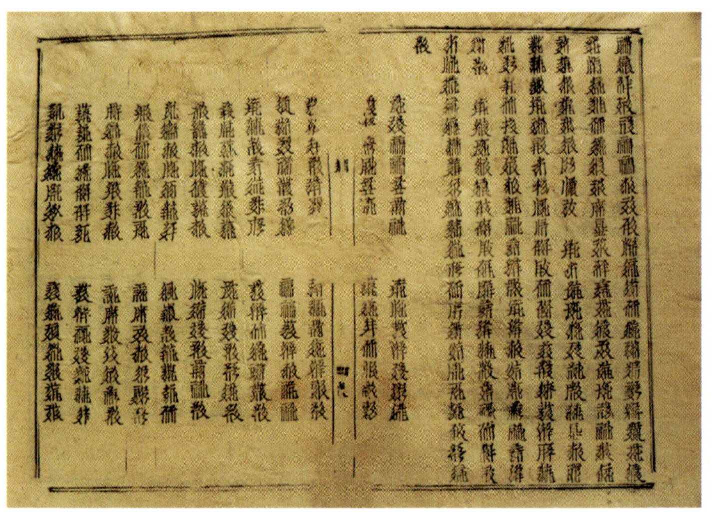

西夏文木活字版印品
Text in the Western Xia language printed with wooden movable-type.

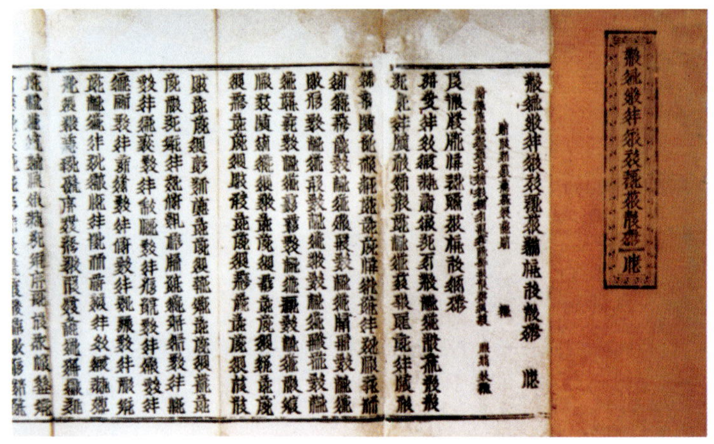

西夏文木活字印本《大方廣佛華嚴經》約 12 世紀後期
The Garland Sutra printed in the Western Xia characters by wooden movable-type in around the latter part of the twelfth century.

造活字印書法

伏羲氏畫卦造契以代結繩之政而文籍生焉注云書字于木刻其側以為契各持其一以相考合黃帝時蒼頡視鳥跡以為篆文即古文科斗書也周宣王時史籀變科斗而為大篆秦李斯損益之而為小篆程邈省篆而為隸由隸而楷由楷而草則又漢魏間諸賢變體之作此書法之大槩也或書之竹謂之竹簡或書于縑帛謂之帛書厥後文籍寖廣縑貴而簡重不便於用又為之紙故字從巾案前漢皇后紀已有赫蹏紙至後漢蔡倫以木膚麻頭敝布魚網造紙稱為蔡倫紙而文集資之以為卷軸取其易於卷舒目之曰卷然皆寫本學者艱於傳錄故人以藏書為

農桑通訣　集之八　四十六

貴五代唐明宗長興二年宰相馮道李愚請令判國子監田敏校正九經刻板印賣朝廷從之錄梓之法其本此因是天下書籍遂廣然而板木工匠所費甚多至有一書字板功力不及數載難成雖有可傳之書人皆憚其工費不能印造傳播後世有人別生巧技以鐵為印盔界行內用稀瀝青澆滿冷定取平火上再行煨化以燒熟瓦字排於行內作活字印板為其不便又有以泥為盔界行內用薄泥將燒熟瓦字排之再入窯內燒為一段亦可為活字板印之近世又有注錫作字以鐵條貫之作行嵌於盔內界行印書但上項字樣難於使墨率多印壞所以不能久行今又有巧便之法造板木作

王禎《農書》中有載《造活字印書法》，是記載古代印刷技術珍貴文獻
In his book *A Treatise on Agriculture* there is an essay on "Making Movable Characters to Print Books," an invaluable document on ancient printing techniques.

木活字版的改革者：王禎

元大德元年（1297年），王禎於旌德縣親自設計製木活字三萬多個，排印了《旌德縣志》。他還設計了轉輪排字盤。所著《農書》中，有《造活字印書法》一篇，記載了他的木活字工藝。

王禎，字伯善，山東東平人，元時曾任旌德縣、永豐縣縣尹。所著有《農書》二十二卷。

Wang Zhen: An Innovator of Wooden Movable-type Printing

In the first year of Dade in the Yuan Dynasty (1297), Wang Zhen designed and made 30,000-odd wooden movable types in Shengde County and used them to print the *Shengde Gazetteer.* He also designed the revolving typesetting plate. In his work *A Treatise on Agriculture* there is an essay on "Making Movable Type to Print Books," which describes the craft of wooden movable-type printing.

Wang Zhen, styled Boshan, was a native of Dongping, Shandong. He served as a magistrate in Shengde and Yongfeng. His book *A Treatise on Agriculture* consists of 22 volumes.

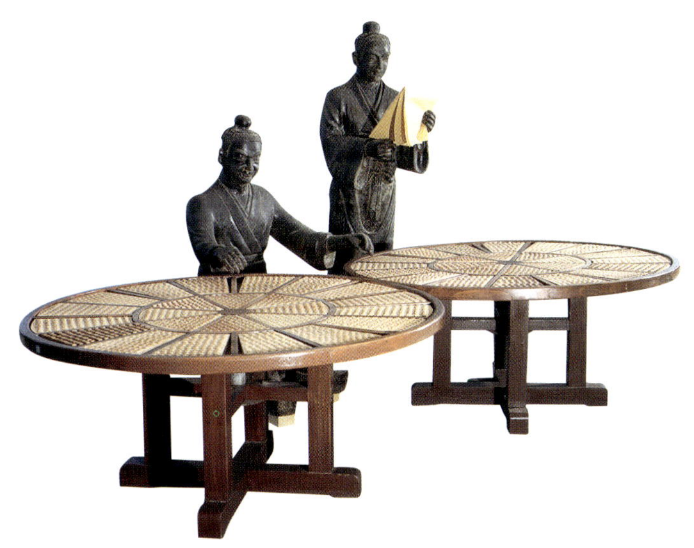

中國印刷博物館展出的轉輪排字盤模型
A replica of the revolving typesetting plate in The Printing Museum of China.

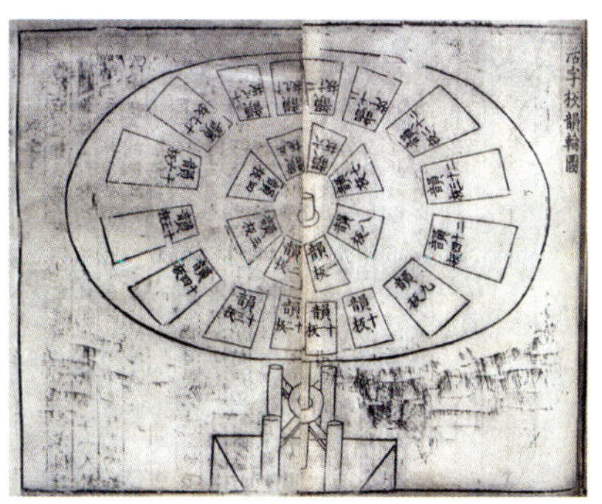

《農書》中的活字板韻輪圖
A diagram of the rhyme scheme used in the movable type from the book *A Treatise on Agriculture.*

最早的金屬活字版

南宋末，曾以錫為活字。元至正元年（1341年）銅活字印本《御試策》，為現存最早的金屬活字印本。

明代銅活字版印刷

明代銅活字版印刷十分廣泛，無錫、常州、蘇州、南京、杭州、建寧、廣州等地，都用過銅活字印刷。尤以無錫華氏、安氏最著名。

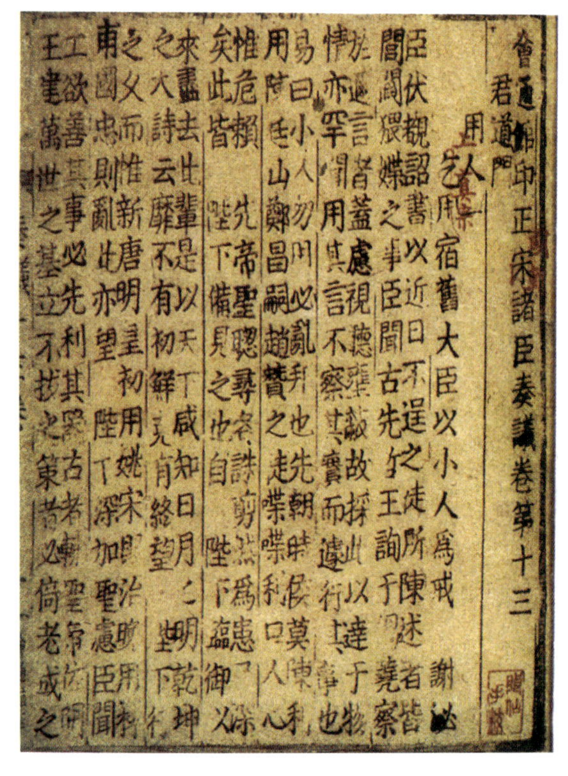

《御試策》元至正元年（1341年）銅活字本
The Imperial Examination Scripts printed by bronze movable-type in the first year of the Zhizheng period of the Yuan Dynasty (1341).

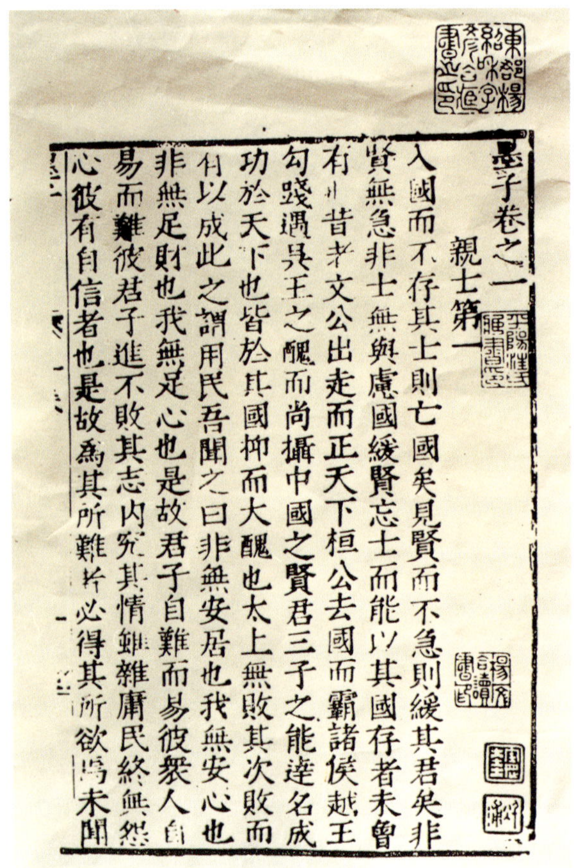

《墨子》明福建芝城銅活字藍印本嘉靖三十一年（1552年）
A copy of *Mozi* printed with bronze movable type in Zhicheng, Fujian in the thirty-first year of the Jiajing period of the Ming Dynasty (1552).

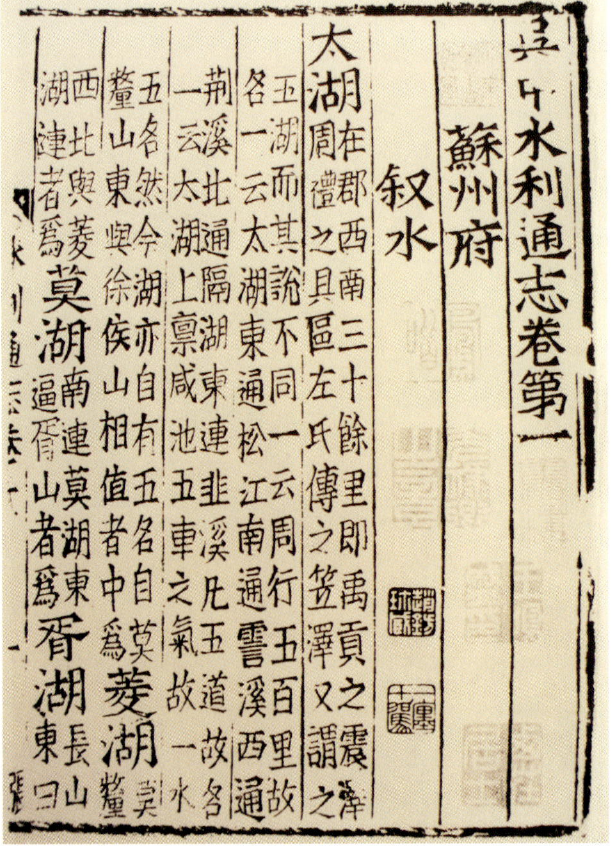

《吳中水利通志》明嘉靖三年（1524年）無錫安國銅活字版印刷
A History of Irrigation in Wuzhong was printed with bronze movable type by An Guo of Wuxi in the third year of the Jiajing period of the Ming Dynasty (1524).

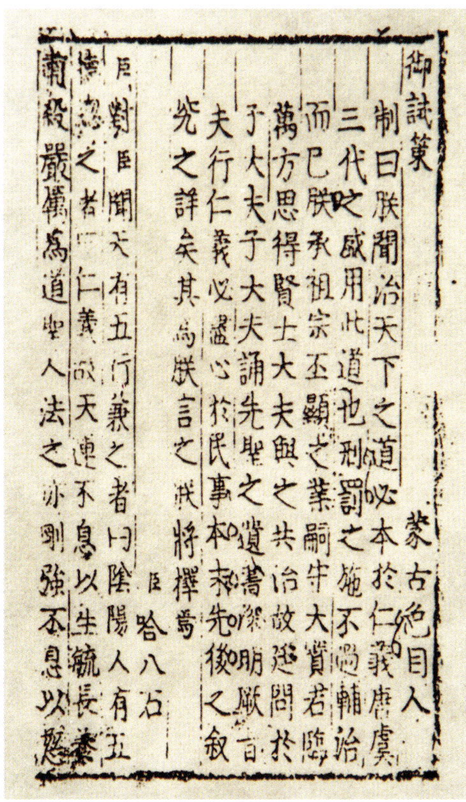

御試策　　蒙古色目人
制曰朕聞治天下之道必本於仁義唐虞
三代之盛用此道也刑罰之施不過輔治
而已朕承祖宗丕顯之業嗣守大寶君臨
萬方思得賢士大夫與之共治故延問於
子大夫子大夫誦先聖之遺書深明厥旨
夫行仁義必盡心於民事和知先後之叙
究之詳矣其為朕言之朕將擇焉
臣荅八石
臣對臣聞天有五行兼之者曰陰陽人有五
德兼之者曰仁義故天運不息以生毓長養
肅殺嚴肅為道聖人法之亦剛強不息以懲

《宋諸臣奏議》無錫華燧會通館銅活字印本　明弘治三年（1490 年）
Memorials of the Song Ministers, printed in bronze movable-type by the Huitong Hall of Hua Sui in Wuxi in the third year of the Hongzhi period of the Ming Dynasty (1490).

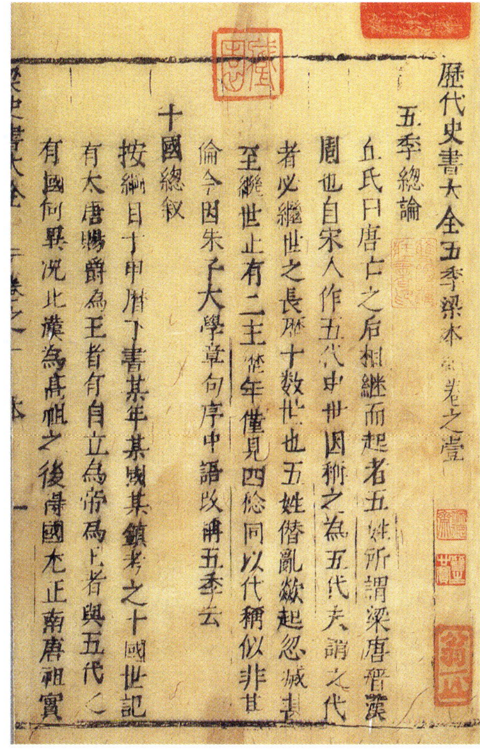

歷代史書大全五季梁本紀卷之壹
五季總論
丘氏曰唐亡之后相繼而起者五姓所謂梁唐晉漢
周也自宋人作五代史世因稱之為五代夫謂之代
者必繼世之長歷十數世也五姓僭亂欻起忽滅甚
至繼世止有二主然年僅見四總同以代稱似非其
倫今因朱子大學章句序中語改稱五季云
十國總叙
按綱目于申朋丁書某年某國某鎮考之十國世記
有太唐賜爵為王者有自立為帝為上者與五代之
有國何異況比漢為高祖之後得國尤正南唐祖實

《歷代史書大全》中國印刷博物館藏明銅活字印本
A Compendium of History Books from Past Dynasties. A copy printed with bronze movable types in the Ming Dynasty in the collection of The Printing Museum of China.

The Earliest Metal Movable-type

In the last part of the Southern Song Dynasty, tin was used to make movable type. In the first year of the Zhizheng period of the Yuan Dynasty (1341), bronze movable type was used in the printing of *The Imperial Examination Scripts*, the earliest metal movable type still extant.

Metal Movable-type Printing in the Ming Dynasty

Metal movable-type printing in the Ming Dynasty was widespread in places such as Wuxi, Changzhou, Suzhou, Nanjing, Hangzhou, Jianning and Guangzhou. The Hua and the An families in Wuxi, in particular, were most well-known.

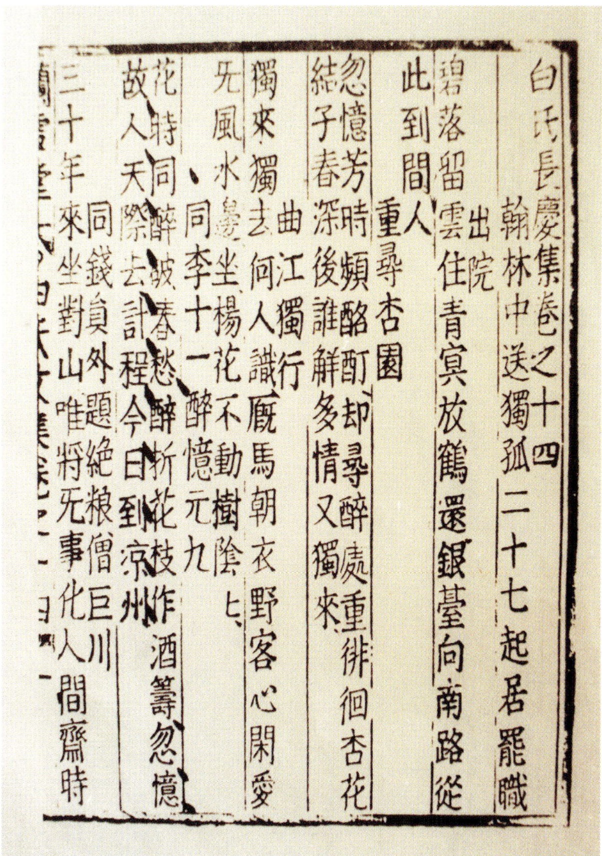

白氏長慶集卷之十四
翰林中送獨孤二十七起居罷職
出院
碧落留雲住青冥放鶴還銀臺向南路從
此到人間
重尋杏園
忽憶芳時頻酩酊却尋醉處重徘徊杏花
結子春深後誰解多情又獨來
曲江獨行
獨來獨去何人識廐馬朝衣野客心閑愛
無風水邊坐楊花不動樹陰陰
同李十一醉憶元九
花時同醉破春愁醉折花枝作酒籌忽憶
故人天際去計程今日到涼州
同錢員外題絕糧僧巨川
三十年來坐對山唯將無事化人間齋時

《白氏長慶集》明正德八年（1513 年）
無錫華堅蘭雪堂銅活字版印刷
Collected Works of Bai Juyi was printed with bronze movable type by the Lanxue Hall of Hua Jian, Wuxi, in the eighth year of the Zhengde period of the Ming Dynasty (1513).

清代活字版印刷

中國古代傳統活字版印刷，到清代達到頂峯。主要標誌是政府大規模用銅活字和木活字印刷了大量書籍。

武英殿銅活字版印刷

康熙四十二年（1703 年），武英殿開始製銅活字，大小各一副，共 25 萬個，到雍正四年（1726 年），排印成《古今圖書集成》，共 10,040 卷，5,020 冊。

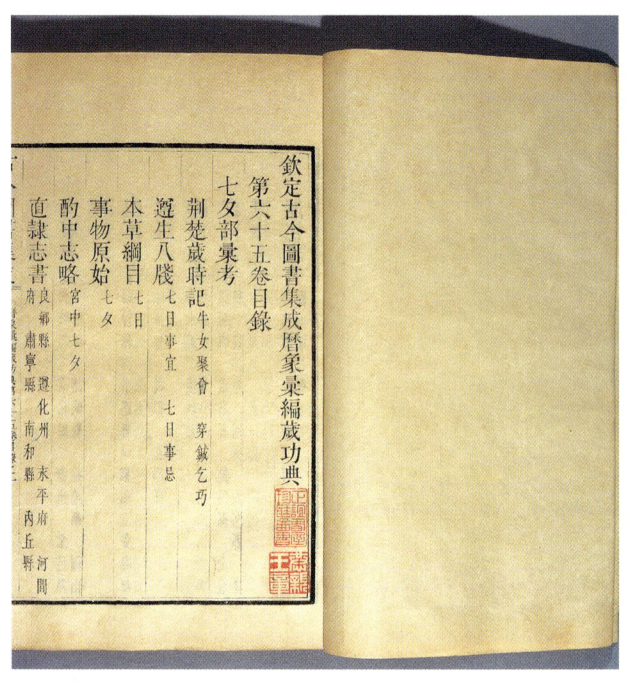
欽定古今圖書集成曆象彙編歲功典
第六十五卷目錄
七夕部彙考
荊楚歲時記 牛女聚會 穿鍼乞巧
遵生八牋 七日事宜 七日事忌
本草綱目 七日
事物原始 七夕
酌中志略 宮中七夕
直隸志書 良鄉縣 遵化州 永平府 河間府 肅寧縣 南和縣 內丘縣

武英殿銅活字版印刷品
Text printed with bronze movable type at the Hall of Military Eminence.

Movable-type Printing in the Qing Dynasty

The traditional movable-type printing in ancient China reached its peak in the Qing Dynasty. The major characteristic was the government printing of large quantities of books with the use of bronze movable type and wooden movable-type printing.

Bronze Movable-type Printing at the Hall of Military Eminence

In the forty-second year of the Kangxi period (1703), the Hall of Military Eminence began to cast sets of big and small bronze movable type totalling 250,000 characters. By the fourth year of the Yongzheng period (1726), the *Imperial Encyclopaedia* was printed. It had 10,040 chapters, in 5,020 volumes.

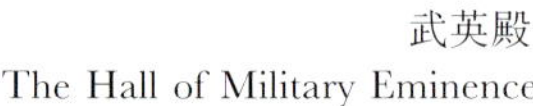
武英殿
The Hall of Military Eminence

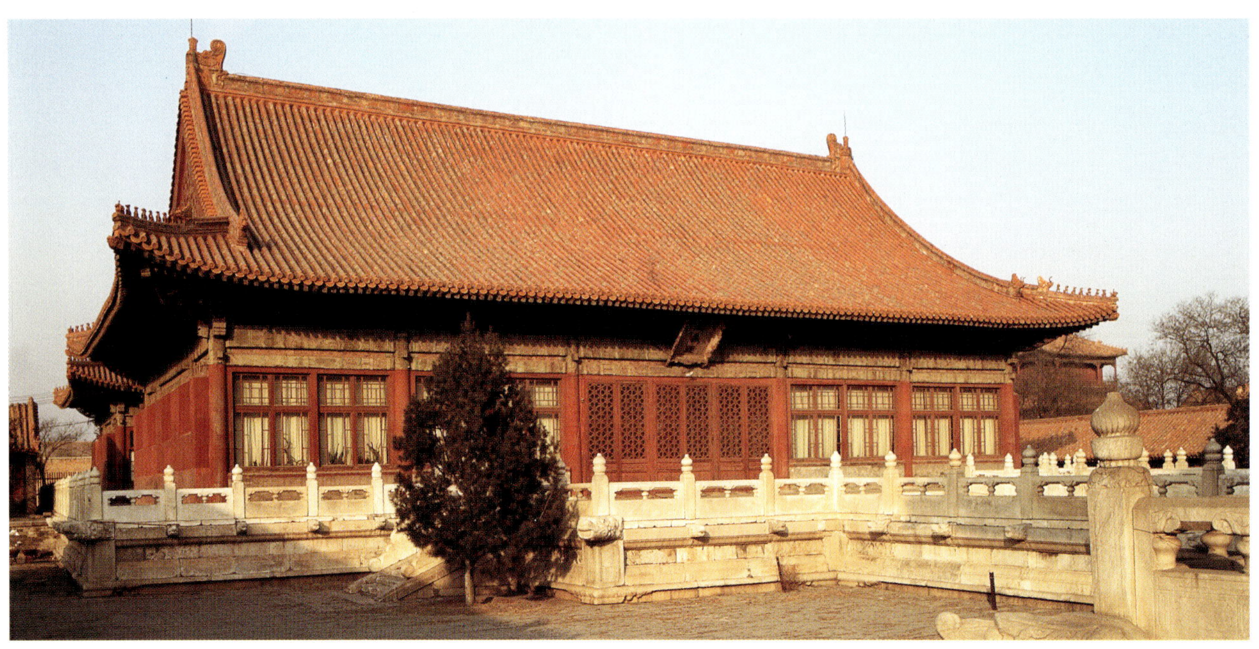

清武英殿木活字版印刷

乾隆三十八年（1736 年），在金簡主持下，武英殿刻製棗木活字大、小各一副，共 25 萬個，印刷了《武英殿聚珍版叢書》。

Wooden Movable-type Printing at the Hall of Military Eminence in the Qing Dynasty

In the thirty-eighth year of the Qianlong period (1736), under the directorship of Jin Jian, the Hall of Military Eminence made two sets of jujube-wood movable type, one large and the other small, numbering 250,000 pieces, and these were used to print *A Collection of Rare Editions at the Hall of Military Eminence.*

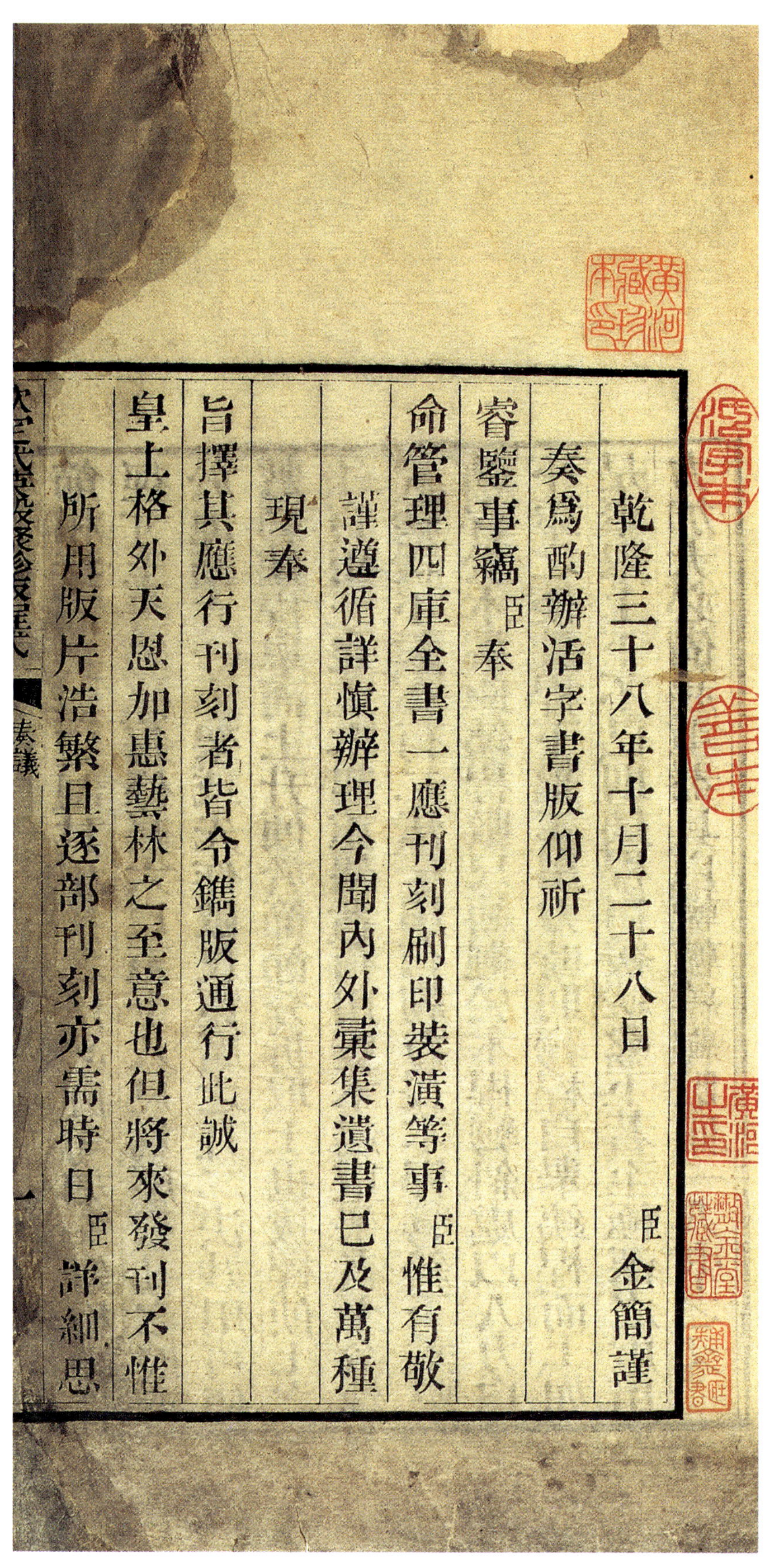

乾隆三十八年十月二十八日　臣金簡謹
奏爲酌辦活字書版仰祈
睿鑒事竊　臣奉
命管理四庫全書一應刊刻刷印裝潢等事　臣惟有敬
謹遵循詳慎辦理今聞內外彙集遺書已及萬種
現奉
旨擇其應行刊刻者皆令鐫版通行此誠
皇上格外天恩加惠藝林之至意也但將來發刊不惟
所用版片浩繁且逐部刊刻亦需時日　臣詳細思

武英殿聚珍版程式　奏議　一

《武英殿聚珍版程式》
（木活字版印本）
Printing Manual for a Collection of Rare Editions at the Hall of Military Eminence
(printed with wooden movable type).

《武英殿聚珍版程式》

這是金簡主持編寫的一本全面介紹武英殿木活字技術工藝的書。包括：活字用料、活字字體、活字刻製、活字規格、排版工藝等。下面是該書的部分插圖。

Printing Manual for the Collection of Rare Editions at the Hall of Military Eminence

Jin Jian was responsible for editing and writing this book which comprehensively introduces the techniques and craft of wooden movable type printing at the Hall of Military Eminence. The contents include topics such as the materials of movable type, typefaces, engraving, specifications and the craft of typesetting. Below are some illustrations from the book.

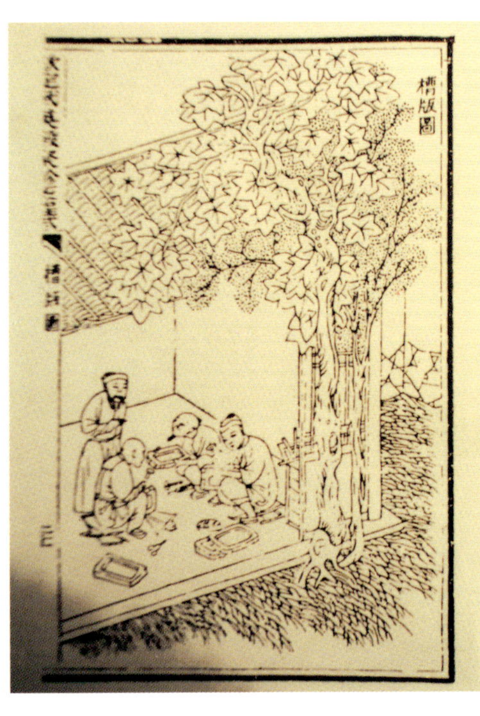

槽板圖
The grid arranged according to a rhyme scheme.

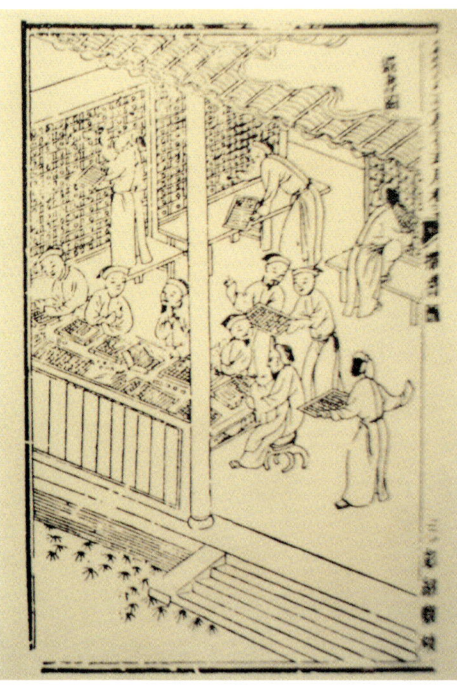

擺版圖
Arranging the type according to the rhyme scheme.

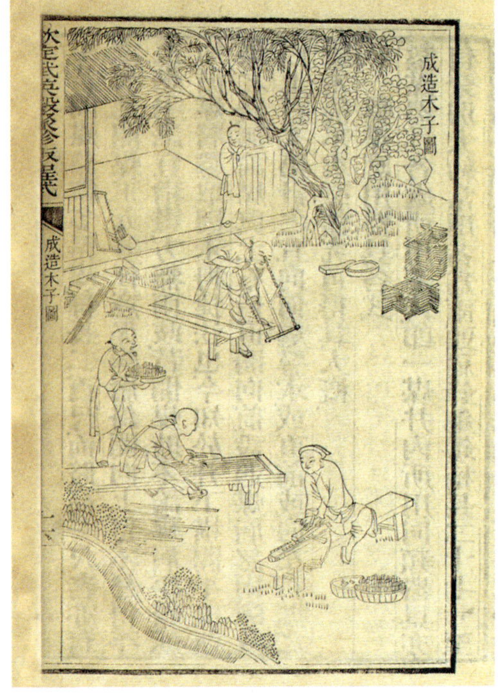

造木子圖
Making wooden type.

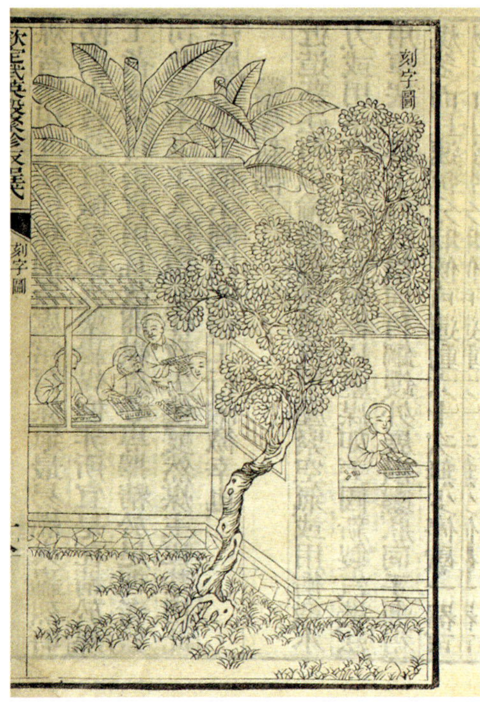

刻字圖
Engraving.

翟金生的泥活字版印刷

宋畢昇發明泥活字版後，歷代都有人用泥活字印書 。清道光年間(1821-1850)，安徽涇縣教書先生翟金生，自製泥活字印書，所印書籍質量較好 。

Clay Movable-type Printing of Zhai Jinsheng

Since the invention of clay movable-type printing by Bi Sheng in the Song Dynasty, this method was used through the dynasties. During the Daoguang period (1821–1850) of the Qing Dynasty, a teacher named Zhai Jinsheng of Jing County, Anhui, manufactured the clay movable type to print books. The books he produced were of high quality.

《泥版試印初編》翟金生泥活字排印

An Experimental First Collection of Books Printed with Clay Movable Type, typeset and printed by Zhai Jinsheng.

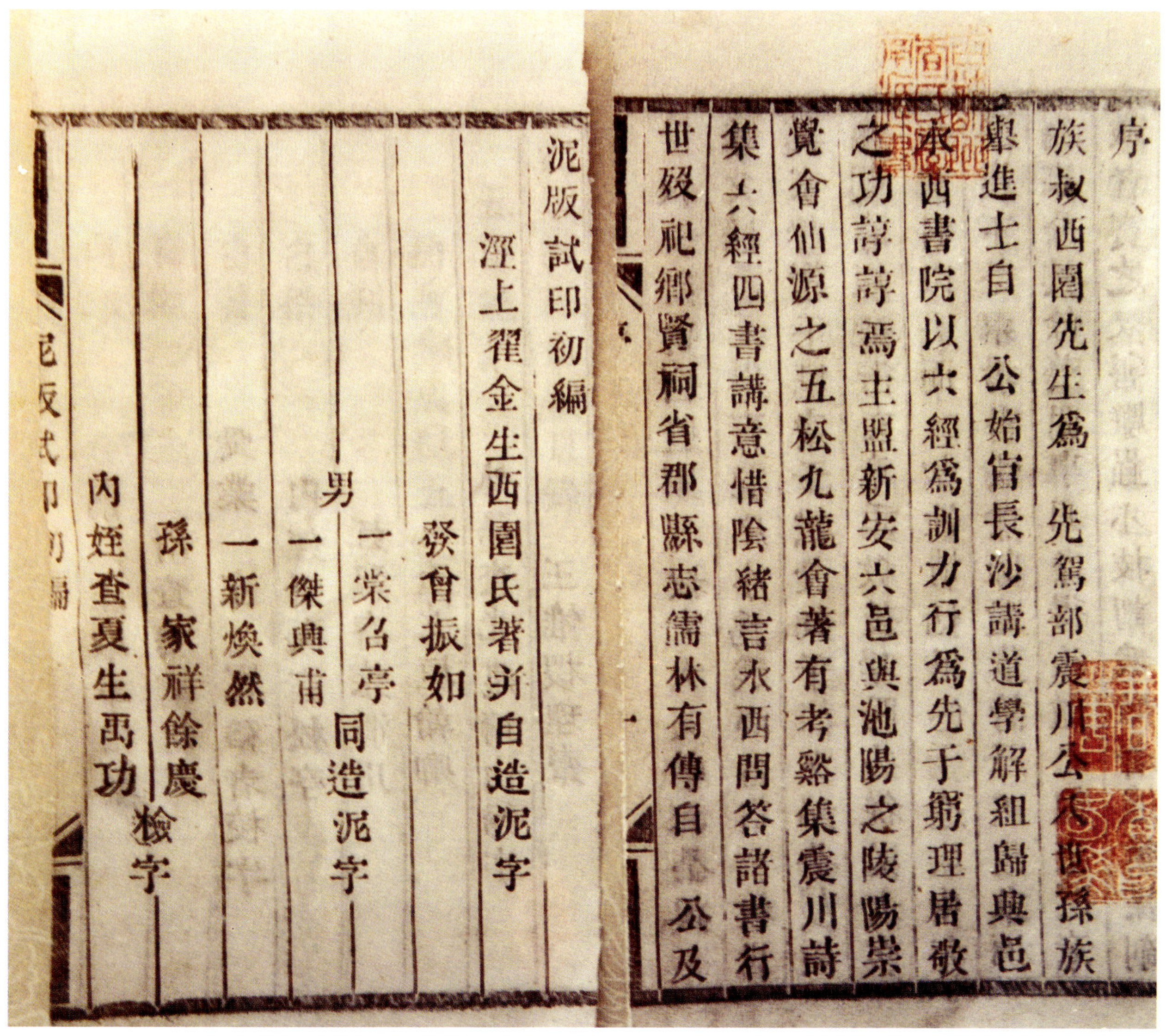

序

族叔西園先生爲　先駕部震川公　世孫族
舉進士自　公始官長沙講道學解組歸與邑
永西書院以六經爲訓力行爲先于窮理居敬
之功諄諄焉主盟新安六邑與池陽之陵陽崇
覺會仙源之五松九龍會著有考槃集震川詩
集六經四書講意惜陰緒言永西問答諸書行
世歿祀鄉賢祠省郡縣志儒林有傳自　公及

泥版試印初編

涇上翟金生西園氏著并自造泥字

男　發曾振如
　　一棠名亭　同造泥字
　　一傑輿甫
　　一新煥然
孫　家祥餘慶　檢字
內姪查夏生禹功

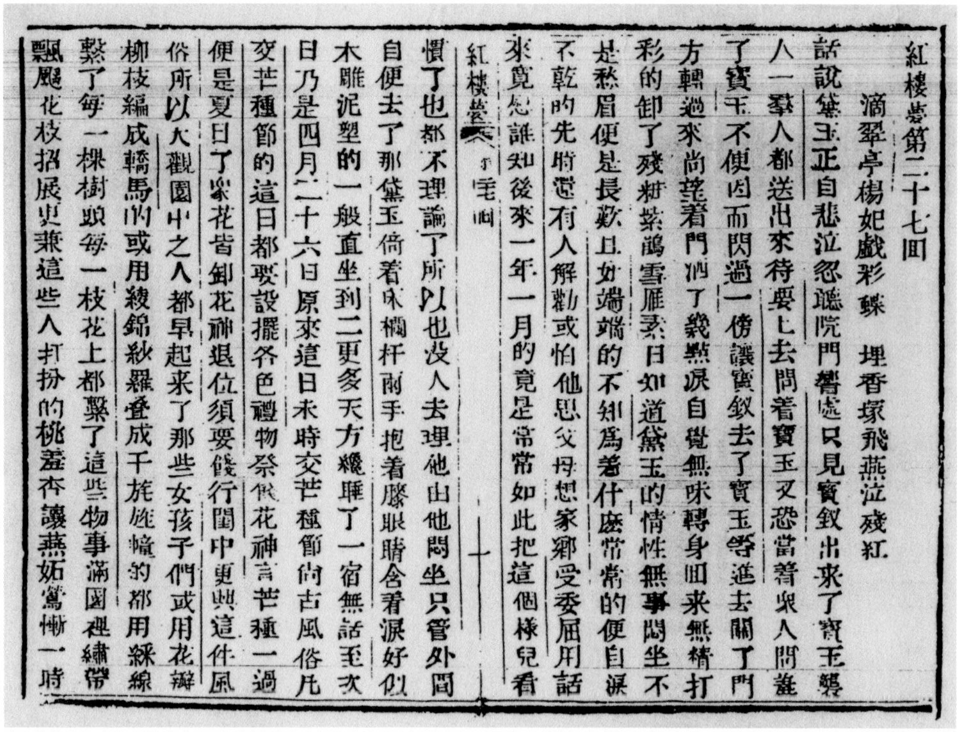

《紅樓夢》清乾隆五十七年（1792 年）萃文書屋活字本
Dreams of the Red Chamber, printed in movable type by the Cuiwen Bookstore in the fifty-seventh year of the Qianlong period of the Qing Dynasty (1792).

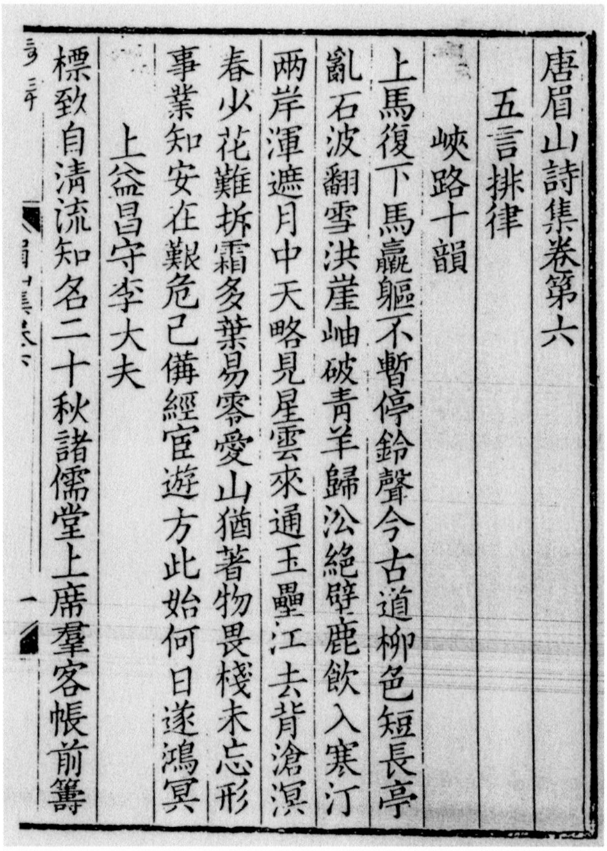

《唐眉山詩集》清雍正三年（1725 年）汪亮采活字本
Poems of Tang Geng, printed in movable type by Wang Liangcai in the third year of the Yongzheng period of the Qing Dynasty (1725).

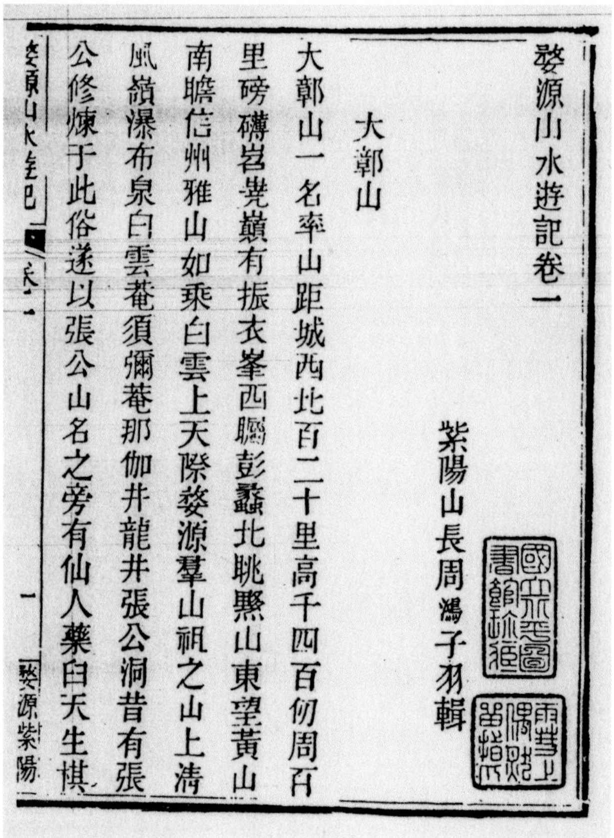

《婺源山水遊記》清乾隆五十五年（1790 年）紫陽書院活字本
A Travelogue of Wuyuan, printed in movable type by the Ziyang Academy in the fifty-fifth year of the Qianlong period of the Qing Dynasty (1790).

書籍裝幀的演變

The Evolution of Bookbinding

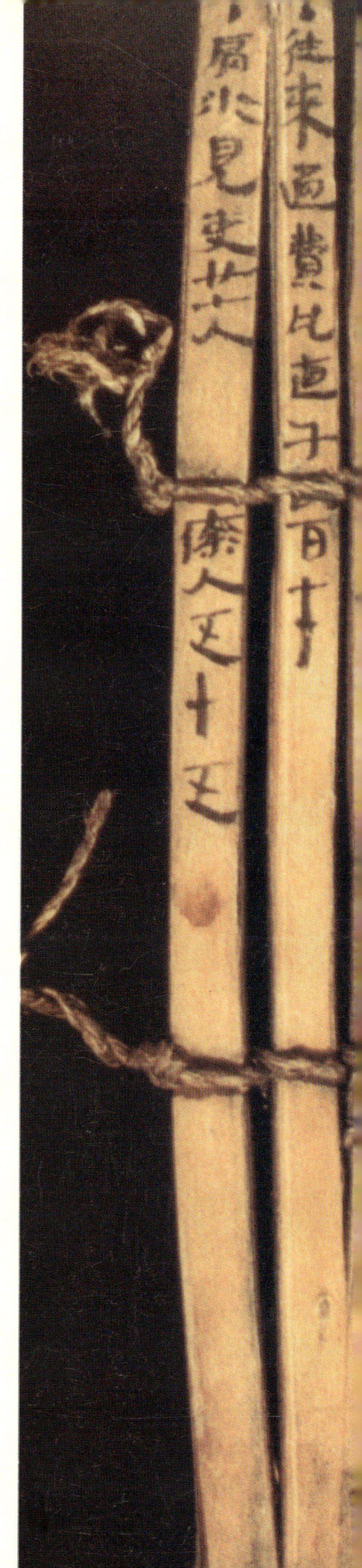

書籍裝幀的演變

中國古代早期的書籍形式之一，是簡策。紙張發明後，書籍的裝幀形式經歷了卷軸裝、旋風裝、梵夾裝、經折裝、蝴蝶裝、包背裝、綫裝和毛裝等。

Early "books" in ancient China were bound in the form of rolled-up slips. After paper was invented, bookbinding evolved through many stages including scroll-roller binding, *sutra* binding, pleated-leaf binding, whirlwind binding, butterfly binding, wrapped-back binding, thread binding, and raw binding.

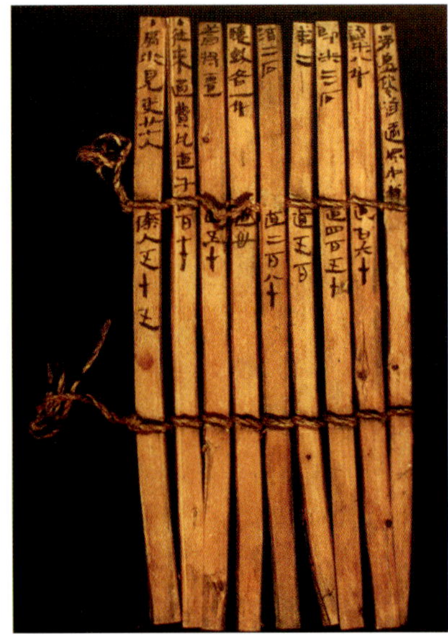

簡策

寫有一行文字的竹（木）片稱簡，將一篇文章的簡用繩順序編在一起稱簡策，捲起後裝入布袋稱"帙"。是中國古代早期書籍形式之一，行用於公元前 700 年至公元後四世紀。

Rolled-up Strips Binding

Characters are written on long strips of bamboo or wood. The strips are sequentially tied with string and then rolled up into a bamboo (wooden) "book". The bundle is placed in a cloth or silk bag called a "wrapper". This format of rolled-up strips is a method of bookbinding in ancient China. It was used from about 700 B.C. to the 4th century A.D.

卷軸裝

紙寫本最早的裝幀形式。南北朝（420–589 年）開始流行。印刷術發明後，最早也使用這種裝幀形式。唐（618–907 年）至五代（907–960 年）最為盛行。

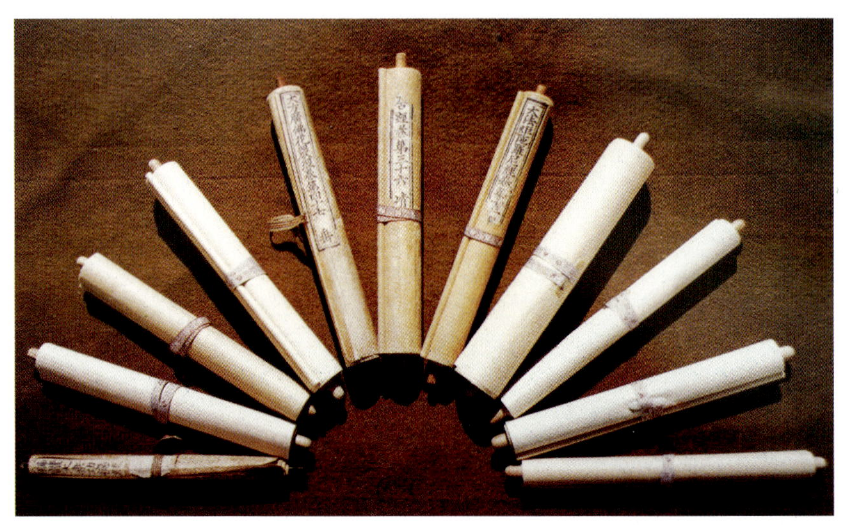

Scroll-Roller Binding

After paper was invented, the scroll format with a roller was the early method for works hand-written on paper. It gained popularity during the Northern and Southern Dynasties (420–589) and remained in use even after the invention of printing. The peak of popularity was reached during the Tang (618–907) and the Five Dynasties (907–960).

旋風裝

將書頁錯開貼於紙卷上，可逐頁翻閱，捲起後外觀如卷軸。故宮博物院藏有唐代王仁昫著《刊謬補缺切韻》，為旋風裝。

Whirlwind Binding

Sheets of paper with words on both sides overlap and are pasted onto a paper roller. When rolled up, it looks like a scroll but allows the reader to flip to any page. There is a Tang Dynasty book by Wang Renxu, bound in that format and kept in the Imperial Palace of Beijing today, called "Errors, Omissions and Supplements of *Qie Yun*".

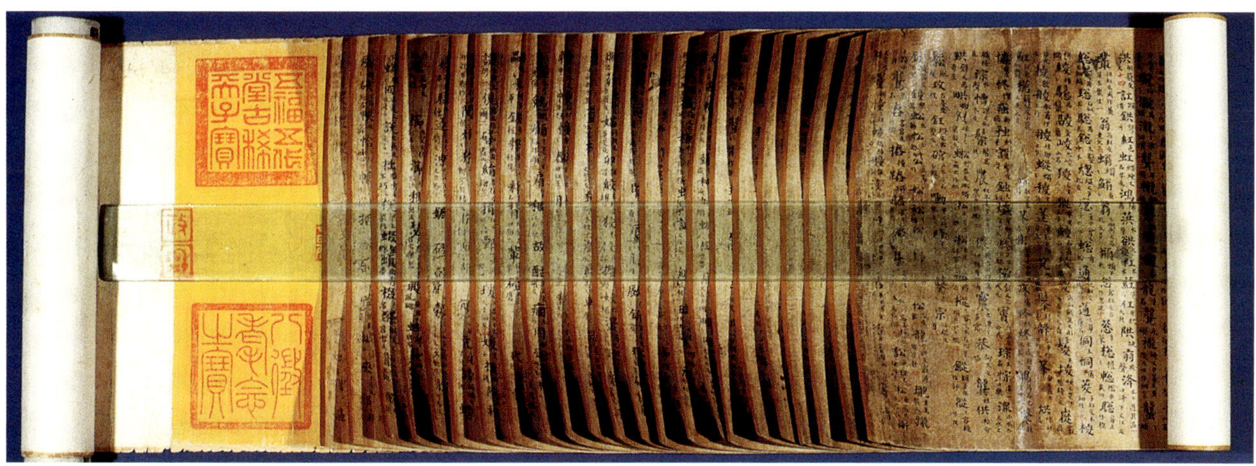

梵夾裝

仿印度貝葉經的一種裝幀形式。書頁為長條形，中有二孔順序穿綫，前後用木板作封。流行於唐、五代。今天藏文佛經仍用這種形式。

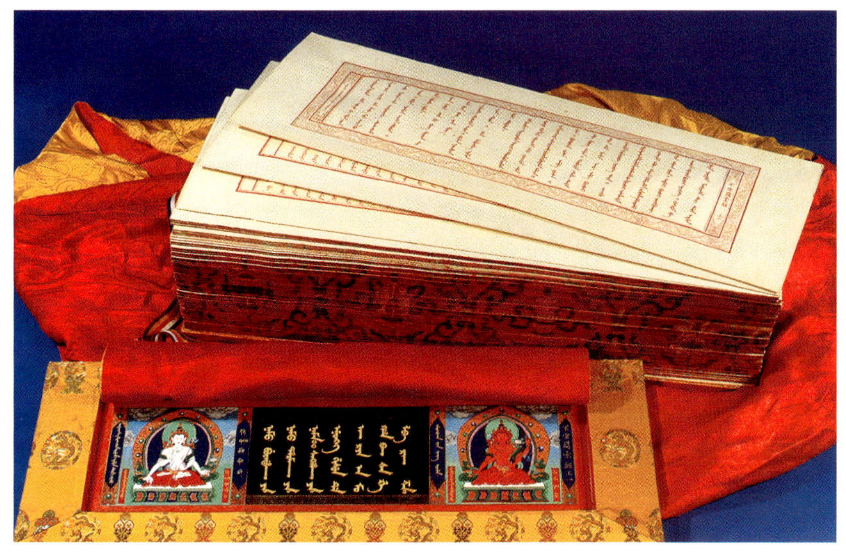

Sutra Binding

So called because it was probably an imitation of a binding method used for Buddlist sutras originating in India. Each page is elongated, with two holes in the middle to thread the pleated leaves which lie between two wooden boards functioning as covers. The format was widely used during the Tang and the Five Dynasties. Today, it is still used for Tibetan sutras.

經折裝

將書頁褙貼成長條後，再反覆折疊，前後用厚紙作封的一種書籍裝幀形式。多用於佛經寫印本。起源於唐代，流行至今。

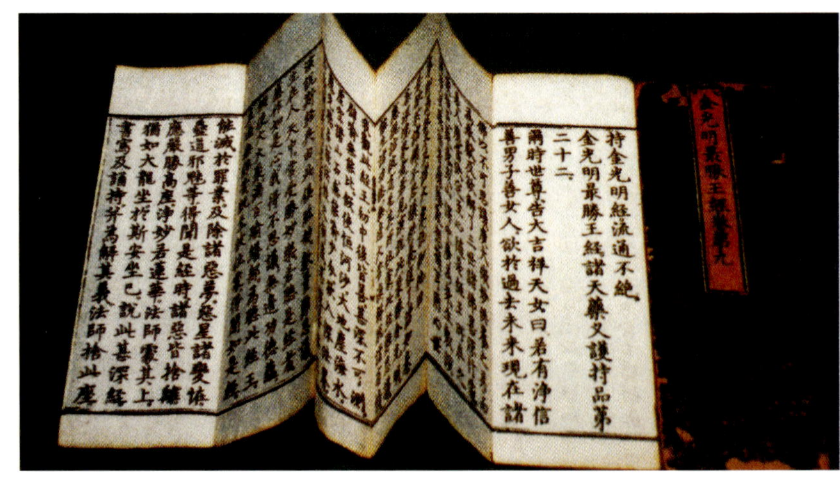

Pleated-leaf Binding

Book pages made of paper are first pasted together to form a very long page. Then pleated pages are formed by folding it repeatedly. The two end pages are pasted to thick paper boards which function as front and back covers. Originating in the Tang Dynasty, this format was used mostly for Buddhist texts and is still being used today.

蝴蝶裝

將印頁沿中縫向內折疊，一本書之書頁順序撞齊，沿折縫一邊用漿糊粘牢，用厚紙（或織物褙紙）包封後三面裁切的一種書籍裝幀形式。起源於五代，盛行於宋元。在書籍史上開創了冊頁裝的時代。

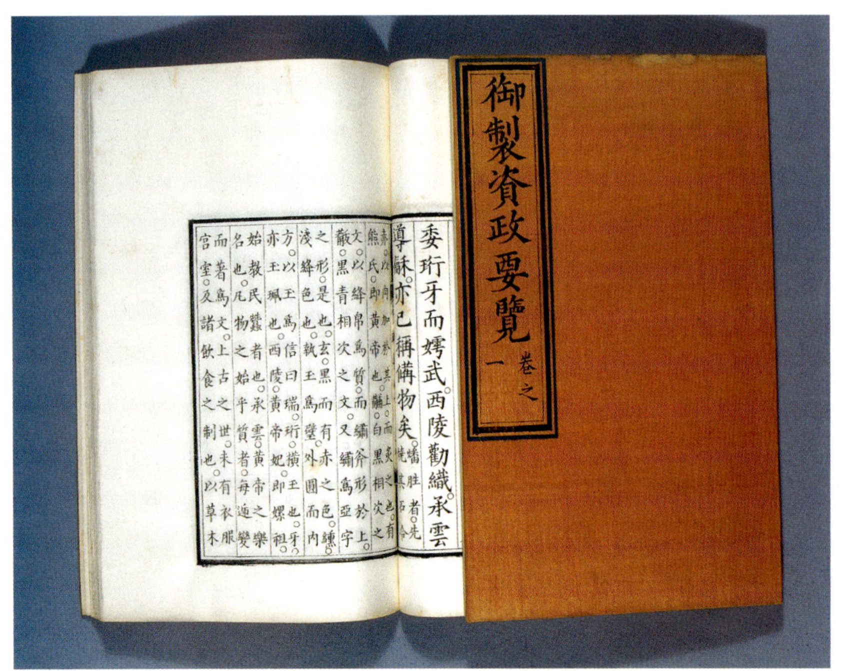

Butterfly Binding

Consecutive pages, with characters printed on one side only, are folded down in the centre and sorted to form a fascicle. The sides with the folded edges are glued and then wrapped with thick paper or cloth. The three sides that are unglued are then cut to form a book. This method began in the Five Dynasties and flourished during the Song Dynasty (960–1279). Its appearance ushered in the era of books printed in separate volumes with separated pages.

包背裝

將書頁沿中縫文字向外折疊，書頁排序撞齊，訂口處訂捻加固，裁切包封而成的一種書籍裝幀形式。起源於南宋（1127–1279 年），盛行於元代（1271–1368 年）。

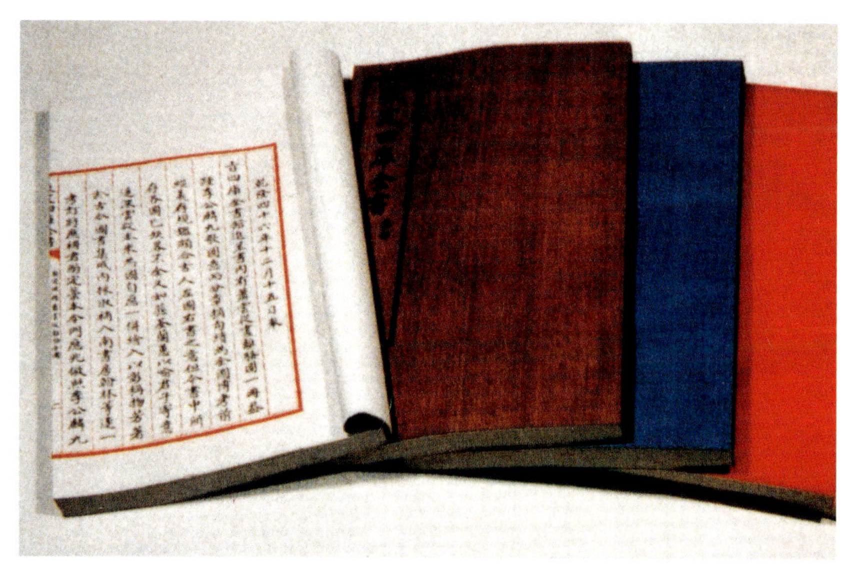

Wrapped-back Binding

Consecutive pages, with words printed only on one side, are each folded "outward" down the centre; then they are sorted to form a fascicle. The edges of the leaves are fastened with twisted threads, then cut and wrapped. This method of book binding originated in the Southern Song Dynasty (1127–1279) and flourished during the Yuan Dynasty (1271–1368).

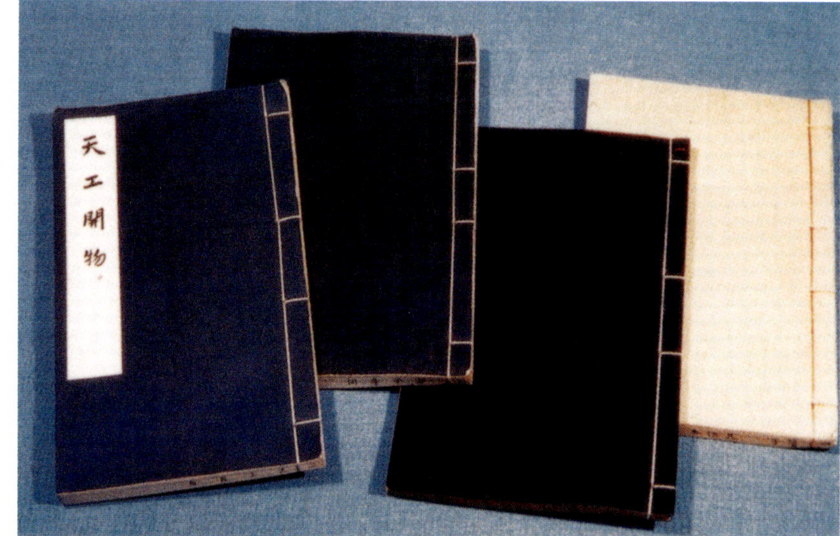

綫裝

綫裝與包背裝相似，只是封皮與書頁同時三面裁切後，再在訂口處穿綫訂牢。綫裝起源於五代（十世紀），但使用較少，明代（1368–1644 年）中期才開始盛行。

Thread Binding

Similar to wrapped-back binding except that after the stack of folded pages (fascicle) is cut on three sides together with covers, the spine side of the book is stitched through several pierced holes with tough thread. Although this binding method dates back to the 10th century, it was not in wide use until the Ming Dynasty (1368–1644).

毛裝

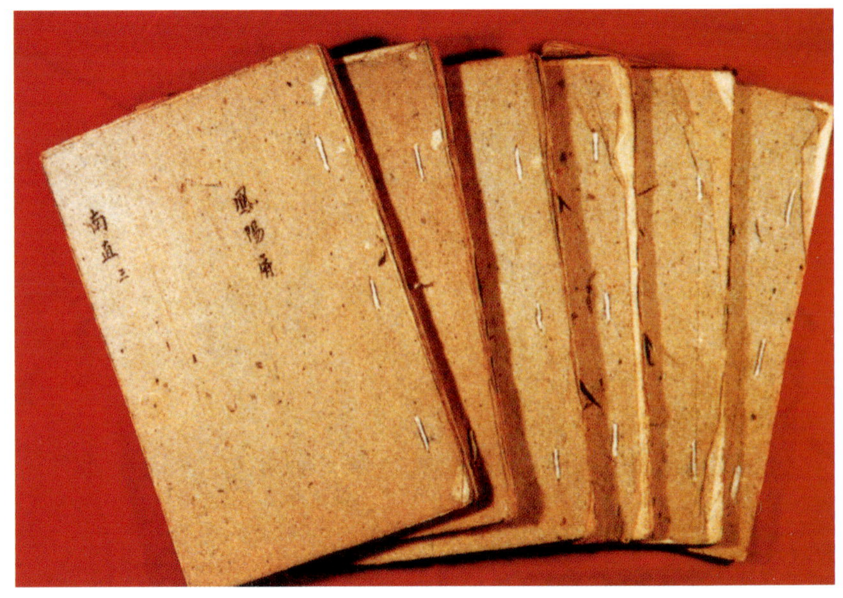

折葉方法一如包背裝和綫裝，仍然是版心所在折邊朝左向外，文字向人。集數葉為一疊，截齊出口，然後右側打眼穿捻，不用綫訂。有的除書口外其餘三邊不切齊，毛邊參差；這種不加封面、不切書口、不用綫訂、而只用紙捻粗裝的形式，就稱毛裝。

Rough-edged Binding

The folding process is the same as the wrapped-back and the thread binding method, with the book mouth (centre of page) facing left and the printed text facing the reader (when the book is opened). Several fascicles are combined with the book mouth (on the left) evenly stacked. The opposite side (on the right) is simply pierced and fastened with paper twists but not stitched with threads. Sometimes the piles are not cut, letting the three edges to expose the sheets sticking out unevenly. This format of binding—without edge cutting or covers and using only paper twists to bound the pages in the raw—is called "raw" binding.

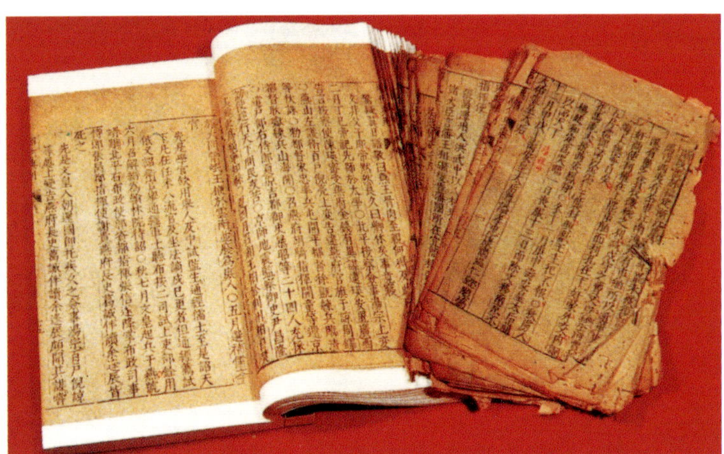

古書修復形式——"金鑲玉"
Restoration of paper manuscripts

索 引

Index

索引

一至五畫

六至十畫

十一畫及以上

Index

中國印刷術外傳圖
Diffusion of Printing Technology from China

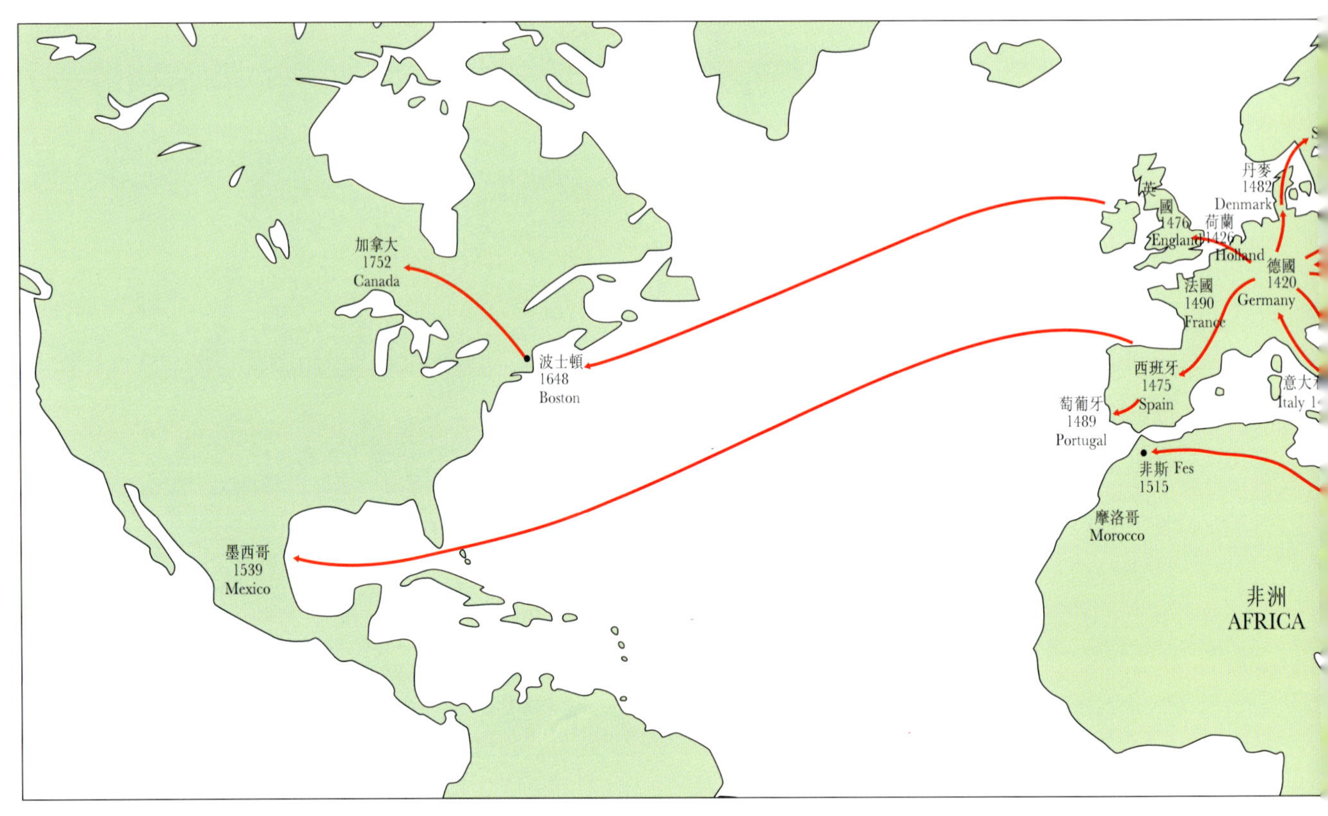

中國造紙技術外傳圖
Diffusion of Paper-Making Technology from China

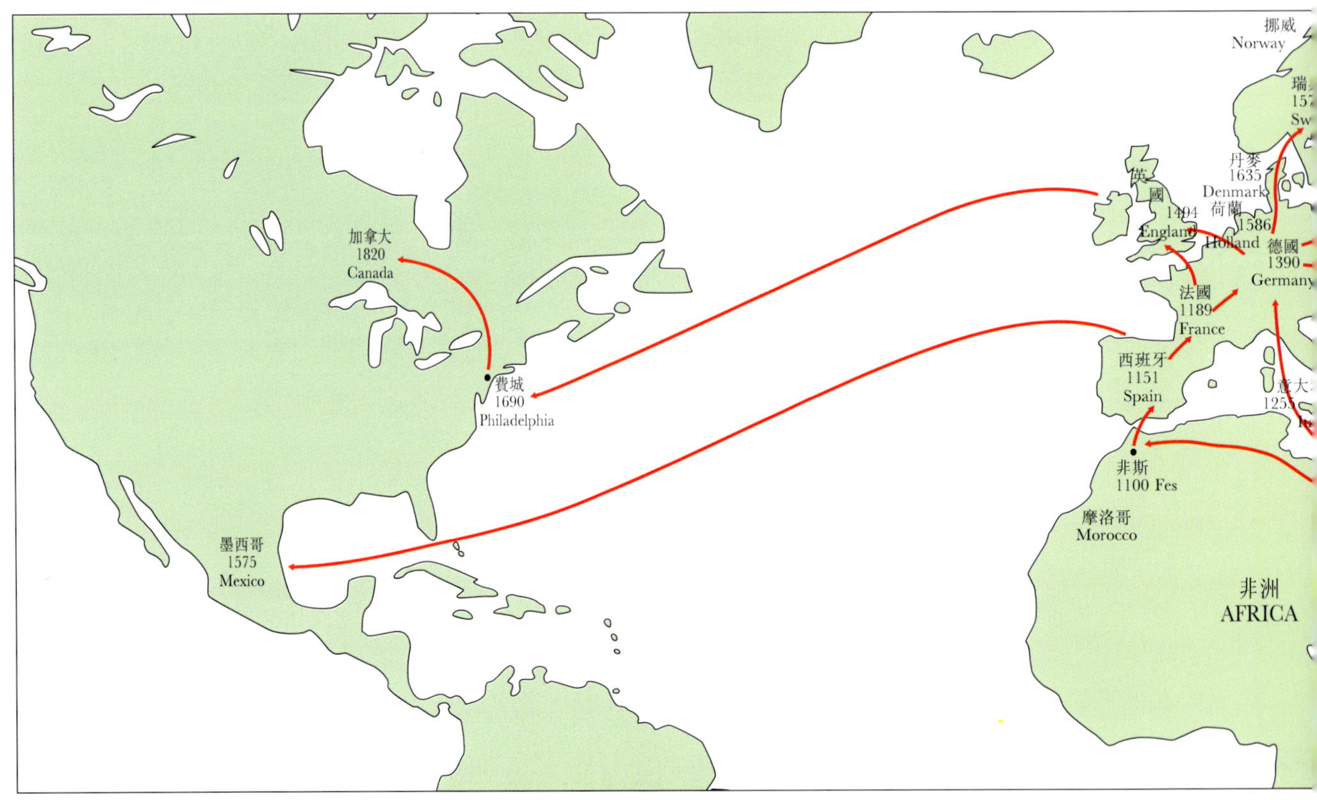

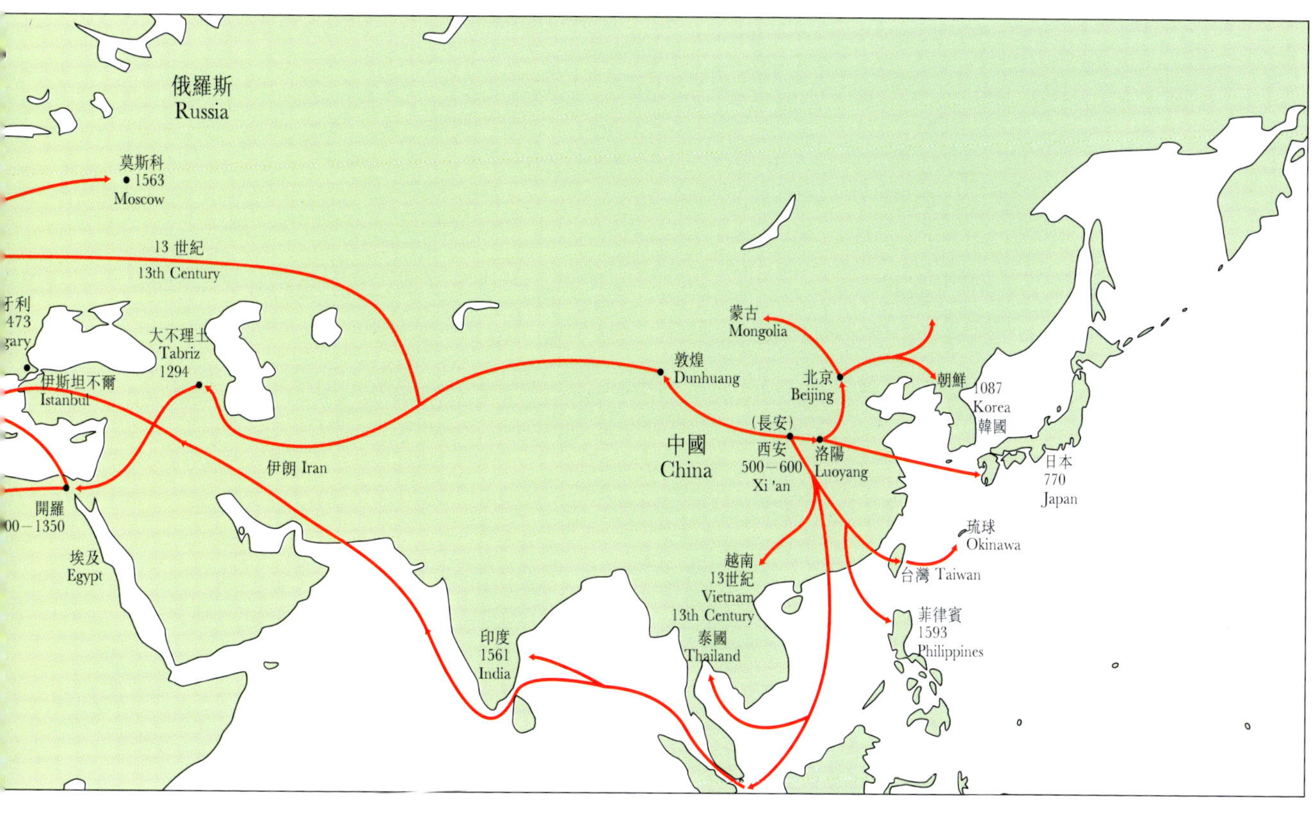
俄羅斯
Russia
莫斯科
1563
Moscow
13 世紀
13th Century
大不理士
Tabriz
1294
伊斯坦不爾
Istanbul
開羅
埃及
Egypt
伊朗 Iran
敦煌
Dunhuang
蒙古
Mongolia
北京
Beijing
朝鮮
1087
Korea
韓國
(長安)
西安
500 – 600
Xi 'an
洛陽
Luoyang
中國
China
日本
770
Japan
琉球
Okinawa
台灣 Taiwan
越南
13世紀
Vietnam
13th Century
菲律賓
1593
Philippines
泰國
Thailand
印度
1561
India

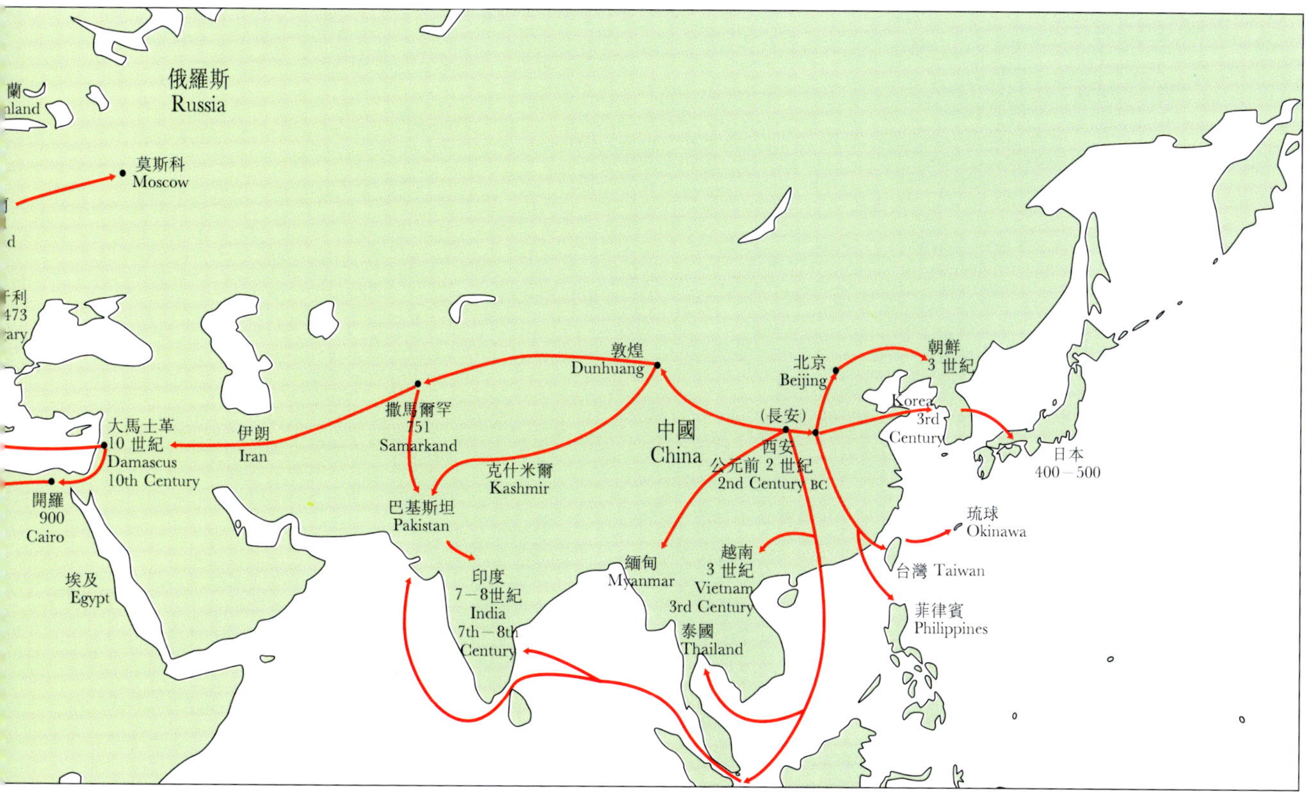
俄羅斯
Russia
莫斯科
Moscow
大馬士革
10 世紀
Damascus
10th Century
伊朗
Iran
開羅
900
Cairo
埃及
Egypt
撒馬爾罕
751
Samarkand
克什米爾
Kashmir
巴基斯坦
Pakistan
印度
7 – 8世紀
India
7th – 8th
Century
敦煌
Dunhuang
中國
China
(長安)
西安
公元前 2 世紀
2nd Century BC
北京
Beijing
朝鮮
3 世紀
Korea
3rd
Century
日本
400 – 500
緬甸
Myanmar
越南
3 世紀
Vietnam
3rd Century
泰國
Thailand
琉球
Okinawa
台灣 Taiwan
菲律賓
Philippines

後　記

印刷術是中國古代的偉大發明，它的發明、發展以及向世界的傳播，對人類文明和社會進步，產生了巨大的推動作用。有鑒於此，研究中國古代印刷史，一直為國內外學者所關注。在中國，這方面的研究者也越來越多，近幾十年來，已有多部中國印刷史方面的專著出版。

為弘揚中華民族古代印刷術的光輝成就，讓國內外廣大讀者進一步了解中國古代印刷術的的起源、發明和發展的歷史，中國印刷博物館組織編印了《中國古代印刷史圖冊》，收入了印刷術的起源、發明、發展過程中有代表性的實物、史料、印刷品、人物等圖片，並附以簡要的文字説明。它形象、生動地向人們展示了中國古代印刷術發明和發展的基本概況，以及古代珍貴印刷品的風貌，有着極高的藝術價值和收藏價值。

編印這本圖冊，是我們一年前提出的倡議，並分別為此做了一些組織工作。近二十多年來，每有機會相遇，我們往往結合各自經歷，縱談於古今中外之間，特別是在中外文化領域裏進行精神遨遊。如今有機會為宣揚中國文化做件實事，這是我們求之不得的。

中國印刷博物館副館長羅樹寶先生承擔了本圖冊繁重的編寫工作，香港城市大學鄺子器先生、文物出版社孟憲鈞先生承擔了本圖冊的編輯任務，中國印刷博物館館長周興華先生，副館長魏志剛先生及文物出版社原社長楊瑾女士等，都為本圖冊的編輯出版出了很大的力。文物出版社、北京圖書館以及其他單位為本圖冊提供了資料和圖片。在圖冊完成之際，謹向為此書作出貢獻的有關人士和單位，表示衷心的敬意。

北京印刷學院　　張伯海

香港城市大學　　張信剛

1998年6月

Postscript

Printing was a great invention of ancient China. Its invention, development and dissemination to other parts of the world contributed significantly to human civilization and social progress. This is perhaps the main reason why scholars in China and in other parts of the world have devoted themselves to the study of the history of printing in ancient China.

In preparing *An Illustrated History of Printing in Ancient China*, The Printing Museum of China has put together a large number of captioned illustrations of representative examples of artefacts, historical documents, publications, and portraits depicting the origin, invention and development of printing in China. The book has graphically outlined the invention and development of printing in ancient China and the original styles and characteristics of valuable publications in respective periods. It has, therefore, a high artistic and collection value.

The idea of publishing this book was raised a year ago and efforts were then made to arrange for its production. For more than twenty years before that, whenever we met, we shared our experiences, talked about things Chinese and foreign, past and present, and had spiritual ramblings in the intellectual worlds of China and other countries. The publication of this book has now given us an opportunity to contribute to the promotion of Chinese culture and this is what we have wished for.

In publishing this book, the writing of the text by Mr. Luo Shubao, Associate Curator of The Printing Museum of China, the editorial work of Mr. Patrick Kwong, Director of the City University of Hong Kong Press, and Mr. Meng Xianjun of the Cultural Relics Publishing House, and the efforts of Mr. Zhou Xinghua, Curator of The Printing Museum of China, Mr. Wei Zhigang, Associate Curator of The Printing Museum of China, and Miss Yang Jin, formerly Director of the Cultural Relics Press, deserve our gratitude. Thanks are also due to the Cultural Relics Publishing House, the Beijing Library and other institutions for the provision of materials and illustrations.

Zhang Bohai
Beijing Academy of Printing

H. K. Chang
City University of Hong Kong

June 1998